ASCENDING THE DREAM

The Life and Climbs of Banjo Bannon

ASCENDING THE DREAM

The Life and Climbs of Banjo Bannon

TERENCE 'BANJO' BANNON
AND LAUREN O'MALLEY

Gill & Macmillan

Gill & Macmillan Ltd
Hume Avenue, Park West, Dublin 12
with associated companies throughout the world
www.gillmacmillan.ie

© Terence 'Banjo' Bannon and Lauren O'Malley 2009
978 07171 4631 4

Typography design by Make Communication
Print origination by O'K Graphic Design, Dublin
Printed by GraphyCems, Spain

This book is typeset in 12/15 pt Minion.

The paper used in this book comes from the wood pulp
of managed forests. For every tree felled, at least one
tree is planted, thereby renewing natural resources.

A CIP catalogue record for this book is available from
the British Library.

5 4 3 2

To our respective parents, Rose and Edward Bannon and Karen and Michael O'Malley, and our families, for all of your love, support and guidance, and to our precious son Conor, for bringing new meaning to our lives.

CONTENTS

ABOUT LAUREN O'MALLEY

Lauren O'Malley originally hails from Melrose, Massachusetts. She graduated from the University of Massachusetts Amherst with a Bachelor of Arts in Sociology and Criminal Justice and went on to obtain a Master's degree in Criminology from Queen's University in Belfast.

She spent time working in the criminal justice system in Chicago, Illinois before moving to Thailand to teach English for a year in a village school in 2003. During her time in Asia, Lauren began rock-climbing and trekking and spent five days completing a 75-mile trek through the Thai/Burmese jungle. She went on to participate in treks and rock climbs in Laos, China, Tibet and Nepal. She was with a small group who travelled to the north face base camp of Mount Everest in the spring of 2003 and met her husband, Irish mountaineer Terence 'Banjo' Bannon, whilst on this trip.

After the chance meeting at base camp, Lauren went on to hike and climb with Terence throughout Ireland and other parts of Europe. Under Terence's guidance Lauren learned the essentials of rock- and ice-climbing and the two trained together in Scotland for an expedition to South America.

In Ecuador, Lauren and Terence completed high-altitude ice-climbs on Mount Cotopaxi and Mount Chimborazo. The following year she become the only female member of the Irish K2 2005 expedition and acted as the base camp manager for the team.

Lauren now works full-time with families of prisoners in the North of Ireland with NIACRO, a community-based organisation.

Lauren and Terence continue to rock- and ice-climb together and have travelled to over 25 countries. They also have a young son named Conor Brendan Bannon.

ACKNOWLEDGMENTS

W e cannot individually acknowledge the countless friends and relatives who have contributed to the writing of this book and been a part of the memories that comprise each chapter, so we would like to collectively thank them all for their support. Special thanks to Peter Jackson, Thomas O'Gorman and Michael O'Malley for their advice and guidance, to Josh Riley for the photographs and to Kevin Quinn and Paul Clerkin for the time they spent helping to make this dream a reality.

INTRODUCTION

The cold that night was unrelenting. My fingers had become stiff and were beginning to lose coordination. My thoughts were fuzzy and with each inhalation of air I could feel ice stinging my lungs. I was frantic to begin moving again, but was also afraid that I was doing irreversible damage to my toes. All feeling in these distant extremities had ceased in the past hour and now they felt detached and foreign in my boots. I knew that I needed to stop and warm them between my hands, but I feared that the pain of exposure on my bare skin would be difficult to endure.

Whilst I was sitting, small crusts of snow and ice began to dislodge from the face behind me and gusts of freezing wind bit against my face. With great effort I dislodged my boot, sat with my back against the peak and began to rub my feet. I was starting to experience pains in my chest and my head was throbbing with a rhythmic pulse that told me my blood was becoming dangerously thick. The limited oxygen in the air was taking a toll on my body and each movement that I made was heavy and laborious. My thoughts began to drift and scattered images passed through my mind. I found myself slightly disorientated at one stage, but then a large chunk of ice broke free beside me and brought me straight back to reality.

I was above camp four at an altitude of over 8,000 metres on the final phase of my ascent of K2, the world's most deadly peak. This mountain had haunted my dreams for many years and now I was just hours away from standing on its prized summit. I had sacrificed considerably to make it this far and I refused to let my freezing feet prevent me from going any further. After a concerted effort to bring the blood back down my legs, I put my boots on and set off again. The sky was still dark but I could see the sun rising up in a purple haze on the horizon. My legs were shaking with each exertion and I was conscious of my isolation and the slow speed at which I was progressing. It was strange to be so completely alone in such a vast expanse of white, but I knew that it would not be long before I reconnected with the Russian climbers.

After half an hour I caught up to Serguey, one of the older Russian men, who had already summitted nine of the world's highest peaks, and the two of us continued on our ascent together. Within a short while, we reached the infamous 'bottleneck' and all of the fear and anxiety that I had harboured about this section of the climb was realised. It was steep and acutely technical, but it was not beyond my abilities. I let my confidence gather and roped into the existing lines laid by the Russians in front of us. Serguey made his way ahead on the icy 300-metre pass that hangs at a vertical incline of 80°. Neither of us was using oxygen and the air had become so thin that our lungs were labouring hard in this physically intense section. Serguey stopped frequently to shake his legs and feet to promote circulation.

We reached the top of the bottleneck together after great effort. The ropes that hung along the route were loose and insecure so each axe swing required great strength and precision. At this stage we were 10 hours into the climb and it was approaching 11 a.m. The sky was still clear and the sun had long since risen. The snow was becoming very soft underfoot, which is unusual at this altitude. I was conscious of the time and of how slowly we seemed to be progressing up this final stage. We pushed on and within an hour we made our way up to the final traverse, leaving only the summit ridge in front of us. We waited in line to complete this pass, as the remaining section was too narrow for more than one climber to ascend at a time.

Serguey and I were alone but Jacek and some of the other men were visible above. I stopped and put a stake into the snow and clipped that stake onto the ropes of the traverse for added protection. I rested my weight against the ropes and looked up to the summit dome on the horizon. I imagined the leading Russian climbers; Yuri, Piotr, Arcady, Victor, Alexander Foigt and Alexander Gaponov must be near the top by now. Serguey and I were nearly celebrating. The hard work was done, we were above the bottleneck and the traverse, and I found my adrenalin rising as familiar thoughts flooded my mind. I remembered this exhilaration well from the moments before I reached the summit of Everest. Whilst I waited on that final section I was convinced that I would stand on the top of κ2.

As I was speaking to Serguey, I looked up to see Jacek fiddling with his ropes above us on the side of the hanging serac; he glanced at me briefly but he didn't move or motion down. Serguey and I continued speaking. He was planning a toast on the summit with a small bottle of vodka that he had packed. Before he could finish his sentence, I heard a sudden swoosh above me and looked up to find only white.

I was confused. Everything was happening so fast and the world seemed to have gone silent. I was knocked off my feet and I was sliding. I was conscious that I had only clipped the karabiner to the rope and not the jumar; this meant that I had no added protection in a fall. I worried that my weight would cause the rope to snap or that I would be buried underneath the crusts of snow coming down upon me. I wrapped the rope around my right wrist as quickly as possible and waited for the sliding to stop. At first my body was in the prone position and then I somersaulted over, landing on my back and looking directly up into the white debris above me.

What had only been a matter of seconds felt like minutes or hours. The climb below flashed through my mind; we had traversed a ten-thousand-foot cliff across the upper section of the bottleneck and now I could see myself free-falling over the edge. I couldn't breathe; my fear was overwhelming and I thought that I was suffocating. For a second it seemed as if I had met my destiny, death by avalanche on the world's most spectacular peak. I didn't feel any pain in those seconds and I wondered if it would hurt when I finally died.

Chapter 1 ∾

| THE EARLY YEARS

'Do not go where the path may lead, go instead where there is no path and leave a trail'
RALPH WALDO EMERSON

In the late 1960s Ireland was a country in the midst of great change. The political and social situation in the north of Ireland was beginning to unravel, whilst the war in Vietnam was raging on and America's civil rights movement was gaining strength. Women across the world were joining in with radical feminist groups to fight oppression and they were burning their bras in protest. The liberal hippie movement that was sweeping the United States was beamed into every Irish sitting room courtesy of the family television, and young men and women throughout the island were beginning to rebel against their traditional Catholic backgrounds. Free love and equal rights for the oppressed became the order of the day—but not at 122 Barcroft Park in Newry, where I was born.

In those days, good Catholic girls like my mother, Rose, married nice young Catholic men and stayed at home, having babies and caring for their husbands. In 1967, the year that I was born, the world was in chaos. Greece was overthrown by a military coup, there was the Six-Day War in Israel, opposition to America's campaign in Vietnam was at an all-time high and the legendary South American revolutionary Che Guevara was killed in Bolivia. But at our home in Newry, Northern Ireland, life was simple. My mother was caring for her five children and patiently awaiting the arrival of lucky number six. She had grown up in a traditional Irish home with seven children and all of the young ladies were taught to be excellent wives and mothers. They learned the value of hard work and were not ever allowed to smoke or drink. In fact, women in my mother's home did not even wear trousers or jeans. They attended Mass every Sunday and prayed together as a family daily. They rarely socialised with boys and when they did it was under strict conditions at the local dances.

It was here that my mother, Rose, met my father, Edward Bannon, in 1947. She was 17 at the time and he was 21 years of age. They dated for quite a while after meeting, but in those days 'dates' consisted of going to Mass together or meeting up for Novenas. My mother was a very traditional woman. Her strict upbringing meant that she wanted a hard-working and religious man who stayed away from drinking and gambling. My father seemed to fit the bill until one evening when they met at Cloughue Chapel for a Novena. The weather was terrible and the rain was lashing down. She arrived late and felt terrible, thinking that my father had been waiting out in the awful conditions. She apologised for being late and my father told her not to worry—that he had gone for a pint in a nearby pub and hadn't been in the rain for very long. My mother was furious. She had never been around alcohol in her life and had been warned that it was a sinful thing. She broke up with my father that night and did not go out with him again for two years.

Luckily, my father was a persistent man and after countless letters and promises to become a teetotaller, he won my mother back. They married on 28 December 1954. The wedding was toasted with orange juice, as my father was a man true to his word! My parents were to have eight babies prior to my birth. Unfortunately only five of them survived. Noel was born first in 1955. He was followed by Eamon in 1956, and then Elizabeth Mary in 1957. When Elizabeth was born she was very premature and weighed less than two pounds. She was baptised in the hospital at my mother's bedside, but sadly only lived for 24 hours. My mother was distraught when she died. She later told us all how she wept non-stop for nearly the entire time Elizabeth lived. However, when the doctors later advised her that Elizabeth would almost certainly have been disabled as a result of her size and weight, my mother became comforted by the thought of her in heaven. She knew that her child had not suffered and was now with God and the angels. After Elizabeth died my mother went on to have a miscarriage and then my sister Geraldine was born in 1959. After Geraldine there was Colum in 1961 and Angeline in 1964, who was followed by a further miscarriage. Finally, in November 1967, I was born and became the final member of the Bannon clan.

My mother remembers my birth vividly. When I entered the world my umbilical cord was wrapped tightly around my neck and I was black from head to toe. Luckily the doctors were able to untangle the cord in time to revive me and from that moment forward my mother was very protective of me. During those days women stayed in the hospital for a week after delivering and for my mother this would have been a welcome respite. All of the new mothers stayed together in a ward, whilst the babies were cared for in a separate room by the nurses. Once the week was over, it was back to the difficult daily grind for my mother. She returned home with me to a house full of children and chores, but she relished the work and loved having a new baby in the house.

As my mother was a staunchly religious woman she had all of her children christened before they even left the hospital. Thus I was baptised Terence Anthony Bannon, after my late great-uncle Terence, at Daisy Hill Hospital. Once I arrived home, my brothers and sisters were all eager to help care for me. My mother laughs as she recalls one particular incident in which she was walking past my Moses basket and noticed something white in my mouth. She quickly reached in and to her horror pulled out a piece of chewing gum. One of my older siblings had given it to me so that I would not feel left out.

My sisters were particularly keen to care for me and Geraldine relished the responsibility of taking me for walks in my pram. She would take me through the streets and up into the fields of the glen. She was fiercely protective of me and always ensured I was well looked after. When I was only an infant and Geraldine was about nine years of age she took me on my first adventure. She carried me through the glen, crossing a stream on the wet stones, and then up a steep embankment. When she reached the top, there was a wall with barbed wire across the top. As she was working out a way to get me over the wall I began to cry. My father had been out in the fields below and heard my wailing. When he realised where I was he carefully took me from Geraldine and led us both back down towards home. Geraldine thought she would be in terrible trouble, but my father was a very easygoing man and he never said a word to my mother about it.

The first years of my life passed by without event but when I was three years old my family suffered a terrible loss. My father became ill and the prognosis was very poor. Within a very short period of time my mother realised that he would not recover, and his final weeks were spent at home with his children and wife by his side. Sadly, this left an indelible impression on me. My first memory as a child was of my father's coffin in the front room of our small terraced house. Although much of my early childhood remains hazy in my mind, the vivid visual memories I have of this day have been with me ever since. All six of us were dressed in our Sunday best, whilst my mum and family and friends gathered around with cups of tea and biscuits.

My father had only lived to be 44 years of age before cancer ended his life. He was a hard worker who had never known privilege or wealth. He himself was from a family of 21 children but most of them did not survive beyond birth or infancy. His mother, Mary Ellen, had three sets of twins but sadly in those days the living conditions were especially poor, causing outbreaks of illness. In fact, when an epidemic swept through Newry, six of the children died within one week. His father, Patrick Bannon, was originally from Cornamuckla, County Louth. He was one of seven children and he and two of his brothers joined the British Army during World War 1. Patrick fought in the Battle of the Somme and then returned to Ireland to work on the canal boats in Newry. While Patrick worked long hours for little money to support his exceptionally large family, his brother Jack went on to become a very wealthy man developing property. He was well known throughout the region and brought great esteem to the Bannon family.

Coming from such a large family, my father knew the value of a hard day's work and he did his best to provide for his wife and children. However, when he passed away, my mother was left with very little. Fortunately we had our home and this gave us more security than some. I can't imagine how difficult those first few years alone must have been for my mother, but she coped remarkably well.

Although we did not have much as children, we were happy. We were always well looked after by my mother, who ensured that we did not want for food or clothing. She took great pride in our appearance and kept the house immaculately clean. I now realise that we were poor, but we were no worse off than any of our neighbours or friends. At that time the entire estate of Barcroft Park was both socially and economically marginalised.

I spent my youngest years like most of the other children on my street. We had adventures in the sprickly begs (a small glen with a river that runs under a bridge above the housing estate) and the barley fields that lined the top rows of our estate and played until the dusk came in or the cold and rain became unbearable. I always returned home to a hot dinner and a warm fire and I have very fond memories of those years. Being the youngest of six, I was spoiled in many ways. My mother and all of my siblings doted over me and I was always given extra treats and special attention, but in other ways I got the short end of the stick. Money was tight in our house so it wasn't every day that we got a hot bath. When we did I was always the last to get in, and by the time it was my turn to bathe the water would be a horrible murky shade of grey. I never came out any cleaner than I went in. But my mother would always put extra coal on the fire to warm us after our bath and I remember happily running into the sitting room naked to dry off.

I also remember the adventures we would have during the summer months as children. All of the boys in Barcroft would group together and conduct raids on the apple orchards in the glen and on Hawthorne Hill. I distinctly remember one particular day when there were at least 60 young boys who were brought together by Eiser McCoy, an older boy from the neighbourhood. He lined all of us up into rows of three and marched us down the road with military precision. He led us on a siege of an apple orchard that was in the back garden of a house on Hawthorne Hill. He instructed us all to take our jumpers off and to make a knot at the neck so that we could hold as many apples as possible. The resultant scene was total chaos. There were boys swinging from branches and violently shaking the trees to get the apples down. The owner of the house must have heard the chaos and raced outside to stop us. When he saw the sheer number of boys in his back garden, he froze. Eiser quickly instructed the man to return into his house and not to come back out. Eiser was only about 14 at the time but, amazingly, the man did as he was told and we continued on until there was nothing left. Once we were done, we departed as we had arrived, in military formation.

Although we were all struggling with our apples, we did our best to maintain step with the fellas next to us as Eiser chanted, 'Left, right, left, right, our boots are heavy, our jeans are tight, our balls are swinging to left and right.' Once we arrived back to Barcroft, we retreated to the barley field, where we ate apples until we were sick and then threw them at each other and the surrounding houses. I remember having 'the runs' for days afterwards as many of the apples were rotten, but it was a great laugh and we staged many more raids like it in the following months.

Once we became confident with the theft of apples, we targeted other estates for tyres to burn on the bonfire nights during the summer. It was tradition at the time for old tyres to be donated to local estates for use in the festivities and the residents would guard their stashes carefully. Collecting tyres required far greater stealth than stealing apples. We used to push the smaller boys into locked garages through the windows and then they would hoist the tyres out to us. Once we had them, we would race back through the streets, struggling to manage our bounty. The easiest way to get the tyres home was to wheel them, and we would roll them right down the road in front of oncoming vehicles and pedestrians. I remember one time we got a huge tractor tyre and had a horrible time trying to get it back. When we rolled it down the hill it bounced off parked cars and probably dented and smashed them to bits, but we never stopped to check.

Another regular pastime in the neighbourhood was a game which we called 'dares or tasks'. We usually played this when a group of us were hanging around with nothing better to do. It involved one of us coming up with a dangerous task, which the entire group would then have to complete. This involved anything from running across the roofs of houses to balancing on beams and ledges. I remember one of the tasks distinctly and to this day I cannot believe that none of us were killed doing it. There was a derelict laundry facility just below the estate and across the roof of this building remained an old exposed beam. The building must have been three stories high and the beam was no wider than a foot across and over 20 feet long. No one liked to complete this dare as there were very few boys who had the nerve to shinny across, but there was one fella who always brought it up as he could walk across without so much as flinching. Gunner Quinn developed quite a reputation for his fearlessness and I will never forget the first time that he dared me to make my way across. I could not stop shaking when I reached the beam and I stood there for ages with my mates shouting abuse up at me. In the end, I just couldn't make myself move and I was forced to retreat to their heckles. However, within a year I had traversed the beam and earned my honour with the fellas.

As a young boy, I attended The Abbey Christian Brothers Primary School in Newry with many of the other kids from my neighbourhood. It was here that I met several boys who would later become lifelong friends. Before I started primary school, I knew little about life outside of Barcroft Park, but once I began at The Abbey I met boys from all over the town and the surrounding countryside. I had no idea that Newry was so big and couldn't believe the stories that the other boys had about their homes and neighbourhoods. However, I never had an interest in seeing these places as I couldn't imagine they had any more to offer than Barcroft Park!

It was in my primary school days that I was first introduced to organised athletics and learned how rough kids' sports could be. When I was seven I was playing in a hurling match during my physical education class and I got hit in the mouth with a hurley. It was brutal. My two front teeth were knocked out and there was blood everywhere. The other kids couldn't believe my injury. They thought I was really tough even though I cried until the end of the school day. Unfortunately this injury occurred a few weeks before my First Holy Communion and thus my mother made me keep my mouth closed tight in all of my photographs.

Every year The Abbey would have a school sports day and all of the boys would compete for medals in the various disciplines. After several years of losing in these competitions, I came up with a plan and vowed to win a medal. The annual champion was one of my friends, John O'Flagherty. He was the top athlete in the school and would win medals in nearly every event. I knew that my best chance of winning was to get him on my team. I convinced John to enter the three-legged race with me. He was bigger and faster than I was but once we were tied together, he carried the extra weight without difficulty. In the end we got the gold for coming in first and I have kept the medal from our victory ever since!

My primary school years were great because I was confident socially and instantly made a lot of friends. However, I struggled with the academics and was taken each day to special classes for extra assistance. At the time there was no negative stigma attached to this and Mr Hollywood helped me a great deal. However, as I grew older I became more conscious of my academic difficulties and found it difficult to keep up with reading and writing in my classes.

Despite my lack of interest in traditional school subjects, by my pre-teen years I became very interested in politics. As I grew older I realised that through my own innocence I had not borne witness to the violent social and political upheaval that was taking place around me. Barcroft Park was almost entirely Catholic and mainly nationalist, and Newry itself was to a large extent a Catholic town, with many of the residents active in the Republican movement. Republicanism was historically strong throughout this region and when the civil rights campaigns and resultant violent political battles began in the late 1960s, Newry became a hotspot for social upheaval.

Despite the violent mistrust and hatred that were forming between the Catholic and Protestant communities throughout the North during my childhood, my parents refused to be sectarian or to become involved in the resistance movement. My father and a number of local residents actually prevented our Protestant neighbours from being burnt out of their home by keeping watch over the property after threats were made to the family on the street by a group of young males. Whilst many others in the area were supporting the IRA, my mother kept a neutral stance and forbade my siblings and myself to become involved. Ironically, her own father, Matt Jackson, had been highly political and was very involved in the local IRA. He joined Sinn Féin in 1916 just after the Easter Rising and became a member of the IRA in 1918. He was in charge of firearms and munitions in the Armagh Brigade Fourth Northern Division and had been involved with ambushes throughout the region during the War of Independence. He even progressed to the rank of adjutant. His commanding officer was Frank Aiken, who later went on to become a minister in Fianna Fáil.

When my father died, my mother had a difficult role to play in managing all six children on her own, but she kept strict rules and constantly watched over us. Many other parents let their children run free throughout the protests and clashes and some even encouraged their children in stone-throwing and petrol-bombing the RUC and army, but my mother was adamant that we remain inside and uninvolved.

Despite my mother's efforts to shelter us, I still managed to see many of the clashes and battles that took place in the streets and will never forget the first time I saw a body, at seven years of age. A bomb that was being constructed by local members of the IRA went off prematurely on the fifth street of Barcroft Park in August 1974. Several young boys from the neighbourhood and I were running towards the smoke and debris that was rising from the Murphys' house when we were stopped in our tracks by a group of older men. They tried to restrict us from the area where the bomb had detonated but, in the ensuing chaos, we were able to pass them.

Barcroft Park had been transformed in seconds to an unrecognisable place. All of the houses and cars in the area had their windows shattered and thick smoke engulfed the streets. Despite being told to stay away from the area, myself and some other boys made our way quite close to the house. We could see body parts around us. I later found out that Patrick McKeown, a young IRA volunteer, was killed during the explosion. His torso was thrown to the telephone wires above the street and the local dogs immediately began to sniff around the scene. It was a morbid sight for a young boy and I remember being intrigued but horrified as well. We waited in the area until the fire brigade arrived on the scene and they began to remove the pieces of the body using an old stretcher covered with a grey fire blanket.

That night I returned home and denied seeing any of the bomb or its aftermath to my mother. I ate quickly and retired to my room to watch the streets below from the window. Many of my neighbours remained outside into the early hours of the morning as the fire brigade, followed by the army, made their way through the streets of my estate.

Despite my mother's resolve for us to remain uninvolved in the war that was being waged on the streets, I was quite interested in the conflict and keen to join in the resistance movement. I was always a mischievous child and by the age of 12 I was sneaking out of the house pretty regularly through the bathroom window. I would go out long after the house had grown quiet and my mother and siblings were asleep and take part in the rioting that had become a nightly affair on the estate. Barcroft Park was a very volatile place and there were frequent bombings and shootings. The IRA had many violent clashes with the army in this area, and I remember playing football and being knocked off my feet by the force of a bomb which the IRA had detonated several streets below. There were cars and lorries hijacked and burnt out nightly, and sometimes I would stay out in the chaos into the early hours of the morning before sneaking back into my bedroom to pretend I was asleep.

Not even my siblings were aware of my nightly escapes and I did a good job of deceiving my mother. It was strange, because most of the adults around me did not work and many would remain outside on the streets until the early hours of the morning. None seemed to notice my presence or that of the other young people; they were so caught up in the nightly struggles that we could pass by without detection. In hindsight it was such an unusual way to grow up, but at the time it all seemed normal. Unemployment was rife in our area and people were really disenfranchised. Most of my neighbours had nothing to lose and thus rioting and resistance became a normal pastime.

Every summer on the night of 8 August, men and women throughout the estate would go from street to street, banging bin lids on the ground, and would light a giant bonfire in the fields around the estate. This was done to honour those who were interned by the British on 9 August 1971. This night always led to rioting and clashes with the army. There would usually be hijackings, and buses and cars would be used to block off the estate. My mother made special efforts to keep us away from the troubles on this date but for my friends and me it was a highlight of the summer.

As a very young boy I participated in the events around me without ever really knowing what we were fighting for. But once I got older I understood the bitterness of my community. When I was 12 and started secondary school at St Joseph's, in Newry, I remember being stopped and searched by members of the British army. Looking back, the 'men' who were interviewing us were only teenagers themselves, but these soldiers did their best to intimidate and terrorise us. There were three of us making our way home from school when the soldiers approached us with their guns drawn. We were made to stand on our tip-toes with our hands against the wall extended above our heads. They spread our legs with kicks from their boots and asked us questions about local residents. They made vile comments about our sisters and mothers and threatened to shoot us as they held their guns to our backs. Despite our anger, all of us knew that the soldiers could be dangerous, so none of us dared to speak back. Once they realised we had nothing to give them they left, and from that moment on I was a changed person.

As I grew older I was more aware of the soldiers' activities in Barcroft and the surrounding areas. My friends and I would hang around together in the fields above the narrow streets of the estate, and on several occasions we saw the army breaking down our neighbours' doors and forcing families onto the road whilst they searched through all of their belongings. One Sunday after Mass when I was about 14 years old, I was coming up the hill from the Dominican Church into Barcroft when I saw a few local lads with rifles. I met some of my friends in the fields and we followed behind the boys to see what they were going to do. After a short while we got bored with following the fellas and began to head back up towards home. As we were walking, the sound of gunfire stopped us in our tracks. We all dropped down so we could not see what was happening, but later that day I found out that two military policeman had been killed. Those were normal days in the neighbourhood.

I remember quite vividly the summer of 1981, when the hunger strikes were taking place in Long Kesh Prison. Barcroft Park was intensely violent during those months. I was at school one day and it was nearly time to go home when we heard a loud bang coming from the hill above the estate. The teachers all raced to the windows to see what had happened. They quickly determined that it would be safest to remain in school, so classes continued on until the usual time. Once the bell rang at the end of the day, my friends and I bolted for the doors. We knew that something big had happened. The sky was filled with thick clouds of smoke and there were helicopters and the sound of sirens everywhere. When we finally reached the fields near Correnshigo, the area above Barcroft Park, it was entirely cordoned off by soldiers. We made every attempt to see beyond them but we could not ascertain what had happened. However, the air had a distinctive smell and acrid smoke was still billowing.

We decided to make our way through the fields, where we met up with other boys from the neighbourhood. One of them led us to the sprickly begs to show us the wheel of a Saracen armoured vehicle that he had found in the tall grass. When we were there one of my friends found a piece of a black leather glove with a finger still in it. We stayed in the fields for hours, searching for debris and hoping to find a gun or weapon that might have survived the blast. By then the rumours had reached us and before I went home for my dinner that night, I knew that the IRA had blown up an army Saracen with five British soldiers in it on the Chancellor's Road. They were all killed instantly.

The next day we all got up early, and before we went to school we went back to investigate the scene. The British soldiers had left the area in the night and taken the remains of the charred vehicle with them. However, a crater the size of Newry Swimming Pool was left behind. It was difficult to make it to school on time as we all wanted to search the area further, but we knew that our teacher would not be forgiving.

Despite all of the chaos around us, my friends and I also did regular adolescent things. Our secondary school, St Joseph's, was on the Armagh Road, a two-mile walk from Barcroft Park. At the time St Joseph's was primarily for those who had failed their 11-plus exams and were not bound for university. There were quite a few of us from the estate going to school there and we all made the walk together in the mornings. It usually took us a while to get there as a result of all the distractions along the way. St Joseph's was an all-boys' school and our walks gave us the best opportunity to see the girls who studied nearby. Many a morning the lads from Barcroft could be found chatting up the nice young ladies of Sacred Heart Grammar, St Mary's School or Our Lady's Grammar.

I was always a shy young man when it came to girls. I was more interested in sports and mischief than I was in having a girlfriend. However, lots of the fellas spent hours trying to get girls to go out with them, and often made plans to meet up after school in the hopes of getting a kiss—or more, if they were really lucky! It was tough for the boys from St Joseph's because many of the young ladies in the area had been warned that we were trouble, and there was a negative stigma attached to the school. But even this did not prevent some of the more persuasive fellas from finding a girl!

I was never a great student and, despite all the extra help I received in primary school, I struggled to concentrate during my lessons. In hindsight I displayed a lot of the characteristics of ADHD but in those days conditions like this were totally unknown. Most of my teachers just labelled me as thick or uninterested. As a result of my academic difficulties, my friends and I were often disruptive and spent quite a bit of time in trouble. Two of my closest friends in secondary school were met in detention, Anthony 'Bubbles' Sloan and Mark 'Ernie' Devlin.

In one particular incident, our music and science teachers had slapped Bubbles and me during lessons, so in our dinner break we decided to seek revenge. In those days teachers still ruled the school with an iron fist, and corporal punishment was the order of the day. They were encouraged to discipline us with a leather strap or a wooden cane. Many of the teachers were Christian Brothers and they brought a staunch form of religious retribution into the classroom. Misbehaviour resulted in six lashes to the palm of the hand.

After a particularly violent lashing from both the music and science teachers for separate incidents, 'Bubbles' and I decided that we would teach them a lesson. We stole a salt-shaker from the canteen and threw it through the glass window in the music room. Then we ran up the stairs and kicked in the science teacher's door. When we were done we ran back down the stairs and into the canteen and acted as if nothing had ever happened. We were questioned at length by the principal but never admitted to anything. We got away without a lashing, as our guilt could not be proven, but by then lashings no longer frightened me.

Myself and the other lads at school used to warm our hands on the radiator, especially during the cold months, when we knew a lashing was coming. This seemed to soften the impact but it did nothing for the pain. I distinctly remember the first time I was hit in primary school and it brought me to tears. It was very humiliating and my teacher seemed to relish it. So from that point on I learned to bite my lip and choke back my tears. I didn't do this to look strong in front of the other boys but to take away the satisfaction that tears gave the teachers. This was my first lesson in defiance.

The first time that I 'bunked off' school was around this time as well. It was coming up to Hallowe'en and some of my older friends decided to go to the quarries at the back of the dam instead of going to class. I was outside the school when I heard their plan, and they let me come along even though I was younger. In those days it was easy to get caught 'bunking off', as adults in the town would always report seeing boys in their uniform during usual school hours. In an effort to hide what school we went to, we took off our neckties and zipped our overcoats over the top of our blazers. I stashed my satchel in the school before I left and this later turned out to be a life-saving decision.

When we left the school we walked into the town and came across some military police. We immediately ducked up into the flats on Water Street and launched an attack against them. As we hid between the entrances, we threw stones down at the soldiers. This led to a chase with the soldiers that took us through the grounds of The Abbey School and up into the quarries. As we passed through the school grounds, teachers in the courtyard also began to give chase. By the time we hit the fields below the quarries, we had several adults on our tails. Although we ran as a group, we were really each scrambling to save ourselves. We jumped over fences and fell in the dirt, but we finally made it to the safety of the vacant quarries and by then all of the soldiers and teachers had long given up.

We collapsed onto the ground and laughed and panted. It was a total adrenalin rush and now that we felt safe, we relived the excitement of it with each other. It was then that one of the older lads decided to make a fire. He told all of us that we would have to use our books and school papers to get it started. I realised then with great relief that I had nothing with me and thus I was spared the horrible lashing that I would have received both in school and at home if I had arrived back with no books. Once the fire was burning away, the oldest boy decided to throw my neighbour, Seán McGivern, into the water. Seán had all of his clothes on, but was pushed in before he had a chance to react. When he finally scrambled out he huddled close to the fire and tried in vain to dry off. I realised then that they were going to come for me next, so I scrambled up the rocks. Luckily they didn't get me, but I could hear another boy hitting the water with a giant splash as I made my escape.

After several more hours messing about up at the quarry, we realised that it was beginning to get dark. We had lost track of time, and it was well after the usual time that we all arrived home from school. As we were walking back towards home I got a terrible feeling in my stomach. I looked at Seán and realised that we were in absolute tatters. My shoes were caked in mud and my trousers were ripped from crossing over the top of a barbed wire fence. Seán was still wet and all of his books were burnt. We tried to be brave, but by the time we reached the top of our street we had both gone quiet and I could tell that he was sick with fear as well.

When I arrived in the house, my mother was livid. She demanded to know where I had been and why I was in such a state. I quickly told as many lies as I could think of and could only thank God that I still had my books. Throughout my mother's interrogation I thought of poor Seán and how much trouble he would be in. In those days schoolbooks were free, but you only got one set. I can't even fathom his parents' anger at having to purchase a replacement set for him. Luckily I escaped with only a stern telling-off. The next morning I had to get a friend to write a note from my mother saying that I had been off sick, and as I nervously handed it in to my teacher, I resolved never to bunk off school again. The stress of the day was too much and school wasn't that bad anyways!

Although I struggled with the academics in class, I loved being with my friends and participating in athletics. I also found great discipline and confidence in boxing. When I was seven I joined the Barcroft Community Boxing Club. My mother was a member of the Barcroft Committee and she thought boxing might be a good outlet for me. I really enjoyed fighting in the ring and greatly admired the boxing coach, Tommy Jones. Ironically, Tommy was an ex-British soldier who had fought in the Second World War. Despite his affiliations, he was well respected in the community and lived safely in Barcroft throughout even the worst years of the Troubles. Tommy was a true inspiration to me. He was a very solid man with a tough character but he was also kind and genuinely cared about the local kids. After I lost my own father at such a young age, Tommy became a father figure for me. He helped me to develop strength and self-assurance, both inside the ring and out.

The other benefit to boxing in the club was travelling. My mother did not drive and we had very little money so we rarely travelled further than the centre of Newry. However, with the club we travelled all over the North and sometimes across the border into Dundalk. Although the places we went were not very far from home, they seemed like a world away to me. The opportunities to get away from my neighbourhood with all of the good friends that I made within the club gave me the motivation to train hard and by the age of 10 I was a fairly competent boxer, winning more fights than I lost.

It was at this age that I gained the nickname that would stick with me for the rest of my life. I was boxing in an outdoor match in the barley field at the back of Barcroft Park when I got into a bit of a scuffle before entering the ring. Myself and another young fella were beating each other up when his mother came over and grabbed me by the ear. She shouted, 'I will banjo you, "Banjo Bannon", if you touch my son.' All of the kids in the area heard her and when it was my turn to fight they all began chanting, 'Banjo'. In the beginning I was embarrassed and remember the blood rushing to my face, leaving me scarlet from ear to ear. Like typical kids, the more I seemed to dislike the nickname, the more my friends used it. However, over time it grew on me and since that day it has been hard to shake.

In addition to all of the training that I did with the club, I also did some fighting at home. When my mother would head out into the town to pick up the groceries or other essentials, my siblings and I would turn the front room of the house into a boxing ring. We moved all the furniture to one side and tied tea towels around our waists with colours to designate which team we were on. It was pretty much an anything-goes fighting arena, where kicks, bites, hair-pulling and punches were all legal. Most often, weapons were not allowed. Although there were four boys in the house, my sister Geraldine almost always won. She was ruthless and a total tomboy and I felt she could have taken on any of the boys in the boxing club without difficulty.

In later years, Geraldine actually proved this to be true. After an incident in the local club where my best friend's older brother insulted my mother, Geraldine knocked him down with a single punch. Ironically, he was a top-class boxer and one of the strongest in the club. She could lift more than most of the fellas at the club's gym and was not afraid of anything. When I was young, it was Geraldine who kept us all in line as she was a force to be reckoned with.

Boxing was a great outlet for me and it not only helped to develop my love for fitness but it also kept me away from one of the biggest problems in my area. By the time I was 14 most of my friends in the estate were smoking and drinking. The older-looking boys would go into the local pub, Fehily Larkins or Nan Rice's, and buy enough Old English cider for all the lads. They would then sneak away up into the fields at the back of Barcroft Community Centre or into the glen to drink themselves rotten. I would always go along with them but I never touched a drop. I watched the boys drink till they were passing out and vomiting all over themselves and wondered what the attraction was. I would sometimes meet them after coming out of the gym and would stay on with them until the conversation turned into complete nonsense.

Once the boys were drunk, they were very brave and trouble usually ensued. There were always fights amongst the lads and stoning the army and RUC was also a regular pastime. Once the drink wore off and the night had passed into the early hours of the morning, we would all return home and my resolve not to touch alcohol would be further cemented.

When I was only nine I went away for the first time as part of a cross-community project. As my mother was on the committee within Barcroft, she and the other members secured grant funding for a few of us to go. We went to a retreat centre in Fivemiletown and we stayed for three weeks. The groups were mixed between male and female, Catholic and Protestant. We did lots of outdoor activities and arts and crafts and we were also taken sightseeing. It was great to get away and meet new people but I was homesick as well. I missed my mother's cooking and the comfort of our house. However, this first trip away broadened my horizons enormously. I got along well with the young Protestant girls and boys and for the first time I realised we weren't that different after all. They too came from socially and economically marginalised backgrounds and many of our experiences were exactly the same.

When I returned home to Barcroft my friends were jealous of my time away and I looked forward to going again the following summer. Throughout the following years I continued to participate in youth club activities. My two sisters, Geraldine and Angeline, had become involved with youth work and thus I was able to go to Shannaghmore and Killowen Outdoor Education Centres to participate in climbing, canoeing and other pursuits. I hugely enjoyed my time away at these centres and was especially fond of escaping into the hills. From these first experiences, I knew that my life would take a different path from many of my friends. Few of them were interested in leaving Barcroft Park. Most hoped for nothing more than an easy job which paid the bills, but I had a love for adventure and hoped to see the world.

Despite our differences, I was fiercely loyal to my friends and had many great experiences with them. There were the boys from the boxing club, like 'Midge' McAllister, 'D' McEvoy and Tommy Jones Jnr, and my friends Mortz, Dusty, Lougho, Kimmo, Clenny, Charlie, Mickey Jo, Raymie, Harpo and Darren, who I spent many a night rioting with. My next-door neighbours, the McGivern family, were also very close to me. In our youth we fought each other on countless occasions but were also great friends. At one stage, I broke my knuckle on Thomas's head when we were in the midst of battle. I called him 'the bull' growing up because he was a stocky fella and would go right through you in a fight. Over the years, we shared many adventures with each other and his brothers, Seán and Eamon. There were football games in the barley field in Barcroft every week and we would all attend and have a great laugh putting together teams and competing throughout the day. Some of the boys would play half drunk but everyone put in 100% and the victors of a match would celebrate for weeks.

My brother Colum was a great footballer. He was faster than almost all the other boys and he was always a great addition to a team. He was a quiet fella, but he played with great determination and everyone always picked him first for their side. I was the opposite. When the boys lined up to be selected I was nearly always the last to be picked. Although I was never good at football, I could get by as a goal-keeper. This was also true of my time playing for the Shamrocks Gaelic Football Club in Newry. However, in this sport I was a bit too small to play goal-keeper and thus my career was short-lived.

I also tried my hand at hurling after my neighbour Eamon McGivern signed me up for the Killeavy team. I wasn't too bad at it but there were a few incidents where my hurley was used as a weapon in fights during practice and the coach was not impressed by this. This brought my career as a hurler to an abrupt end, but it did not diminish my mother's pride in my participation. She was a keen supporter of the Killeavy team as her father had once played for them.

My brothers Eamon and Noel were not really into sports. Eamon was always a quiet lad and mostly kept to himself. However, he played a bit of Gaelic football and rugby at school and enjoyed these experiences. Eamon's real passion was cars, and when I was young he decided that he would become the first person in our house to learn to drive. He signed up for driving lessons with a local instructor and eagerly awaited his first time behind the wheel. However, on the day of his first lesson the weather conditions were terrible. The instructor drove first to help Eamon get a feel for the car, and when it was Eamon's turn to have a go the instructor pulled over and Eamon opened the door. Just as the car door swung open there was a terribly strong gust of wind and the door was ripped right off its hinges. Eamon stood frozen as the car door was laid flat out on the ground next to him. He never took another lesson after that and to this day he has never driven a car!

Noel and I did not spend a great deal of time together growing up as he moved to my maternal grandmother's farm when I was only young. However, we saw each other once a week, as we would visit him and my granny every Sunday after Mass without fail. It is strange now to think of siblings growing up apart or with such different lives but at the time many other families were living in similar circumstances. My mother was struggling financially to feed and house all six children in a three-bedroom house, and my granny was alone and in need of someone to work the farm, so it worked out well for everyone. I know that Noel probably found it difficult to be away from our mother and his siblings but he loved my granny dearly and thrived at her house.

Noel was a natural with the hard labour and early hours that farm life required and I remember when we would go up to visit he would take us on walks over the fields and to another farm several miles away, where he worked as a part-time labourer. When it was time to bring the cows in for milking, Noel would put me on their backs and I would ride them in like horses. He taught me a lot about caring for livestock and how to work the land.

My granny's farm was on the Dublin Road on the outskirts of Newry, in a place called Cloughue. We would take the bus from outside the market in Newry to Fathom's Cross and walk the short remaining distance. I will always remember how my mother would buy one and a half tickets for her and me. The bus driver eventually got to know us and sometimes, when the weather was especially poor, he would stop just outside the house for us. In those days neither my family nor my granny had a phone so the weekly visits were a time to catch up on the whole week's events.

Whilst our house in Barcroft was fairly new, my granny's cottage was nearly 200 years old. It had been the family home of the Jacksons for generations and had seen countless births and deaths since its construction. It was a typical Irish stone cottage with one entrance and small windows with sills over two feet deep. The front door was made of solid wood and to lock it there was a drop bar at the back of it. This was an unusual feature in an old cottage, but my grandparents had put it in to protect the family if the RIC or army ever arrived at the door. My grandfather was officially 'on the run' until the time he died. Although the security forces probably knew where to find him in the later years, they did not bother with him in the end.

The ceilings in the cottage were very low and the thick smoke from the open hearth would blur your eyes when you first entered. The cottage always smelt damp and seemed dark even on the brightest days. The white stone wash on the outside was overgrown by honeysuckle and windbush. The house had only two bedrooms and no indoor plumbing. There was an old water pump in the front, which would draw icy water from the deep well. For the toilet you had to trek out into an old long-drop outhouse in the field. It was rustic, to say the least, but my granny loved it there.

I had many of my greatest adventures as a child in this house and the surrounding fields. My granny loved cats and dogs and there were always plenty of animals to play with. I remember that the place always seemed to be overrun with chickens, and have a sad but vivid recollection of a day one summer when we took my granny away for the afternoon. Whilst we were gone, a fox got into her chicken coop and went into a frenzy. When we returned we found all the chickens dead, but only one had been eaten. I could tell it broke my granny's heart. She loved animals and hated to see the chickens killed so senselessly.

A few times I stayed the night at my granny's when Noel was away, so that she wasn't left on her own. I remember being afraid to go out to the toilet at night and would wait inside until I felt like I would burst before finally heading out into the fields. Even then, I stayed very close to the cottage, as the land was unimaginably dark, and I worried about what lurked in the shadows. My grandmother and mother were both very superstitious women and they would tell us old stories of ghosts and banshees. They also greatly feared the devil and would tell tales of him being spotted on the roads below the house and in the hills surrounding the cottage. I was not very brave as a boy and spent most of the night awake on the occasions that I stayed with my grandmother.

As I grew older I came to appreciate the peace and serenity of the cottage. I was always particularly fond of a tree at the front of the garden. It was a massive oak tree with huge branches and a knotted, bumpy trunk. I would climb as high on the branches as I could manage and then challenge myself to get back down. It was my first real exercise in overcoming a fear of heights. My grandmother remained in the cottage until the time she died, at 94 years of age. She was a very important part of our family and we all loved and missed her dearly.

After my grandmother died and as we all grew older, my family and I spent more time apart. My sisters were both married by then and my three brothers all eventually emigrated to various countries. Eamon went to Canada to look for work, whilst Noel and Colum headed to England, and then Colum moved on to Holland. The North's unemployment rates were soaring and politically and socially it was worse than ever. In my younger years it was still relatively easy to get by on the limited social benefit payments that we received, but as we all grew older and the cost of living went up my mother desperately needed wages to come into the house. My brothers always sent money home to my mother. We would wait excitedly to hear from them by letter or the occasional phone calls to the house of our neighbour, Mrs Mathew.

With my brothers away and my time at St Joseph's drawing to an end, I began spending more time in the mountains and doing outdoor pursuits. At this stage, I was very involved in the Barcroft Youth Club activities and took advantage of any opportunity to get away. A young man named Dermie Russell from Rostrevor had taken over the role of warden for the club and was skilled at engaging the young people. I really enjoyed spending time with him as he was into physical fitness and body-building. We all admired his toned physique and his great personality. He did a lot for the club and played an important role in encouraging me to pursue outdoor education.

At around 15 years of age I began to attend the 'unemployed club' in Barcroft, which was run in conjunction with the youth club. They would take the young men who attended on trips to Rostrevor, Warrenpoint and Craigavon to go water skiing, pier jumping and canoeing. We also went rock-climbing and to the mountains for hill-walking. At this stage my sister Angeline was a voluntary youth worker in the club and she further encouraged my participation. These trips gave me great respite from the chaos of the world around me and I developed a real fondness for the beauty of this escape.

Unfortunately, that same year I suffered one of the greatest tragedies of my life. A good friend of mine, Brendan 'Cindy' Watters, was killed when a bomb he was carrying exploded prematurely. Cindy and I had met each other in the 'unemployed club' and immediately became close friends. He was a lot older than me but we had many things in common. He was very popular with the ladies and had a great sense of humour. All of the boys in the club liked to be around 'Cindy' as his personality really drew people in. He also had a passion for motorbikes and loved getting away on trips with the club. Unbeknownst to his friends, Cindy was also very interested in politics and had become involved with the IRA.

I remember the day that Cindy was killed with perfect clarity; it was 8 August 1984. I had seen him late in the afternoon on a 'silver dream' motorbike going through the streets of Barcroft. He stopped and offered to take me for a spin. We raced up and down the hill and then he gave some of the other boys a go. After I left him, I continued on down the street to meet up with some other friends and to make plans for the evening. As it was bonfire night, I knew that there would be a lot of action in the neighbourhood that night.

Cindy had a sister who lived on the third street of Barcroft Park with her husband, and sadly her house would be the site of Cindy's death. After I left Cindy that evening he had been involved in an IRA operation to attack the RUC. He was given a nail bomb to carry in a satchel, which he was meant to throw at an RUC Land Rover when it opened its doors. However, the operation was compromised when the RUC and soldiers descended upon the estate on foot through the fields rather than in Land Rover vehicles. As Brendan did not want to be caught carrying the bomb, he quickly hid with it at his sister's house. When he entered the residence, his sister and her husband had no idea that he was involved with the IRA and no indication that anything was wrong.

When Cindy arrived at the house, his nephews had just gone to bed after having a bath. In those days the water was heated through a fire in the main sitting room and Cindy had not anticipated the heat that he would encounter. The fire in the sitting room caused the gelignite in the bomb to weep, making it fragile and intensely volatile. As the bomb began to make a whistling sound, Cindy quickly realised the danger they were in and advised his sister and husband to stay back whilst he ran towards the door with the device. He had made it as far as the hallway when the bomb went off. He quickly threw himself on top of the satchel to protect his family.

Cindy's abdomen took the full impact of the blast and although he lived for a short while after the explosion, it was quickly apparent that he would not survive his injuries. I was at home when I heard an explosion and ran out to see what had happened. I could see smoke above Cindy's sister's house and I heard chaos on the street. I raced down to find Cindy lying in the entrance to his sister's house. His sister and brother-in-law were with him and there were crowds of people in the street, staring on in shock and disbelief. I didn't know what to do and I couldn't believe what I was seeing. There was blood and metal everywhere and suddenly everything became a total blur. I stood by Cindy in a haze as the ambulance came and the paramedics tried to resuscitate him. He kept asking us for help, and I think in those last moments he knew he was going to die.

Helicopters soon began to buzz overhead and all of my friends had descended on the scene. I think that Cindy was still conscious when he was finally taken away but I knew that he did not have very long to live and that this would be the last time I would ever see him.

Cindy died that night in the hospital. The RUC and the army arrived on the scene quickly after Cindy was taken away and my friends and I all returned home so that we would not be taken in for questioning. I did not sleep at all that night. It was tough to be alone with my thoughts and I found my anger and sadness overpowering. I lay awake and tried to block out the images of Cindy in his final moments that kept coming into my head. The next morning I was out on the streets with my friends when an RUC Land Rover passed us with a 'Sindy' doll hanging from the grille that covered the window. The soldiers and police took great pleasure in Cindy's death and their celebrations sickened me.

Cindy's funeral was one of the biggest I have ever seen. He was given a full military burial with a volley of shots over his coffin at his home in Derrybeg. Myself and all of the other boys from Barcroft were there to pay our final respects to a great friend. After Cindy died we were astonished to learn the extent of his involvement with the resistance movement. He never spoke publicly about being in the IRA and his family had no idea until the time of his death.

The day after Cindy's funeral my mother took me away to Cranfield Beach in County Down, where we stayed in a caravan for a week. I am sure it was tough for her to afford this trip but she worried constantly about the number of boys becoming caught up in the Troubles and feared that I would be next. During that time I thought a lot about my life and all of the carnage that I had witnessed, but I also thought about the times that Cindy and I had spent away on the club trips, swimming in the sea and hiking in the mountains. After that tragic summer I made every effort to visit the Mourne Mountains and the hills around South Armagh as frequently as possible. I spent a lot of time alone on these walks and thought about my friend often. I loved the solitude of the hills and the strength and confidence that my time in the wilds gave me. It was during that year that I realised mountains would play a pivotal role in my life.

Chapter 2 ∾

DISCOVERY IN THE MOUNTAINS

'The adventure is in the journey, not the destination.'
UNKNOWN

When I was 14 years of age I borrowed my brother Colum's boots and took the first bus of the morning from Newry to Newcastle. I had passed through Newcastle before on one of Barcroft's community youth trips and was vaguely familiar with the area. When I got off the bus at the station in Newcastle the air was cool and the morning dew still glistened on the grass in the fields below Slieve Donard. There were low clouds and a mist around the summits of the higher Mournes, but I knew that as the day progressed the cloud would lift and it would become fine and dry. I set off with my rucksack strapped to my back. I was carrying an extra sweater with a hat and gloves as well as my lunch and a heavy flask. I was wearing an old pair of corduroy trousers and a thin, plastic-lined jacket. I had no map or compass and no experience in the mountains on my own, but I was determined to make it to the top of Slieve Donard.

A few weeks earlier I had learned in school that Slieve Donard was the highest mountain in the north of Ireland and this inspired me to climb it. I had mentioned casually to my mother the day before I set off on this big adventure that I was going to Newcastle to climb, and she dismissed my comment as a childish notion. However, my determination was steadfast and as I began the rocky hike through the lower forests on the mountain, I was confident in my abilities. At that time, there were no other hikers or tourists around on the mountain, so I was alone on my ascent. I was comforted in my solitude by the stark beauty all around me and by the noise of the meadow pipits that circled low overhead. I remember the cool breeze blowing through the branches of the pine trees and the smell of damp soil. When I reached the clearing at the top of the forest, I stopped for a rest and was overcome by the beautiful views. The sea was directly behind me and there were uninterrupted views of blue waves with white crests crashing into the shore. I drank from the stream that flowed down from the upper slopes and watched as the water raced over the rocks and dropped towards the tree line below. From here, it was a clear path to the col below the summit, where I met the famous Mourne Wall.

I followed the old dry rock wall right to the top of Donard and sat down next to the stone hut marking the summit to admire the scenery around me. I had had no idea how vast the Mourne Mountains were, but now I could see the rocky hills extending for miles. I had originally planned to hike to the summit and back down into Newcastle, where I would take the bus home, but once I saw the peaks that extended to Rostrevor, I was inspired to continue on my journey straight through the mountains.

I made my way back down to the col, where I met an old farmer. He was wearing a yellow plastic raincoat, similar to my own, which was tied with twine over tweed trousers and a pair of ancient-looking wellies. He was surprised to see me up there on my own. I told him of my plan to hike to Rostrevor and he advised me to follow the wall all the way along the Brandy Pad until I reached Kilbroney Forest in Rostrevor. There was one road to cross and it was a simple journey to navigate. His most important advice was to keep the wall in front of me at all times. With his directions in mind, I set off on the long hike through the Mournes.

I was so excited at points that I was running. My ambitions of a great adventure were being fulfilled beyond the extent that I had imagined. I could see myself that night at dinner. I would relive the trip to my mother and siblings and couldn't wait for the shocked expressions on their faces. I dreamt of telling them the distances that I had travelled and how I had done it all alone. The afternoon was warm and dry and I enjoyed every moment of my solitary hike. Although I saw some other hikers and farmers in the distance along the way, I never crossed paths with another person directly. I loved the feeling of remoteness and spent a lot of the walk dreaming that I was in a distant mountain range, surviving on my own against the elements. I envisioned myself in a desert or on a mountaintop covered in snow and I let my imagination run wild.

By the time I reached the Deer's Meadow and the point along the route where you cross over a road, my legs were tired and my feet a bit sore, but my daydreams kept me going. As the afternoon passed into early evening I finally arrived in Rostrevor and could no longer fight my exhaustion.

The trip had been longer than I had expected and towards the end of the hike I wondered if I would ever make it into Rostrevor in time for the last bus home. I was beginning to worry that I would arrive back to Newry very late and be in trouble with my mother. However, once I made it onto the main road into the village, I was able to hitch a lift and made it home in time to escape a telling-off. The man who drove me into the town asked where I had come from and when I told him of my adventure, he laughed and looked at me with scepticism. I could tell he didn't believe a word of my story and at that point I knew that no one would truly believe what I had achieved.

When I finally arrived home, my mother asked where I had been for such a long time and I just laughed and said that she would never believe me if I told her. After a massive dinner, I retired to bed that night and dreamt of the peaks throughout the world where I would climb. I had no idea where the world's highest mountain was located at that time but before I fell asleep I promised myself that I would be the first man from Ireland to climb it. My thirst for adventure was now insatiable.

Over the following year I was involved with a program run through Shannaghmore Outdoor Education Centre in Newcastle. It was a course for aspiring mountaineers where we learned all of the basics of mountaineering. It was a mixed programme comprising Catholic and Protestant and male and female participants. One weekend every month we were taken to the Mourne Mountains, where we were taught the essentials of rope work, camp craft, navigation, hill-walking and equipment use. One of these weekends in particular stands out in my memory. It was the middle of winter and the Mournes were covered in snow and ice. The instructors took us up through the gullies, into Cove Cave and onto the upper cove. We completed this ascent in crampons and used a single ice axe each. This was my first experience with winter mountaineering and it definitely inspired me to continue on in my mountain training. Whilst some of the young people in our group were frightened during the climb, I welcomed the difficult physical nature and was not afraid of the dangers.

After nearly nine months in the course, we were each required to complete an expedition component in order to graduate. This section was conducted over Easter week in Connemara, in the west of Ireland. It was here that I completed my first leading rock-climb. I led Andy Carden, who was my instructor at Shannaghmore, on a cliff ascent. It was a previously unclimbed route and, since that day, it has been named after me. This gave me tremendous confidence and by the end of the week I knew that I would not only pass the course, but would go on to pursue even greater challenges.

After I completed the mountaineering course in Connemara, I returned home to Barcroft a more self-assured young man. My first goal upon return was to climb in the quarry on Camlough Mountain and to show all my friends my new skills. I was excited to introduce them to rock-climbing and mountaineering and led a group of boys on a hill-walk in the area. As a result of my success on the course, Andy Carden approached me about bursary grants that were available for young people to go on a three-week Outward Bound course in Loch Eil, Scotland. The application procedures were stringent and the applicant was required to undergo a lengthy interview with a board before they could be accepted. I was immediately interested in applying, but I was anxious about the interview. However, both Andy and Dermie Russell encouraged me through the process, and in the end myself and one other boy from the North were accepted.

Within a few months, I set off for Scotland and the Outward Bound course. It was the first time I had ever travelled any real distance alone and I was apprehensive. I took the bus to Belfast and walked out to the docks, as I could not afford the taxi across town. I took the ferry over to Scotland and then got on a train to Glasgow. As I got off the train in Central Station, a young man who I had noticed on the ferry and the train approached me. He and I were both wearing rucksacks and when he saw my name tag, he realised that I was the other Northerner who was on the course with him. John Kennedy ('Jacko', as we called him) and I got along well straight away. He was from Lurgan and was working as a voluntary instructor at Shannaghmore, where I had attended my course. He was very interested in outdoor pursuits as well and had spent a good deal of time training in the Mournes.

After our meeting, John and I travelled together up to Loch Eil. I remember our first night at the Outward Bound centre very well. It was late summer and the sky was black and cloudy. As we bunked down for the night, the sound of thunder rolled in off the hills and I experienced my first real thunder and lightning storm. It seemed to last for hours and bright white flashes rained down close around us. The building itself was an old Scottish gentry house and it felt haunted that night. Although I was 16 years of age, I felt a bit lonely and frightened as I tried to get to sleep.

The following day we began our training. The young people who were involved in the course came from all over England, Scotland, Wales, Ireland and Holland. Most of them came from a military training background and were preparing for the armed forces. All of the young people were divided into clans, and John and I were put into separate groups.

My clan was named the McPhersons. There were 12 of us in the group and we were all male. We were told that we would spend the remainder of the three weeks living and working together. Our daily routine involved rising at 6 a.m. for a run and a swim in the loch, followed by breakfast. After breakfast, we would be given different tasks to complete throughout the day. These tasks included team-building and problem-solving as well as rock-climbing, sea kayaking, white water kayaking, wet bouldering, hill-walking and navigation. We were also taught first aid and rescue procedures. As my time in Scotland progressed, I became more convinced that my future career was in outdoor pursuits. I excelled in all of the disciplines and thrived within the group. I admired the instructors and could see that they were all dedicated to their work.

As a component of the Outward Bound course, all of the clans had to complete a weekly expedition into the hills and on the loch. The length of time you were away on these expeditions increased progressively with each week, so that in our final week at the camp we were expected to complete a four-day trip on our own. During the expeditions, clans would have to work together as a team under their own initiative and without adult guidance. The groups were shadowed by instructors, but these leaders were not visible and did not actively participate in the process. My clan was fortunate because all of us worked well together and dissent within the group was minimal. However, like most of the other clans, there were a lot of chiefs and very few Indians.

For our final expedition we set out into the hills around Loch Eil and established a camp for the night. We had been assigned several tasks to complete in order to pass the Outward Bound course and we were pleased with our progress thus far. The following day passed without difficulty and by the third day we were well on our way to completing our final expedition and looking forward to graduating from the course and returning home. That morning we set out on a walk across a high ridge in the Scottish hills and as we were making a traverse, one member of the clan, named Richard, tripped over on the scree slope. I remember hearing him fall and I looked back to see what was happening. As I turned my head I could see him sliding and realised that although he had originally fallen forwards he had then somehow rolled onto his back. He was wearing a metal-framed rucksack and it acted like a sleigh, pulling him straight off the ledge. Myself and the other boys stared in horror and disbelief as Richard plunged over the edge and out of sight. There was total silence as he disappeared from view. We were all frozen with shock and fear but within seconds everyone began descending towards where he had disappeared to look for him.

At this stage the instructor who was shadowing us emerged and grouped all of us together to lead us off the ridge. We were taken to a safe place and told not to move, whilst the instructor went back to try to find Richard. I could tell by the instructor's face that he was very worried, but none of us knew what we could do to help. I remember as we sat waiting some of the boys became hysterical. They were worried that Richard could be seriously injured or could have even been killed. I tried to talk to the others and keep their spirits high whilst we waited, but over time I too began to think the worst.

After what felt like hours, our instructor finally returned and silently led us down to a mini-bus which was waiting to collect us. Several of the boys were questioning the instructor about what had happened to Richard, but he told us very little. He added that we would be updated on his condition when we arrived back at the centre.

The return journey passed in a haze and everyone sat silent and stunned in the bus as the realisation that Richard's injuries must have been very serious set in. When we arrived at the centre we were taken in to a large room with most of the programme's staff and directors. They told us that Richard's injuries had been fatal. The RAF had tried to stage a rescue but he had died instantly and there was nothing they could do to save him. Everyone was numb and just listened with disbelief. When it was over, we all returned to our bunks. That night there was meant to be a céilí in the camp as a celebration of the course's completion, but this was cancelled and grief counsellors met with each of us instead.

The next day, letters were sent from Outward Bound to each of our families, telling them what had happened. We arranged in our final days there to place a cairn in the grounds of Loch Eil Outward Bound Centre commemorating Richard's life, and when our time in Scotland was complete, John and I set off on the journey home. Many of the boys and girls who we met on the course were deeply saddened by Richard's death and I got the sense that some of them would never return to the hills again. Although the course had come to a tragic end, I found great inspiration in what we had achieved and I personally felt no fear about returning to the mountains.

I think that Richard's accident was very traumatic for many of the young people on the course because it was their first experience with death, but after Cindy's death one year earlier, I was numb to the pain of losing friends. When Cindy died, I was very emotional and angry but in the long year since he had passed away, I had become hardened. I realised then how different my background was to that of most other young people my age. Growing up in Barcroft had exposed me to a lot of violence and carnage and I was detached from the emotional side of loss.

When I returned home my mother had received the letter from Outward Bound and she was very concerned about the impact that this tragedy would have on me. I think that she expected a lot of grief or fear and was relieved to see that this tragedy had not changed me in any way and that I was still committed to climbing in the mountains.

Over the following year, 1986, I continued my studies in mechanical engineering at Newry Technical College and did a placement at

Milbrook Tool and Gauge. I also remained active in boxing and I won a few national titles during that time. I was chosen to box in England for the first time and travelled with an Irish Select team to Stoke-on-Trent, where I boxed in a welter-weight match. All the while I persisted with the hill-walking and climbing and still made frequent solo journeys to the Mourne Mountains. My participation in youth club activities continued as well and I became a member of the Newry and Mourne Youth Council. I was elected to represent Barcroft Park and as a result of this, I was sent on an exchange program to Bavaria in Germany with students from all over the Southern Education Library Board area.

The 10-day trip took us to Munich and on to the lovely village of Berchtesgaden, where Hitler famously kept his holiday cottage in the mountains, known as the Eagle's Nest. Whilst we were there we did a lot of hiking and hill-walking and spent time getting to know the German exchange students.

It was on this trip that I met my first girlfriend, Sabina Harms. We met on one of the hikes into the German/Austrian mountains and we hit it off straight away. She was a student from Erlangen in West Germany and she spoke excellent English. Her mother was a keen rock-climber and Sabina enjoyed rock-climbing and hill-walking as well. She had blonde hair and blue eyes and I remember being attracted to her straight away. As I got to know her better, I realised that she was very well educated and worldly. She had a keen interest in politics and was a left-wing socialist. She had very progressive views and was empathetic towards the situation in the north of Ireland. At the time Germany was still divided into two countries, and although Sabina lived in the privileged West, she was also eager for the reunification of her nation.

The trip was designed to introduce the Irish students to German culture in all its forms. We went sightseeing, learned a bit of the language, were educated in their political systems and were exposed to song and dance. At the completion of the 10 days, the German students returned to Ireland with us and spent 10 days in our country. We were based out of Shannaghmore and went sightseeing and hiking as well as attending concerts and dances. Sabina and I spent much of the trip together and by the time the exchange came to an end, I had arranged to go back to see her the following summer in Germany.

Over the following months, Sabina and I wrote to each other often and I continued in my studies and began a one-year 'stage one' mountaineering leadership course. I was the youngest student in the programme. For the expedition component of this course we travelled to Scotland. Being back in Scotland reminded me of my time at Outward Bound and I thought of how Richard had tragically lost his life at such a young age. Despite my memories of that day, I did very well with the course and completed a winter ascent in the Highland Monroes. It was my first true experience in snow craft and winter mountaineering.

Once the course was over, I returned to Germany to see Sabina again. I stayed with her family in Erlangen, near Nüremberg, and we went rock-climbing on the limestone cliffs with her mother and sightseeing throughout the country. I was there for a total of 10 days and when it was time to leave, Sabina and I were already arranging our next meeting. She planned to visit me in Ireland later on that year. I returned home to my studies and looked forward to seeing her again.

As the months passed, the political and social situation in Ireland continued to deteriorate. It was 1987 and the Republican movement's fight against the British occupation was as strong as ever. I remember the spring being particularly volatile. The RUC and army presence was at an all-time high on the streets of Newry and there were frequent clashes in Barcroft Park. One day, as I was driving my mother and sister home from the visiting the graveyard, the army stopped us. The soldiers made all of us get out of the car and, despite the fact that Geraldine was heavily pregnant at the time, they began to give us abuse. They called us Fenians and one of them took my photograph, which he told my mother he would send to a Loyalist death squad. They called my sister a 'slag' and when I could no longer stand their antics, I lashed out at the soldier who had taken my photo, smashing his camera to the ground. The soldier responded to this by swinging at me with the butt of his rifle. Thankfully, I saw the blow coming and was able to avoid the impact. This led to a bit of a scuffle between myself and the soldier but another patrol landed on the scene shortly after and a senior officer stopped the melée. He allowed us to set off again but I had to comfort my mother for hours afterwards as she found the entire situation very distressing.

Not long after the soldiers stopped me, the army ambushed and killed eight IRA volunteers and one civilian in Loughgall, County Armagh. The social situation felt like it was near total collapse and many of my friends and neighbours were caught up in the struggle.

The country was in turmoil and my dreams of a peaceful, united Ireland seemed further away than ever. I continued to pursue my ambitions in the mountains and enjoyed the quiet serenity of the hills. The mayhem and chaos in the streets of Northern Ireland were overwhelming and the escape of the mountain slopes beckoned to me with every free moment.

As the year drew to an end, I completed my studies in mechanical engineering and began to look for work. A job opportunity became available at Short's Aircraft Factory in Belfast and I went for an interview. I was required to do a variety of tests over a one-week period to see if I was suitable for the job. The day I arrived at the factory I found myself in a completely foreign environment. There were Union Jacks everywhere and the workers' lockers were covered in stickers and patches with British emblems. I knew on that first day that this was not the job for me and I left before the week was out to look for something else.

It was difficult to find paid employment in Catholic areas and thus I decided to pursue further training to enhance my career opportunities. I completed a course at Newry Training Centre in welding and fabricating. After this I went to work at Mor Play Steel, where I was a welder and fitter. I was there for roughly two years and then went onto Public Works Signs, where I remained for several more years.

During this time Sabina and I continued to see each other once every year, when she would come back over to Ireland to visit. However, our long-distance relationship was too difficult to maintain and I eventually met a girl from Newry who I began to date more seriously. Geraldine and I travelled to Spain together with a large group of friends and spent a lot of time travelling around and dancing at the discos.

As the years passed and I grew older, my responsibilities became greater and I was not able to spend as much time in the mountains as I would have liked. However, my love of adventure, hiking and climbing had not diminished and I began to consider more challenging climbs throughout the world. I worked each day as a welder but I was more involved than ever with youth work and was now leading groups on hikes and climbs each weekend. Although it was my day job that paid the bills, I had not given up hope that one day my aspirations would be fulfilled and I would work and travel in the mountains.

Chapter 3 ✑

| THE ACCIDENT

'I find hope in the darkest days, and focus in the brightest. I do not judge the universe.'
HIS HOLINESS THE 14TH DALAI LAMA

In May 1989 I was still working with Public Works Signs. My job as a welder and fabricator paid for my climbing excursions and I enjoyed the work. My primary role was to cut steel for signs and to weld base plates for light poles. I worked long hours but had great workmates and really liked the atmosphere within the factory. We were based in the Greenbank Industrial Estate in Newry and every morning I walked from Barcroft Park across town to work.

PWS was a large operation which manufactured steel signs and posts for roads and businesses throughout the country. There were roughly eight of us working together on the floor and we had a foreman who oversaw the production line. It was a family-run business and the father, Tom, was the most senior director in the company, with his two sons and one further man running the daily operations. Most of the work that we did was loaded up onto lorries with forklifts on site and then transported out of the factory by another team of men.

On the morning of 10 May my day began like any other. I arrived at work and got into my welding gear. I spent the morning working as usual and shortly after 12.30 I left the floor to bring in some poles from behind the factory. As I was walking along, a forklift passed beside me. Suddenly, as I stepped closer to the door, the machine accidentally veered onto my foot. I was wearing steel-toe-capped boots, which saved the bones in my foot from being crushed outright, but I could feel the weight of the machine upon me and I was immediately aware how serious this was. I screamed as loudly as possible but the driver could not hear me. Suddenly everything seemed like it was in slow motion and although I could hear my fellow workmates shouting at the driver to stop, I knew it was too late. As the forklift continued to progress forward, it twisted my leg, causing my tibia and fibula to snap in a compound fracture. Once the forklift shifted and I was free of the weight, I felt an overwhelming sensation of sickness and pain. I collapsed to the ground and although I was wearing jeans and my welding overalls, I could see red splashes of blood soaking through my clothing and seeping onto the floor. I felt short of breath and dizzy and I nearly vomited. My co-workers quickly raced over to me.

The first person to reach me was Paddy McCabe. He grabbed me from behind and tried to lift me but I screamed in pain for him to let me go. My body had moved but my foot, which was nearly detached from my body, had stayed in the same place. Before he could attempt to lift me again, Mac McKenna raced over and instructed everyone not to touch me. He cut open my jeans and overalls to see where the injury was and he looked away in disgust when he saw my skin. I could see his face turn pure white and then I looked down myself to see the bones in my shin sticking out of my leg. They had broken with jagged white edges and I became lightheaded and nearly passed out. Jimmy Taylor, the foreman on the floor, soon realised how serious the situation was and raced outside to get a car. At that time you could wait for quite a while on an ambulance from Daisy Hill Hospital and he knew that I might bleed to death if I wasn't moved immediately.

By the time the men loaded me into the car, the amount of blood on my jeans and the floor around me was substantial. The mere sight of my injuries made me ill and I was trying to cling to consciousness as the men spoke to me and attempted to keep me calm and alert. Someone had given me a belt to bite for the pain and I remember the dry leather in my mouth as we raced to the hospital. Somehow I maintained consciousness and as the car came to a halt outside the casualty department and doctors and nurses came racing out with a stretcher for me, I felt slightly relieved. My workmates had rung into the hospital to inform them of my accident and this meant that they were well prepared for my injuries.

I was rushed straight to the operating theatre and I distinctly remember the stretcher being stopped for a priest to come and give his blessings. I was given my last rites and within seconds was put under anaesthetic for the operation to begin. Throughout the procedure the surgeons worked to save my leg. They repaired the compound fracture and gave me a blood transfusion to compensate for the serious amount that I had lost. When I regained consciousness after the procedure I found my mother and sisters at my bedside. My leg was swollen to three times its normal size and they had cut a hole in the back to alleviate the pressure arising from the volume of fluid. As I lay there, I could tell that my mother and sisters were very concerned about my condition and although I was hazy from the morphine, I somehow knew that my life was still very much in danger.

As I began speaking to my mother, a student doctor came into the ward to check on my condition. My breathing had begun to accelerate and I felt tightness and pain in my lungs. He immediately noticed blotches on my chest and diagnosed me as having an embolism. This blood clot had travelled from the site of my injury to my lungs and now posed a serious risk to my life. I was transported immediately back to the operating theatre and remember being quickly wheeled past my mother and sisters as they wept helplessly. The same priest returned to my side for another blessing and I went back into theatre wondering if I would come out alive.

The rest of that day and the next are very hazy in my mind. I slipped in and out of consciousness and the morphine and pain kept me from being lucid. However, once a few days passed, I gained a greater sense of clarity and was told that the embolism had been treated effectively but I was still at serious risk of further clots. My leg was plastered but the blood had seeped through the open hole they had cut at the back and had stained all of the white bandages red. It remained strapped in traction high above me for over a week whilst I was treated in intensive care. The pain was agonising and although I was on constant morphine, it never fully relieved it.

After my condition improved, I was transferred to the general ward. It was here that the doctors informed me that the catastrophic injuries to my left leg would require skin grafts to heal. They told me that the grafts are usually taken from the buttocks but, in light of my condition and the fact that I would be spending several months in a sitting position, they instead elected to take the skin from the thigh of my right leg. The grafts were performed in the operating theatre and they removed three patches, which were several layers deep and nearly six inches in length. The pain after the procedure was more intense than the initial break. It felt like someone had ripped off my skin and left me entirely raw.

A few days after the skin graft, my mother was in visiting and noticed a putrid smell in the room. I was so dazed with pain and medication I hadn't really noticed, but it was coming directly from the site of the graft. I was quickly transferred back to intensive care and told that the wound from the graft had become severely infected. This was treated with intravenous antibiotics and I was kept in isolation. After a week the infection cleared and I was taken back down to the general ward where I would spend the next several months.

Emotionally and physically the accident was very demoralising for me. I had been in peak condition in the months leading up to that day and I had great aspirations for upcoming climbs in Scotland and the Alps. When I regained full consciousness after the forklift struck me, I knew that the damage would be irreversible. I immediately worried that I might need an amputation and felt that my climbing career could be over before it had ever really begun. Fortunately the doctors had been able to save my leg, but their prognosis for my future mobility was poor.

In the first few weeks after the accident the doctors advised me that it would take great effort and rehabilitation to be able to walk again. They felt that it would take me quite a long time to walk without support and that I would never regain the ability to run or climb. However, even in those first difficult days, I knew that they were wrong. As the weeks passed, I was able to come off the pain medication entirely. I felt stronger and more focused when I had a clear head and I set small goals for myself from the outset. In the beginning these goals were very simple. They involved things like lifting my head off the pillow for a few minutes at a time or lowering my leg to the ground slowly. I remember that the first time I stood up I became so lightheaded that I nearly passed out, but I was determined to make it to the bathroom on my own. I hated the dependence of being bedridden and wanted nothing more than to take a hot shower and go for a walk. Eventually, with the help of the physical therapists who met with me daily, I was able to crutch up and down the stairs and the length of the hospital corridor.

Although my long hospital stay took a toll on me physically and psychologically, it was not all bad as I made several friends on the ward and got along well with all of the nurses. Myself and the other patients played pranks for entertainment and tortured the staff to pass the time. We would use our small toiletry mirrors to direct the sun onto the nurses' desk or their faces as they were passing. On other occasions we would get one of the men to pretend that he was very ill and when the nurses would rush in to assist him, we would tell them how good-looking they were and ask them out on dates. Thankfully most of the women had a great sense of humour and had a laugh along with us.

Having a bit of fun with the other patients lightened the atmosphere in the ward and luckily I had excellent support from my girlfriend Geraldine, my friends and family. I was never without visitors and could not keep count of all the cards and good wishes that I received. My friends from the neighbourhood were especially supportive and made sure that I was well looked after. Andy Carden and Fred McCann from Shannaghmore also came to see me and encouraged me to fight hard in my rehabilitation so that I could return to climbing once again. Emotionally all of the support really kept me going. It would have been very easy to become defeated lying in that hospital bed but I gained strength from all of the encouragement.

When I finally regained enough mobility to get about on my own, the doctors allowed me to return home. I was told that I would have to remain on crutches and in plaster for one year and that I would not be able to bear weight on my leg at all during that time. I also had to continue with regular physical therapy at the hospital and at home. On the day of my discharge, I said goodbye to all of the friends I had made and headed home to begin the long, slow process of recovery. I will never forget some of the other patients and how humbling it was to know them. Many of them were very ill or far more seriously injured than myself and all of them faced their plights with amazing resilience and bravery. When I finally got home after all those weeks in the hospital, I was like a new man, just happy to be alive.

It was late summer, the sun was shining and everything felt fresh and warm. My friends and family arranged a 'welcome back' party in the Granville Arms in Newry. Although I was exhausted and still crutching around, it was great to get out and return to normal life. Lots of friends and relatives attended that party and we stayed out most of the night celebrating my recovery.

In the weeks and months that followed I set about the real work: regaining my strength and mobility. Within a few weeks of getting out of the hospital, a friend of mine, 'Ham' Cunningham, took me out for the day to Slieve Gullion. I remember that the sky was clear and the sun was shining down on us as we parked the car. I told Ham that I was going to crutch all the way to the top and he just looked at me in disbelief. It took me ages and my hands were very sore by the time I reached the summit on the rocky path, but I made it. I was soaked in sweat and constantly had to fight to free my crutches from the boggy peat, but my determination paid off and I was able to make it all the way up and back down on my own.

Once I achieved that first summit after the accident, I was more convinced than ever that I would regain full mobility. I was strong-willed and steadfast and set out to prove the doctors wrong. From that day forward, I started to train regularly in the gym. I focused primarily on developing the muscles in my upper body and midsection and would lift weights for hours until I was exhausted. My leg was still in the plaster cast and I was registered as disabled, but I did not let this get in my way. I went climbing at the quarry in Castlewellan with the assistance of friends and continued to hike with my crutches. When I would rock-climb, my partners would hook me onto a top rope and I would use my upper-body strength and my right leg to do all of the work. I cracked the plaster on multiple occasions but the hospital was well used to me coming in for recasts after the first few weeks.

I hated being labelled 'disabled' and saw first hand the discrimination and hardship that people face. I remember being in nightclubs where people would walk right into me and drop cigarette butts on my foot. I found it difficult getting in and out of shops and restaurants, but bars and discos were the real nightmare. Fellas would always torture me after they had a few drinks and many a night they would knock my crutches away from me on the dancefloor or take them whilst I was sitting down. Thankfully, my girlfriend, Geraldine, had a worse temper than my own and would smack any guy who came near my crutches! I also had good friends from my boxing years who worked as bouncers and many a night a drunk would get chucked out on their ass after harassing me!

In the year that my leg remained in plaster, I toned and strengthened every muscle in my body so that when I was eventually allowed to walk again, I would have greater endurance. I remember many long days, particularly in the cold winter months, when I felt down about my leg and wondered whether things would ever really be the same again, but somehow I kept going and will never forget the day I was told that the plaster was coming off. It was nearly spring again and my injuries had healed enough to allow partial weight-bearing. When they cut the massive white plaster off, the leg that I saw before me was like a withered old man's. It was so thin and wasted that all I could see was the sharp edges of my bones. The sites of the skin grafts had healed but remained a vibrant pink and purple colour and felt tight and itchy. I was afraid to touch the smooth skin that seemed so misplaced on my shin and I had no feeling throughout much of the lower leg.

The first thing I did after the plaster was removed was head to the swimming pool. I felt weak walking on my bony leg and was intensely fearful of banging it or causing further injury, so I completed a lot of my training in the pool. I was still using my two crutches but no longer moved about with as much speed, as I worried constantly about falling.

Once I was able to rebuild some of the muscle, I returned to the hills and eventually progressed to walking with one crutch. The rehabilitation was slow, but I persevered and after a long road, I was able to come off the crutches entirely by summer. During the year after my accident I had been unable to return to work and was subsisting only on social disability benefits. The money was limited in those days and any savings that I had were quickly depleted. Not long after my accident, my workmate Mac McKenna had moved over to New York with some friends of mine from childhood. The McClelland brothers had grown up in Newry but were born in the US and thus had American citizenship. They left Newry when the economic situation was at its worst and Seán, the oldest in the family, had established a construction business in New York City. Seán was always looking for workers and once a few of the Newry clan headed over, many more decided to follow as the pay was good and the nightlife was even better!

Geraldine and I had split up by the spring, but we remained close friends and during the summer she decided to move to America and live with a friend in Queens, New York. With so many of my mates heading away to the States, I decided to join up with her and then move on to the Bronx to complete some work for Seán.

We arrived in JFK Airport in New York City on a very hot summer's day and I could not believe the heat. I had never experienced anything like New York. I felt like a lost child with the endless sprawl of skyscrapers before me. Geraldine and I made our way by taxi through the busy streets to Queens and I remember the sweat running down my face the entire time. I spent a week or so touring around with Geraldine before heading up to the Bronx to meet up with Seán's brothers, Kevin and Musky. It was strange to be so far away from home and in such a vast city and yet to be surrounded by so many of my friends. There were literally tens of thousands of Irish at that time working over in New York and a night in one of the local bars felt just like being home in Newry.

The first day that I arrived at the boys' apartment off Broadway in the heart of the Bronx is a day that I will never forget. Kevin McClelland collected me and on our way from Queens we had driven through Manhattan and up Park Avenue. I was amazed by the wealth and the sheer size of the buildings and the boys laughed as I leaned out the window, snapping countless photos. However, as soon as we crossed over the Harlem River, I could not believe the difference in the landscape. The poverty and chaos were unreal. Everyone we saw came from a different ethnic background and coming from Ireland at that time, with virtually no cultural diversity, it all seemed very strange to me. I had heard about the 'ghetto' but had never seen such an area until we drove through Harlem and I saw homeless men with only jeans on and no shirts or shoes. The summer heat was relentless and they were ducking out of the sun into doorways and eating out of tins of cat food. My whole perception of New York quickly changed. I had imagined the streets to be wide and sprawling with fast cars and big buildings but I had not realised how poor many of those who lived in the boroughs were.

When we finally arrived at the apartment, I was exhausted, but the boys had planned a big night out to welcome me to America. That night was like most others during my time in the States. We went to the local bar, The Punch Bowl. This was an Irish bar, frequented almost entirely by Irish customers. They played Irish songs, showed Irish sports on TV and even sold Irish food. Every Sunday there was Gaelic football on in Gaelic Park and we would all head down to the match after late nights out on the town. The boys drank like fish whilst we were away. They were all working for Seán at Erin Construction and, despite the long and demanding work hours, they partied hard almost every night of the week. Everyone in the house had to be up at 7 a.m. for work, but no one returned home from the bars before two or three each morning. They would crash wherever they fell and Seán would waken everyone each morning with a phone call to make sure that no one was late.

Whilst I was there I spent most of my nights out with the fellas but I eventually got sick of the monotony. I wanted to sightsee and I dragged the boys around to the tourist attractions of New York. They had lived in the city for nearly a year before my arrival and yet most had never seen a thing! Our adventures in New York were endless and the little things amazed and amused us. We couldn't get over the vast subway networks or the endless chaos in the city. The Americans who we met would comment on how dangerous life in the North must have been with all of the bombings and shootings, whilst there were about 10 murders a day in New York! In fact, in 1989 alone there were over 2,200 murders in New York City and in the entire span of the 'Troubles' in Northern Ireland (between 1969 and 2002) there were under 3,500 people killed. The Bronx was such a ghetto at that time that all of us were very conscious of our safety. We stayed together as much as possible and constantly looked out for each other.

In light of our safety concerns, the boys all took advantage of the lax American gun laws and purchased handguns and rifles for protection in the neighbourhood. However, what we really needed was protection from ourselves! There is one incident in particular that I will never forget. We had been out on the town all night and in the early hours of the morning I returned home alone, as I was wrecked. Our apartment was in the basement of a 10-storey brick building block. There were not enough bedrooms for all of the lads living there, so I slept each night on a pull-out couch in the front living room. I had just gotten into bed when I heard the fellas coming in through the door. I could tell that they were wasted and was surprised when they passed by without harassing me. I pulled the covers over my head and was trying to get some sleep when suddenly I heard the boys burst out laughing. I knew that they were up to something but was too tired to get involved. Then suddenly I heard the sound of guns being locked and loaded. Before I could even take cover, they began shooting like crazy at a partition wall that we had decided to remove to extend one of the rooms. The whole place shook as the bullets ripped through the plaster and the sound was absolutely deafening. The only thing I could hear over the gunshots was the boys' 'yee haa's and laughter. I was afraid to move in case one of them accidentally shot me and I waited in the bed until the dust settled and the final spent shell hit the floor. After several moments of silence I got up to survey the scene and found the wall looking like a piece of Swiss cheese, with massive gaping holes littering the plaster. The boys just went to bed after their escapade and I finally went to sleep myself, laughing all the while in disbelief. Not long after I finally dozed off, a loud banging on the door awakened me. None of the boys even stirred, so I got up to see who it was. When I looked through the window, I could see two cops outside the door. I quickly ducked back and went to wake up Kevin, as he was the only American citizen. Kevin was still drunk at this stage, but we raced around the apartment, hiding the guns and shells, before he finally responded to the officers' bangs on the door.

When Kevin opened the door they stated that neighbours had phoned about the sound of gunshots and they wanted to know what had happened. Kevin said that we had had a party and set off some fireworks, but they wanted to come in and have a look around. We were really worried at this stage but had no choice but to let them in. When they saw the state of the apartment and the wall shot out from top to bottom they laughed out loud. It turned out that both the cops were of Irish descent and when Kevin told them that we were friends with a sergeant in the New York Police Department who came from the North, they let us off lightly. They told us to hand over a few of the guns and to keep it quiet in future.

We had a lucky escape that night as the cops let us off without charge. None of the other fellas had even awoken during the police visit and on our journey to work the next morning we had quite a laugh embellishing the episode to the others!

Whilst I was in New York, I continued to rebuild the strength in my leg. I went training daily in Van Cortlandt Park, where many of the NYPD officers run, and eventually I went rock-climbing in upstate New York. I also went on a kayaking trip in the Delaware River. All of the boys were supposed to come along with me and we scheduled the trip several weeks in advance, but the night before we were due to set off, they all got drunk and wouldn't get out of bed the next morning to go. A mini-bus sat outside our apartment blaring its horn for ages on the day of the trip, but in the end I was the only one who went. When I got out to the river, the guides asked what my sleeping arrangements were for the night. I realised then that the boys had never booked this part of the trip and I was left without a hotel or even a sleeping bag or tent! Luckily it was a warm night and I was able to get food and a bit of shelter from some other campers who were on a similar trip.

My experiences in New York were fantastic and I felt stronger and fitter after my time there. The heat helped my leg to heal and by the time I returned home to Newry for the court hearing about the accident, I was nearly back to the man I had been before that terrible day. Unfortunately, after I had cut my time in New York short to be home for the trial, it was postponed and did not take place for several more years. In the end the factory was held responsible for my injuries and I received a small settlement to compensate me for the damage to my leg as well as my time off work and the resultant pain and suffering. It was nowhere near what it should have been, but it gave me some money to put toward future adventures. Once I arrived back from New York I had a serious taste for travel and was looking forward to returning to winter mountaineering. Nearly two years after my accident, I set about planning a technical solo climb in the French and Swiss Alps. I was now ready to return to the mountains and felt more confident than ever in my abilities.

Chapter 4 ∾

| THE ALPS

'There are many paths to the top of a mountain but the view is always the same.'
CHINESE PROVERB

In the months after I returned home from New York, I completed the post-'stage two' mountaineering course at Shannaghmore and once again I returned to Scotland to complete my expedition component. During this course I met Kevin Quinn, a fellow climber and outdoorsman. Kevin was a married father of two living in Hilltown and, although he was nearly 20 years older than myself, he and I immediately became good friends. We spent a great deal of time together during the course and also went rock-climbing and hill-walking independently. Kevin was a great asset for me. He was an instructor at Shannaghmore who had previously worked at the Mountain Centre and Ardnabannon Outdoor Education Centre. He had vast experiences in the mountains and on the rivers and was a top-class rock-climber and canoeist.

Kevin was also a very solid man with a strong ethos about mountaineering and a great sense of humour. He had an 'old-school' philosophy when it came to outdoor pursuits and firmly held the notion that if a climber was not capable of making an ascent on their own, they should not be on the mountain. He was dead set against using fixed bolts on rock-climbs or employing guides or Sherpas on expeditions. He was also very conscious of the impact that hill-walking and rock-climbing have on the environment and fully supported trace-free climbing. Kevin took me under his wing. He saw my potential from the outset and guided me in the advanced techniques of rock-climbing and mountaineering. Within the year that we spent together on the course, my climbing abilities improved tenfold. I gained immense experience and knowledge from Kevin and was privileged to become his protégé.

Once we completed the course, we set about making plans for future climbs. However, I had no high-altitude experience and needed to spend some time on the larger peaks before I could attempt an expedition with Kevin. The French Alps were the best place logistically for me to gain this experience and I organised two climbs that summer in the Mont Blanc Massif. In the Massif I would be able to introduce my body to high-altitude snow- and ice-climbing and would also gain vital experience in technical ascents. There is a year-round snow cover on these mountains and they can be rather icy and dangerous throughout the summer months, so it would be great training for me. Although it would have been ideal for Kevin to accompany me on these trips, he was working and had family commitments, so I set off alone.

For the first of these ascents, I arranged to get a lift to France with Kevin McClelland, who had just recently returned home from New York. Kevin was travelling with Marty 'Ham' Cunningham and Seán 'Hunch' McKevitt over to France on holiday and they agreed to take me with them to Mont Blanc. It was a long journey overland in the car and we were on a tight budget, so we camped every night. The quarters were a bit cramped but we had a great time sightseeing and meeting new people. When we finally arrived in Chamonix and I got my first views of the towering peaks around the village, I could not contain my excitement. The boys thought that I was nuts to be attempting to summit alone, or to be heading into the mountains at all for that matter, as their only interest was visiting the French bars and meeting the local ladies!

That first afternoon in Chamonix I spent organising my gear and provisions for the ascent, and the boys went touring around. With Kevin Quinn's guidance I had mapped out the route I planned to take and was confident that I would be able to complete the entire climb in two days. I went to bed very early that evening and when I awoke to depart, the boys were only returning home from their night on the town. I said goodbye and headed off to the local bus station, where I would get a lift to the village of Les Houches and from there a cable car to La Chalette. After the cable car journey I took a train to the foot of the glacier, where tourists are transported for photographs. Once I reached this point, I began my ascent on foot to the Tête Rousse hut.

The first few hours of the hike were fairly easy. It was a rocky scree slope along the ridge of the mountain until I reached the hut at 3,167 metres. After a short rest and feed at the hut, I moved on towards the snow line, where I put on crampons and began to use a single ice axe. This section of the route can be dangerous due to rock-fall and although it was still early in the day, I was conscious that conditions in the late morning and afternoon are treacherous. Once the sun begins to melt the snow and ice from above this section, known as the *grand couloir*, climbers are at serious risk of being battered by rock-fall. Mountaineers are often killed here and I was quite conscious of my timing. Thankfully I was able to move quickly through this area and encountered no difficulties along the way. Once I ascended beyond this section, the route returned to rock and scree and I was able to make the standard level rock-climb to the Goûter Hut without any great effort.

Kevin had stayed in the Goûter Hut on previous climbs and advised me that it provided an excellent base for making the ascent. I was looking forward to arriving at the hut and offloading some of my gear. Even at this early stage in the climb, I realised that I had seriously over-packed and with each step, the weight of my gear was taking a toll on me. As I made my way closer to the hut, the strong midday sun was shining down upon me and I began sweating with each exertion. The effects of the altitude suddenly hit me and I experienced a headache and pains in my stomach. The hut looked like an oasis in the distance as I made my final approach and I couldn't wait to stop for a rest and to reorganise my gear.

However, it wasn't long before the 'oasis' image of the hut was entirely dispelled. Once I reached the plateau where the structure is based, I was quickly disgusted by the smell of human waste rising up from the toileting facility. It was a long drop toilet over the ice coloir located directly in front of the building. Once I made it past the putrid odour and entered the hut, I was told that there were no more places available that night. The hut was packed with climbers and their gear, and there was not even a place to sit down!

This was when I began to realise how ill-prepared I was for this climb. I had not looked into reserving a bunk in the hut in advance, I was laden down with excess gear and I was feeling sick from the altitude. I knew that I desperately needed to rest, so whilst I was there, I took off my pack and used their facilities to boil water for drinking and soup. I was conscious that I needed to rehydrate before I moved further up the glacier. The sun was now quite strong in the afternoon sky and I could feel my muscles cramping up from the heat. Once I took a short break and refuelled, I felt slightly stronger and decided to continue towards another hut that I had read about, further up the mountain.

This hut was not actually a bunkhouse but, rather, a very basic aluminium structure that was mainly used for emergencies. It lacked the essential facilities of the Goûter Hut but it was my only other option for shelter. The hut was located a few hours further up the ridge but was directly below the route used for the summit, so it would still provide a valuable place to rest before making my final ascent to the top. I set my hopes on arriving there in the late afternoon and sleeping for a short while before making an attempt on the summit that night. However, once I began climbing up in the direction of the hut, I felt the full weight of the altitude come down upon me. I was moving very slowly and my pack was a constant annoyance. I began to feel ill and stopped frequently for rests. After several hours the day progressed into night and, with the disappearance of the sun, the temperatures began to plummet. I had borrowed all of my gear from Andy Carden at Shannaghmore and I was feeling bursts of cold and wind through the old Gore-Tex jacket. The altitude and freezing temperatures were taking a toll on my strength and I found myself leaning for support on the heavy hickory ice axe that Andy had lent me. I could barely make my legs move at one stage and I was now stopping frequently with doses of diarrhoea.

I became frightened at that point and recognised that I was out of my depth. Although I could see head-torches at the hut in the distance, it seemed to be very far away and my motivation was rapidly diminishing. I sat down in the snow to think through the situation. I was convinced that I could make it to the hut if I left my pack behind, but I worried that this would jeopardise my attempt on the summit and could actually mean losing all of my gear. On the other hand, I worried that if I continued on at the slow pace I was moving, I might freeze to death on the exposed slope. I cursed myself for being so naïve and egotistical. I had assumed that the climb would be straightforward or even easy on the basis of my past experiences and had not properly prepared for the conditions I would encounter. I was completely inexperienced with altitude and had not heeded Kevin's warnings about taking adequate time to acclimatise. I guess it was young bravado but I thought I was fit and strong and could make the ascent without feeling any ill-effects. The reality of how wrong I had been was now resting on my shoulders like a two-ton weight. After a long break weighing up my options, I decided that I had no real choice but to continue on with my pack until I reached the hut.

The final section of that climb was fairly steep and icy. I was so tired it took great effort to make my body move. At times the only thing that I could think about was the warmth of my sleeping bag and how badly I needed a rest. After an exhausting journey, I finally arrived at the hut and immediately offloaded my pack. I took a long drink from my flask and a combination of aspirin to thin my blood and paracetamol for the pain in my head. Once I gathered the strength to go inside, I was devastated to find the hut totally packed. There were climbers asleep on the floor in every corner of the small metal building and there did not appear to be enough space for even one more person. As I opened the doors, I could hear men groaning with annoyance at the disruption I was causing to their sleep; no one made any efforts to allow me in. I was forced to push my way past the sleeping men until I made my way to the middle of the floor. I knew that my gear was inadequate and that if I stayed near the door I would be freezing cold, so despite several of the men cursing me in French, I continued on until I had wedged myself in the centre of the room. Within seconds of resting my head on the floor, I was unconscious, but my sleep was short and fitful. Only hours after my arrival, the other men were awake and preparing for their summit bids. I was still too tired and weak to move, so I lay on whilst the first groups departed. I briefly went back to sleep but awoke again a short while later, knowing that if I did not get up to go for the summit soon, I would miss my chance entirely.

When I finally arose it was after 2 a.m. and the night air was bitter. With all of the other men away up the mountain, the hut had suddenly become unbearably cold and draughty. I packed my things and decided to leave a good deal of my gear behind in a bin liner, which I stashed in a corner of the hut. I took only the most essential items with me and began to ascend the steep slope above. Fortunately, it was a clear and starry night and although I had planned to navigate my way to the top using a map and compass, I could see the line of climbers in front of me illuminated by the glow of their head-torches. Their tracks were still fresh in the snow and I could walk along the route with ease.

The lead group were all climbing in single file and thus everyone behind them had followed suit. This made the climb very enjoyable for me. The men at the front of the climb had broken the trail and I was able to catch up with the climbers ahead of me in no time. My brief period of sleep had restored my strength and the aspirin and paracetamol had effectively cured my headache, so I was nearly back to full steam.

I took time to look around me as I climbed up the towering mass of snow and ice and was overcome by the stark beauty of the white landscape. I stopped for brief periods of rest and reviewed the glacier below me. I could see lines of head-torches ascending from the lower hut and the climbers looked like an army of ants as they made their way up towards the summit. Just as the dawn began to break, I ascended onto the Bosses Ridge, which is the final section below the summit. This area is a narrow ridge which becomes progressively steeper and more tapered as it reaches the final dome on the top. As I made my way up through this section I could hear men arguing above me on the ridge. I stopped for a rest and could see in the distance three Englishmen ascending whilst a French guide and his clients were descending in the same section. Apparently the French guide had physically pushed one of the Englishmen out of the way for his clients to get through. The Englishman would have fallen to his death had one of his friends not been there to break his fall. Despite the danger that the French guide had caused, he simply ignored the English climber's shouts and continued to progress downwards. I quickly realised that I too would be crossing paths with this group in a narrow section of trail. I became frightened that they would push by me in a similar manner and I would plunge off the mountain. I was not using rope and had no one else with me to break the fall. I decided to stop and steady myself before they passed. I kicked a platform in the snow and drew my ice axe up like a weapon whilst I waited for them. Once they made their way to where I was standing, the French guide took one look at me and urged his clients quickly around me without incident.

After the French climbers passed, I remained a bit shaken, but continued on up the slope and within 10 minutes, I was standing on the summit dome. When I reached the top it was packed with other climbers who had ascended from both sides of the mountain. They were all celebrating their success. It was well below zero but no one even seemed to notice. There were men attempting to drink from bottles of Champagne that had frozen solid and others who were unveiling flags and banners. I stopped for a good while to reflect on the journey and to take in the scenery all around me. The sun had risen high into the sky at this stage and the clouds seemed to be miles below me. I could see straight across the Alps and was amazed as the mountains reached endlessly towards the horizon. I sat quietly for a while, breathing in the joys of my success, before my inadequate gear left me cold and shivering and I knew it was time to descend. I asked a few Italian climbers to take my photograph and then began the return journey down.

The descent was very quick. I felt strong and confident and once I began to warm up with the morning sun, I was able to move without difficulty. I arrived back at the hut with astonishing speed and packed my bags for the final section. Whilst I was in the hut I met two English Royal Marines who had just completed the climb as well. They were young like myself and full of energy and excitement after their success. We spoke briefly and then agreed on a little challenge to make the final section of the descent more interesting. We would race each other back to the train station at the base of the mountain. There was no prize involved, just pride. Once our bags were packed we burst through the doors of the hut and ran like crazy down the fixed ropes that traverse the upper section of the mountain. I was wearing leather gloves so I had excellent traction on the rope and thus never even bothered to clip on. I was so intent on beating the soldiers that I just let the rope run through my hands and used it only to keep myself steady. Once I reached the glacier and the rocky moraine at the bottom, I began sprinting. My pack was extraordinarily heavy and it was pulling me down, but I pushed on with all of my might. One of the soldiers was very close behind me and I knew that I had to move quickly if I was going to beat him. I was still wearing my plastic Koflach boots from the summit and I could feel the upper edges pushing into the skin on my shin and causing my scars to bleed, but I no longer cared about the pain. I was so full of adrenalin and renewed strength that I kept moving. The possibility of beating British soldiers fuelled me on!

In the end I reached the train station a sweaty, bloody and exhausted mess but I had beaten the two Brits by a few hundred metres. It was a moment worth celebrating for years! They were really gracious and offered to buy me a drink back in Chamonix but I politely told them I didn't drink and declined their offer to meet up again. Although they weren't bad lads, I couldn't imagine bringing two British soldiers back to meet the boys and didn't want to raise too many questions about a group of fellas from the north of Ireland!

When I finally made it back to the campsite where the boys were staying, they were astounded to see me. They told me that they were convinced I would freeze to death or die trying to get to the summit! Once I told them that I had actually made it all the way to the top, they decided to celebrate, but only after viewing the photographic evidence! It was a great excuse for the boys to take to the bars again and I joined them, downing Cokes and orange juice until the early hours of the morning. I didn't have long to recover from my ascent, as we set off for Ireland the next day, but I had learned a great deal in my short time climbing on Mont Blanc.

My naïveté on the mountain could have cost me my life and my poor preparation took the enjoyment out of my ascent. Kevin always spoke about climbing with temperance and I often wondered what he meant by this, but now I clearly understood. There is no room for ego on the mountains. I realised now that mountaineering is less about physical strength and speed and more about planning, preparation and patience.

After the climb I returned to work with PWS, where I had had my accident two years earlier. At first it was strange being back in the factory, but I had no animosity towards the forklift driver or the company and still had many good friends working in the facility. My body had recovered surprisingly well from that day and with each climb I was feeling stronger. I worked as many hours as possible to earn the money and time off that I required to get away climbing. I was also doing work with the Southern Education Library Board at this stage and was now being paid to take youth groups hill-walking and canoeing. I earned good extra money doing these weekend trips and was using all of the cash to fund my further climbs.

When I returned home from New York, I went back to living with my mother in Barcroft Park and continued to hang around with most of my childhood friends. Many of the fellas who had travelled to New York with me were now back in Newry and we frequented the local bars and discos together each weekend. It was on one of these nights out that I met a girl named Lisa from Camlough, who I began to date. Initially she was not into the outdoor lifestyle but I soon got her camping and hiking and we spent many weekends together on the mountains.

Once I was able to get enough money together for a return trip to the Alps, I set off again in August to do some technical rock- and ice-climbing in the Massif. This time I got a lift from a lorry driver who was heading over to France from Newry. A friend of mine knew him and made all of the arrangements for me. The driver was a nice fella who took me all the way to the Mont Blanc Tunnel. This tunnel goes directly through the mountain and into Italy. From here I walked to Chamonix and set up again in the local campsite. My plan was to spend time in the valley below the mountain, making short day trips up the peak to allow my body time to acclimatise to the altitude. I had learned a valuable lesson on the last trip and was not going to suffer from altitude sickness this time.

Whilst I was at the campsite, I met some Scottish climbers who were planning to climb the Index and the Cathedral. There were three of them climbing together and that can be an awkward number for making ascents, so I agreed to join them; the four of us would make the climbs together. We had great weather and the climbing went very well. For the first time in my life I was climbing routes with fixed bolts and could not believe how easy this made the progression between pitches. There are no fixed-bolt climbs anywhere in Ireland, so it was a real novelty for me. The Scottish climbers were very strong and each of us took turns leading. I was shocked by how quickly we were able to complete the routes and gained a great deal of confidence from these ascents.

After we completed these two climbs we were all feeling very strong and decided to attempt a more difficult route, known as the Aiguille du Peigne. This route consists of 19 pitches and is incredibly steep. By comparison, the previous routes that we had completed were only about seven pitches long, so we knew this would be an exhausting climb. The other challenges with this route were the altitude and the fact that it has snow and ice at the top. We set off quite early to reach the base of the climb and were well on our way up the rock face by noon. We stopped for brief breaks during the ascent to refuel on food and water and to take in the scenery around us. On one of these rests, I noticed a bit of cloud coming in our direction, but we continued to progress up the rock face regardless.

Then suddenly, with only about four pitches remaining before we reached the top, we found ourselves caught in a lightning storm. The temperature dropped quickly and thick clouds rolled in, blackening the sky entirely. We had no time to seek shelter and were forced to abseil down as the rain and lightning came down around us. It was extremely dangerous due to our high level of exposure on the rock and as the thunder blasted around us, I wondered if we would make it to the bottom without incident. Fortunately, we reached the base safely and quickly packed our gear before heading back towards the campsite. Although we had not completed the route, it was a powerful climb and also a valuable lesson for us all about the changeable weather conditions on the mountain. We cursed ourselves for not getting a detailed weather forecast before making our ascent and vowed not to be so foolish again in future.

After resting for the remainder of the day, the Scottish climbers decided to take the following day off to sightsee, whilst I headed back into the mountains for some ice-climbing. I went to the Petite Verte, which is a stop on the cable car route where climbers can either traverse along a route to the ridge or complete two pitches of ice-climbing for faster access onto the upper slopes. I elected to do the latter. It was fairly steep and I was a little shaky at first, but I quickly found my rhythm and was able to make it onto the ridge without difficulty. After this short climb, I was forced to return to the campsite as there was a weather front moving in over the upper slopes of the mountain and I did not want to be caught out in bad weather again.

Once I was back at camp, I arranged to meet up with the Scottish climbers again two days later at the top of Aiguille du Midi, which is a pinnacle on Mont Blanc. I planned to climb two of the peaks in the Massif (du Tacul and Mont Maudit) and then to complete the Cosmiques Ridge, where I would bivy for the night in the Midi Station. This facility is used during the day as a viewing station for tourists and at night many climbers bunk down here, as it is sheltered and warm. I soloed these ascents without difficulty and met up with the Scots again after camping at the station. From here we headed to the Chere Couloir, where we split up into two groups, with my partner and me leading the ascent. It was a great ice-climb. The route was frozen solid and we did not have to use our own gear as there were chains fitted into the ice. Once we completed this climb we abseiled down the mountain and after completing a further six climbs on my own over the following week, I again returned home to Ireland.

The French Alps had given me an excellent base for high-altitude climbing and the combination of rock and ice routes was perfect for honing my technical skills. I learned a great deal from each ascent and looked forward to tackling climbs in the Swiss Alps. The following year, after a solid winter ice-climbing season in the Scottish Highlands, I set off for Switzerland.

I was now climbing competently at grade four/five and was able to make solo ascents without difficulty. Once I arrived into Zermatt in Switzerland, I set about two weeks of high-altitude ice-climbs. I was alone on most of these ascents and based myself out of a campsite in the village. For the first few days I completed short treks and rock-climbs on the Riffelhorn to acclimatise to the altitude. Once I felt strong enough, I set off for the Monterosa, where I would spend three days climbing and navigating.

In hindsight, I took the wrong approach to ascending this peak. I travelled across the glacier which traverses the mountain unaccompanied and unroped. I did not realise at the time how vast and dangerous this glacier can be. It is littered with deep crevasses where many climbers have lost their lives and, with no rope or gear to break a fall, I would not have survived if I had accidentally broken through a snow crust.

Thankfully, I managed to make the ascent without incident and I reached the two summits of the Monterosa feeling strong and confident. As I descended back towards the base at Zermatt, I passed three Czech climbers who were making their way up the mountain. They immediately struck me as ill equipped. They were wearing thin plastic coats and old, battered leather boots, but they seemed like strong men and were making good time despite the condition of their gear. As we crossed paths, they stopped briefly to speak with me and to borrow my map. Once they had a look at it, they thanked me and moved on. I returned to Zermatt for a brief rest before I set off into the mountains again.

This time I attempted the Breithorn. It was a technically challenging climb but despite the extreme cold, the weather was clear and pleasant. The final ridge on this peak was quite steep and narrow and I hit a few spots that were icy and dangerous but, on the whole, it was not an overly difficult climb to complete. I moved very quickly and was able to finish the ascent more quickly than I had planned and thus returned again to the campsite for a day of rest.

Whilst I was resting in the camp, I heard rumours from other climbers that there was a team of Czech men missing on the mountain. I was shocked by how unimportant the situation seemed to the others. No one spoke of staging a rescue or sending a search party and no one appeared to be particularly concerned for their safety. I remembered crossing paths with the men a few days earlier and felt sorry now that I had not asked them if they knew where they were going. It did seem strange at the time that they did not have a map, but in those days Eastern European climbers often came with only the most basic gear and supplies. I heard nothing more about the Czechs until a few days later, when another climber told me that they were now 'presumed dead'. To this day I do not know what their ultimate fate was, but it has haunted me since how callous life in the mountains can be.

Despite the bad news about the Czech climbers, I continued with my scheduled climbs and went on to complete the Weisshorn and the Matterhorn. For my ascent on the Weisshorn I joined forces with a Welsh mountaineer and we spent three days completing the climb together. He was a solid climber who had vast experience in the Alps and made an excellent partner. Once that climb was complete, I made my final ascent of the season on the highest and most beautiful peak in the Swiss Alps, the Matterhorn. I completed this ascent alone over two days and although it was primarily a straightforward climb, there were constant risks of rock-fall from other climbers dislodging stones on the route above me. Thankfully, I made the summit and descent without any difficulties and once the climb was complete, I returned home to Ireland.

In the months that followed I began a rock-climbing course at the Mountain Centre in Tollymore, where I met Dawson Stelfox, a Belfast climber, who was the director of this course. He worked as an architect and was one of only two qualified mountain guides in the whole of Ireland at that time. Dawson was a top-class rock-climber and a very solid man. Whilst I was on the course, he was in the process of organising an expedition to the north ridge of Mount Everest for the spring of 1993, where he hoped to make the first successful Irish summit. There were eight climbers on the team and they were looking for a support group of trekkers to accompany them as well. As soon as I heard about the expedition, I was keen to take part. Although the cost of participation was quite high, I was able to procure sponsorship from the Credit Union and did local fundraising in Newry, using my past climbing experiences to establish credibility.

Once I had my finances in place, I arranged all of the details with Dawson and became a member of the second trekking party, which would ascend to Advanced Base Camp on the mountain. Although we were advised that advanced base camp was the limit for this trekking group, I remained hopeful that once on the mountain I might be allowed to travel as far as the North Col on the basis of my experience. I spent the following year training hard in the gym and set off in March 1993 for one last climbing trip to Scotland before our scheduled departure to Nepal in late April.

Chapter 5 ∿

| A FALL ON POINT FIVE

'Live as if you were to die tomorrow. Learn as if you were to live forever.'
M.K. GHANDI

In February of 1993 I set about organising a week of climbing in the Scottish mountains. I planned to go with Kevin Quinn and Paul Clerkin, another climber from the North who I had met in previous years whilst rock-climbing in Donegal. Paul was from Rostrevor and had a strong climbing background. He and his cousin Paddy Clerkin were renowned within the Irish climbing community for the vast number of routes that they had established throughout the country. This trip would be the first time that Paul and I ice-climbed together and he was especially keen as it had been six years since his last winter ascent.

In addition to Paul, two friends of Kevin's, Steven Ferris and Jim Milligan, also agreed to come along. Steven worked at Ardnabannon Outdoor Education Centre as a full-time instructor and was a top-class rock-climber. Jim was a friend of Kevin's who had suffered a terrible hit and run accident and was just making his return to climbing. Once the five of us came together, we worked on selecting routes. We planned to spend one week climbing, with technical ascents in Glencoe and Anochmore as well as on Ben Nevis. We were unsure what the conditions would be like, but we set off with high hopes and arrived to find solid snow and ice throughout the West Highland region.

For the first few days of the trip we based ourselves out of Ballyhoolish, which is a small village near Glencoe. We spent our days rising early and making the long treks into the inner gullies and ridges along the peaks. The conditions were ideal and we completed our climbs with astonishing speed and precision. After our time in Glencoe we decided to move over to Fort William to begin ice-climbs on Anochmore and Ben Nevis. It was on one of the routes up Anochmore that I led my first grade four ice-climb. It was a tremendous feeling to accomplish this route as it had a large overhanging cornice and was technically difficult due to the heavy snows that had fallen in recent days. After completing this particular ascent, I felt a real sense of confidence and knew that I was ready to progress to more difficult climbs.

The following day we set out on Ben Nevis to complete the 'observatory ridge', which was a fairly straightforward route, but had high levels of exposure on either side and was not for the faint-hearted. We were all in good form that morning as we awoke to find perfect weather conditions for the long afternoon climb. I remember the sky was clear and bright and the sun was shining down upon us as we set off from our bunkhouse at 7.30 a.m. The hike to the CIC hut on the mountain was easy and enjoyable. We were all planning to stop once we arrived at the hut to rest and eat before setting off together on the ridge. However, as we passed by a highly technical and sophisticated route known as 'point five', our plans changed.

Paul was the first to notice the route and he immediately remarked that the long vertical gully appeared to be in perfect condition for an ascent. He had been eager to attempt the climb on many previous occasions but had always experienced bad weather or threats of avalanche, which had thwarted his ambitions. Paul was a talented climber and his enthusiasm was contagious. Once he suggested abandoning our original plans for traversing the observatory ridge and tackling this route instead, I was sold. However, the others were not so keen. Kevin seemed especially hesitant and I sensed he had concerns about tackling such a difficult route after a season with little climbing. In the end Kevin, Steven and Jim opted out of climbing point five and instead decided to stick with their original plan to climb along the observatory ridge. However, the five of us agreed to meet at a refuge hut on the summit once we completed our separate climbs and to make the descent together as a group. We wished each other well and parted ways.

As our original plans involved traversing a ridge, we were ill-equipped for a gully climb. Paul had no helmet with him and we only had one 9-mm rope between us, but we were confident and excited and without any further consideration, we began the long and arduous climb. I remember taking one final look at the route above me as we stood at the base of the climb. I admired the perfect white snow and ice that had set throughout the gully and had to arch my head back to see the steep upper sections of the climb, which led directly onto the summit. I knew from the outset that the route would be difficult for both Paul and myself as it is infamously technical, but I was excited about the challenge and felt energetic as we made the first few moves. We had begun the climb quite late as it was after 12.30 p.m. by the time we set off, but we were both strong and moving quickly, so I did not let this worry me. We anticipated that the climb would take a total of six to eight hours because we only had the one rope and we knew it would be well after dark by the time we reached the summit, but the conditions were the best that either of us had ever seen on Ben Nevis and we were not going to let this opportunity pass us by.

Paul led us up the first pitch, which was about 80 feet of sheer vertical ice. We were using a waist belay system, which essentially means that you wrap the rope around your waist, rucksack and one arm and then use your free arm to take in and push out the rope. Once Paul reached the end of the rope, I made my way up to him, taking out his gear along the way. I also completed the first pitch without difficulty and then led us up towards the second pitch. I felt strong and competent as I moved up through the ice and snow and I could hear Paul behind me, shouting up instructions and words of encouragement. However, not long after I began moving up through the gully, a spin-drift avalanche came down upon us and I was forced to stop and duck my face in against the ice for protection. I could taste the powdery snow in my mouth as debris flew down around me. After taking a quick glance back, I found that I could no longer see or hear Paul.

Paul had no helmet on so he had put his axes in the ice above his head and ducked into them as the avalanche progressed. After several moments the spin-drift stopped and I continued my progression onto the second pitch. However, I had not been moving long when another avalanche came down upon us. This one lasted for nearly half an hour and I remember feeling cold and sore as I waited in a strained position along the vertical face. When it finally ceased, I tried to put an ice screw in for protection but I could not get the gear to go into the thick ice mass beneath me. I decided to move on despite a nagging concern about the lack of gear that I had in place. I could hear distant shouts from Paul, telling me to stop and place some gear, but I wanted to keep moving until I reached a safer place in the gully before I attempted to place an ice screw again.

At this point I had about three quarters of the rope out and was 80 feet above the last placement of protective gear. I was moving with astonishing speed and precision and kept a strict focus on the route ahead. I have a strong stomach for heights but even I felt slightly sick when I looked down, as the route below me was so severe. Suddenly I reached a point along the gully where I could no longer see above me. There was a thick cornice of snow and ice and I was forced to swing my axe in above my head without a view of where it was going. However, I was fortunate and my first swing hit the ice hard and held. Once the axe was in, I leaned back and began to swing with my second axe to make a placement. There was still a bit of spin-drift coming down around me and I closed my eyes for protection as I swung out with the second axe. Just as I felt my shoulder rotating in, the first axe broke free from the snow and ice and I lost all contact with the gully. I flew backwards and let out a deafening roar as my life passed by in a blur of snow and ice. I hit nothing for what felt like minutes and then suddenly the rope tightened and I stopped. I had fallen 180 feet and was now dangling upside down after smacking against the hard ice wall in the gully. My leg was above me and I was tangled in the rope. I was overcome with panic. Paul was at least 80 feet above me and would not be able to see or hear me. He would be suffering terribly from the initial exertion of my fall and now, with my dead weight resting on his waist belay, he would be in terrible pain and would almost certainly think I was dead. I struggled for what felt like hours to right my body and relieve the tension on the rope. I was conscious that Paul would have to free the dead weight at the end of the rope in order to survive and I knew that he would not have long to do this before it became an issue of life and death for him as well. I felt sharp pains shooting through my chest and couldn't catch my breath at all, but I continued to fight against the awkward tangled mess that I was in and miraculously managed to get an axe placement into the ice to relieve some of the tension. Once the first placement was in, I found it much easier to right myself entirely and managed to get my body upright with my crampons dug tightly into the ice.

I was overwhelmed with pain and fear but I knew that I was safe, at least for the moment. The rope was still intact and Paul had not cut me free, but I was also worried that the damage caused by my fall would make the rope unstable and unreliable and was very conscious that a single slip at this stage would kill us both. I started the slow and painful climb up towards Paul and when I reached him we rejoiced in our survival. The impact of my fall had been severe on Paul. Before I broke free from the ice above, Paul had the rope wrapped twice around his waist and the force of my weight in free fall had pulled the rope so tight it nearly cut him in half. We had no waist plates for protection because at that time they did not make any that were suitable for ice-climbing, and Paul's ribs and internal organs were so quickly constricted that he did not even have a chance to take a final gasp. His feet had smashed through his stance and he was knocked upside down and immediately deprived of oxygen. His lungs were so restricted that he could not breathe in or out and he later said that he found the pain totally incapacitating.

Paul was losing consciousness as I struggled to right myself below him. He had little time to react and save his own life and thankfully before he was able to make the decision to cut the rope and release my weight, I created the slack he needed to live. Paul was convinced that I was dead below him and, in those terrible moments before I reconnected with the ice, he was in absolute agony but also overcome with fear and shame. He reflected on this moment many years later and told me that he was in such pain that he was only five seconds from cutting the rope. He knew that if he didn't free himself quickly, he would have died along with me, and he couldn't bear to think about the impact this would have had on our families.

Luckily, when the rope loosened and my placements became secure, Paul was able to breathe and the pain decreased as quickly as it had taken hold. He did not know at this stage if I was dead and had just broken free from the end of the rope or if I was alive and had begun climbing, but either way his physical relief was considerable. Once Paul was free he righted himself and began to pull in the slack rope. To his relief he found me climbing up at the other end of it. When I finally reached him, I was exhausted and so weak that I was nearly numb, but I was alive and eternally grateful for that. I told Paul that I was okay because I did not want to alarm him. I knew we still had a very difficult battle ahead for our survival and I wanted him to have confidence in me.

We had only two options at this stage. One was to abseil off the route using the stretched and weakened rope and the other was to continue to climb up, making as many gear placements as possible because we knew that the rope could not withstand another fall. In the end, the decision was made for us. As Paul continued to reel in the slack rope, we reached a frayed and dangerously worn end that was about 10 feet short of the original length. When I had fallen and the rope had raced out around Paul, it must have cut across the razor-sharp edges of his crampons, severing the end. This left us with no other option than to continue climbing up the steep and treacherous route, and we prayed that we had the strength and gear to make it to the summit.

Although I was doing my best to conceal my pain and terror, Paul knew that I was seriously injured and thus he took all of my gear in with his own and led us back up the route. The first section was very steep. It was the third pitch, known as the 'crux', and as Paul made his way through this narrow chimney, a large block of ice broke free beneath him and struck me hard against the knee. Paul had shouted down as the ice raced in my direction, but there was very little time to react. I was in a sitting belay and my only measure of protection was to push my feet out in front of me to block the ice. Despite my best efforts, it smashed against my kneecap with great speed and the pain that followed left me breathless. Paul felt terrible, but I roared up to him that we could not stop and to go on.

It was now dark and the cold came in around us very quickly. I could feel pins and needles throughout my entire body as the icy dampness seeped in through my clothing. I was shaking uncontrollably and could taste blood in my mouth after each cough. Although it was getting difficult to see in the twilight, the bright red and black clumps that I was spitting stood out against the pure white snow. I was afraid my body would begin shutting down and I tried desperately to cling to consciousness despite my urge to sleep. I was slumped against the gully when I heard Paul roar down for me to begin climbing. I struggled to move and could feel my knee swelling and my mobility decreasing.

It took me a few minutes to find a position that I could climb in without further injuring my knee, but finally I was able to begin the slow process of ascending. Then, just as I reached the most difficult point in the crux, I slipped again. Luckily, I did not fall this time, as Paul was keeping the rope tight and had placed a lot of gear. With every move I had to clench my teeth to overcome the pain. My mouth was completely dry and I did not even have the energy to suck on a piece of snow. I finally reached Paul and we rested briefly whilst assessing the situation. Although I did not realise it at the time, my speech had begun to slur and my face was stony white. Paul was very conscious of my physical deterioration and knew the danger that we were in. He later recalled the circumstances at that stage as dire.

Despite my failing state, we had no choice but to continue and Paul again began to lead us up the route. He was nearly at the fourth pitch when I heard him curse loudly above. He then shouted down for me to get moving and to make every placement count. He advised that each axe swing and kick must be totally secure in the ice and that I could not let myself slip again. This warning heightened my awareness. I was fading in and out of focus but Paul's sharp command brought my mind back to the danger that we were in and I moved up the gully with great precision. When I reached Paul, he pulled me in tight against him. He looked me directly in the eye as he spoke and told me how strong I was and how well I was doing. He went on to say that the remainder of the climb would be more dangerous than what we had encountered thus far and our survival would depend on total focus. He shouted, 'Do you want to live or do you want to die?' and it hit me like a bucket of cold water in the face. He words left me suddenly wide awake and aware. It was then that he hit me with a bombshell. His ice axes had broken and he needed mine to lead the climb. This would leave me with only his broken wooden shafts to stab into the thick ice. At this point it was completely dark and I was terrified at the thought of climbing this steep route without the basic protection of my axes, but I knew that we had no other option.

Paul took my axes and quickly set about the ascent towards the fifth pitch. I watched intently as his silhouette disappeared beyond the glow of my head-torch and began to shiver uncontrollably again. Each time I stopped moving, my teeth would chatter so loudly I could hear the noise echoing off the gully walls. It was -10°C already and it was a totally clear night so I knew that the temperature would continue to fall. Thankfully, the stars were shining brightly above and they illuminated the steep upper slopes of the route. At this point Paul began shouting down for me to release more rope, but there was no more to give him. I could see him in the middle of a sheer vertical pitch with both axes and crampons dug deeply into the ice. He was about 30 feet away from the next safe belay spot and, unbeknownst to me at the time, he was out of ice screws.

Paul was forced to use rock pitons that he was carrying on his harness to create a belay. In a fall, the pitons never would have held as they can only be used in solid rock, but I think they gave Paul a sense of reassurance. He kicked in a narrow platform on the sheer vertical face and used all his remaining strength to belay me up. Before he began the process, he again repeated to me how important each placement was and I knew then that a single slip would send us both plummeting down the gully to certain death. When I finally reached the first ice screw along the pitch, I realised it was solid enough to support a belay. I hooked the sling, which was connected to the harness around my waist, onto the screw and then kicked out a deep, triangular platform to rest my weight on. At that point the muscles in my calves were burning and my knee was swollen to the point that I could no longer bend it. I rested my weight forward so that my kneecap was directly against the cold ice, in order to help reduce the swelling.

This allowed Paul enough slack in the rope to continue along the route until he reached the safety of the rock 30 feet above. When he finally made it to that point, we both took a moment to breathe and rest our tired bodies. We had been climbing for over 10 hours without food or water and both of us were exhausted. I took this moment to suck on a piece of snow and I let the moisture run down my dry and scratchy throat. I was having trouble breathing and had a vice-like feeling in my chest. My lungs would occasionally push out deep and painful coughs that brought up clots of fresh and dried blood, and the salty taste of this phlegm never left me.

After only a very brief rest, I stabbed my way through the ice to reach Paul again. With the temperature dropping as night progressed, the ice was becoming impenetrable and the thick wooden shafts were useless in providing any real traction against the slippery face. By the time I made it to Paul my mitts had frozen solid and my hands were raw and numb. Paul knew that I was in a bad way and for the first time he saw the bloody clots that I was coughing up. He worried that my internal bleeding could be life-threatening if left untreated and again urged me to sharpen up and continue moving as quickly as possible.

Paul persisted in climbing and made it as far as the seventh pitch. Throughout the climb there had been traces of old gear in the gully but after the seventh pitch there was no more gear in place. From that point, he was forced to find his own belay areas and to navigate the route entirely on instinct. This was a very difficult task because there was a huge cornice directly overhead and he was unsure where the best place to approach this giant ice precipice was. Just as Paul stopped to ponder his next placement, I heard the sound of a helicopter approaching overhead.

Initially, I was overjoyed. In my exhaustion and delirium, I thought that a rescue party had been sent to save us. I was so tired and in such constant pain that all I could think about was being winched to safety. I immediately began shouting and waving up at the helicopter but my joy quickly turned to fear as the downdraft from the rotor blades nearly swept the two of us off the mountain. The spindrift of snow and ice that the helicopter brought up felt like glass cutting against our faces. At this stage I still thought they were there to save us, but Paul shouted down to me to 'shut the fuck up'. He told me that there was no way we could be rescued off this gully as we were too exposed on the vertical face and that the helicopter was only moving low overhead, not stopping for us. I was devastated, but I knew in my heart that Paul was right. We had to rescue ourselves at this stage and I worried that I might not have the energy or confidence remaining to do that.

However, once the helicopter had moved away and the snow had settled again my thoughts turned to the fact that Paul had seen head-torches on the observatory ridge and that meant that the others might still be climbing as well. Initially any thoughts I had about the others were spiteful. I imagined them resting at the refuge hut and waiting for our arrival and I was annoyed by the notion of them being warm and comfortable. However, now I was worried that something might have happened to them and hoped that their circumstances were better than our own. I remembered for a second that the helicopter often comes to collect severely injured climbers or to retrieve their bodies, but I could not allow myself to dwell on this thought.

We moved on and at the next pitch I noticed that Paul had placed a sturdy steel piton into the rock and had also backed it up with a 'friend' for extra support. For the first time all day, I felt confident in the placement and took a brief psychological break from my fear. I allowed my body to rest and leaned back to take in the route above. The sky was completely clear and the stars illuminated every last corner of the blackness. The conditions for ice-climbing were ideal and in any other circumstances I might have relished being out on the mountain. I could see the pitch above but beyond that there was only a solid white wave of snow and ice that jutted out from the mountain for over 10 feet and was over 20 feet deep.

This cornice was so vast; I had never seen anything like it in my life. It looked like an ocean wave ready to roll onto the shore and I felt a sense of dread rising up in my stomach as I realised that it could come down upon us at any moment. This dread was worsened by the realisation that it was far too wide to traverse on either side and it came out too far to climb over. The only way to the summit on this route was to cut a chimney through this massive expanse and hope that it held solid as we passed directly through the middle of it.

Although it seemed an impossible feat, I knew that Paul would have to muster all of his remaining strength and use his axes to cut the chimney through the cornice. He hesitated before he set out on this mission and I sensed his apprehension. I shouted up to him that he needed to go for it and that I had the strength to support him if he fell. With that he set about the difficult task of cutting through the ice—but he was careful to place a 'dead man' just below the cornice before he began. A 'dead man' is a metal plate that climbers use for belays in the snow when there is no rock or other solid placement. He was confident that this piece of gear would hold if he fell and shouted down to me that he was secure. The temperature had dropped even further in the past hour and it was now roughly 20 below. My hands were freezing in my soaking mitts and I could tell that one of my fingers had already progressed into frostbite. The cold made the ice as solid as rock and I could see Paul straining with the difficult physical labour.

I was cold and tired but my mind had become incredibly sharp. I was annoyed at myself for the situation that we were in. I had made a catalogue of errors and I knew in my heart that I should have stopped to place more gear before the fall, but after I was unable to get the first ice screw in, it had been easier to continue on. I worried that Paul and I might not survive this night and I felt guilty that my family would never see me again. It was a Friday night and I should have been in a bar or disco with my friends, not dying on a mountain in Scotland. My mother had suffered so much when I had my industrial accident and she worried constantly for my safety. I hoped that I would not cause her further pain and prayed that this night would end and we would both be alive when the sun rose the following morning.

It was not long before ice and snow began to rain down upon me. I was stationary on a small ledge below Paul and the deeper he cut, the more the chips began to accumulate around me. By the time he was three quarters of the way through the cornice, I was nearly buried in snow and ice, but I was grateful to be alive and astonished that the wave of ice had held solid throughout. After a few more swings, I saw light begin to break through the dark ice overhead. Paul worked furiously until he could put his entire arm and axe through the opening. Then he widened the hole, put in a placement and climbed up onto the top of the cornice. He walked about 20 feet, put in some more gear and stood on the summit. Once the gear was safely in place on the solid snow of the summit plateau, he came back to the hole in the cornice and shouted through, 'Banjo, I am in heaven.' Words cannot describe my relief. Paul pulled in the slack on the rope and I quickly pulled out the remaining gear before climbing up through the cornice and onto the summit myself.

As I crossed through the tunnel of ice, I took one final look below me and was stunned by the sheer vertical incline of the route. It was as if we had climbed directly up the face of a skyscraper and the darkness below me made it all the more haunting. I was overwhelmed with relief and I immediately embraced Paul until we fell into the snow together, laughing and crying. The night sky was perfectly clear and we lay in the snow looking up at the stars and thinking about all that we had overcome.

However, this joy was short-lived, as we still had to survive the night before we could descend to safety. It was now after 2.30 in the morning and we had to make it to the refuge hut to meet the others before deciding what to do next. Paul dragged me across the summit plateau to the hut and when we arrived we were shocked to find that the others still had not arrived. Although we were rather concerned, we were both freezing and my pain was growing unbearable. Paul pried open the frozen metal door and we entered the small tin hut. This facility is rarely used as it is only for emergencies and upon entering I worried that it might not be large enough for all five of us to stay the night. I lay down on the floor and again began to shiver uncontrollably. Paul emptied out his pack and covered me with everything he had. He even put the pack itself around me for added warmth and he then elevated my leg. Once I was stabilised, we ate what remained in our packs and chewed the glucose and dextrose tablets that we had packed. We drank the remaining water but it was freezing cold and I found it difficult to swallow.

Once we had refuelled, Paul set out to look for the others. Within a few minutes he located their head-torches on the end of the observatory ridge below the summit. He threw them down a rope and once Kevin made it onto the top, he pulled the others to safety. The men were all exhausted and weather-beaten. They had spent the entire 12 hours completely open to the elements. The wind and cold were horrific and they had been extremely slow to progress as they had three climbers on one rope and one of them was struggling with the exposure. Once they were all safely on the top, they returned to the hut, where we crammed in together to escape the cold. This was a bit ironic, because the hut is nicknamed 'the fridge' for its freezing temperatures. A standard home freezer is set at -18°C and this metal hut was below –20°C. It was no bigger than a tent and the ceiling was so low that we were unable to stand. It was difficult for me to breathe with the others packed in tightly around me but I got a slight relief from the cold with their body heat.

Initially we had the door to the hut open to allow us enough air to breathe, but soon the cold became unbearable and one of the men shut the metal door tightly. Within seconds, Paul screamed at him to open the door. We were all becoming a bit claustrophobic and we feared that if the door froze shut, we could become trapped or run out of air. It was a miserable night and none of us slept. I was in agony with my knee and my frostbitten hand and by the time day broke and we packed our things up to depart, I was almost entirely immobile. The men took my gear and literally had to push me through the small door of the hut as my leg was massively swollen. The conditions on the mountain were horrific. It was a total whiteout and the snow was blowing in every direction. I hobbled and slid across the summit with the help of the others and then began the long and tedious descent down the rocky access route on the mountain.

It took us hours and was excruciatingly painful, but we finally made it to the van which we had left parked at the base of the peak. The men had to literally lift me into the vehicle. They drove me straight to Fort William Hospital and although I worried that I had done significant damage to my body, I was eternally grateful that I had survived the terrible fall and the ensuing epic climb. Images of my upcoming trip to Mount Everest kept flashing through my mind but I refused to let myself think about what the repercussions of this climb would be.

Chapter 6 ∿

THE FIRST IRISH EVEREST EXPEDITION

'The greatest glory in living lies not in never falling, but in rising every time we fall.'
NELSON MANDELA

When I awoke in the hospital bed in Fort William, I was groggy and confused. I remembered arriving at the hospital after we came down off the mountain but everything after those initial moments was a blur. Now I was suddenly alert and alone. To my horror, my right leg was in plaster from toe to hip and I had an intravenous drip in my arm. The gravity of the situation immediately hit me. I became furious with myself for climbing so close to the scheduled departure for Mount Everest and cursed my stupidity as I frantically buzzed the nurses' station. When one of the nurses finally responded, she informed me that my right patella was fractured and that I would need to remain in plaster for several months and have follow-up treatment at the hospital in Newry once I arrived home. Furthermore, she told me that I had suffered a protrusion to my lungs, which had caused an internal bleed that would also require follow-up care. In addition to this, I had frostbite on one of my fingers, but thankfully it appeared that the tissue would recover. I was devastated. I felt like crying. I had only just recovered from the industrial accident and now my mobility was again in jeopardy. More importantly, I had had such high hopes of being part of the first Irish Everest ascent and would now surely lose out on this opportunity.

When the boys arrived at the hospital later on that morning, they were astonished to see me already attempting to get up out of the bed and move about. I decided to ring my mother and break the news of my accident to her. As soon as she answered the phone she asked me what was wrong. She said that she had had a terrible feeling all during the night that something had happened to me and she had been waiting for me to call. I told her about my broken knee but assured her that I was fine and would be home late that evening if they allowed me to be discharged. I did not tell her anything about my lung injury, as I knew it would be too upsetting for her. Luckily, I was fit to be discharged that afternoon and I made the long journey home in the van and on the ferry with the others. It was an exhausting journey but we were all grateful that the climb was over and that the outcome had not been worse.

Over the following weeks I attended several appointments at Daisy Hill Hospital, where the injuries to my knee and lungs were monitored. I had not told Dawson or the Irish Everest Committee about my injuries and the date for our departure was approaching rapidly. Much to the shock of my friends and family, I was still intent on being a part of the expedition. I had not mentioned to the doctors that I would be setting off on a climb within a matter of weeks because I knew that they would vehemently object to this plan. I was unsure how seriously the injuries would impact my ability to complete the trek, but I had no intentions of missing out on this enormous opportunity. When the Everest committee convened a final meeting two weeks before our scheduled date of departure, I cut the plaster off my leg at home with a Stanley knife and scissors so they would not know that I was injured.

After removing the cast, I initially found it difficult to bend the knee and had great pain in the joint as I walked, but this subsided over several days. I knew that I had very little time to recover, so I went to the hospital and told them of my plans with the hope that they would begin my physical therapy treatment. Despite their concerns, they agreed to fast-track the therapy and I began working on strengthening the muscles and increasing my mobility each day. One day when I was out walking in Newry centre, I met a man on the street who recognised me from the media coverage of the Everest expedition. His name was Jim Morgan and our chance meeting that afternoon had a very positive impact on my recovery.

As Jim and I spoke, we discussed my recent accident and how little time I had to recover. I told him about the exercises that I was using to promote healing and said to him that my main difficulties were joint pain and stiffness. Jim's wife was suffering from multiple sclerosis and also had great difficulty with pain and stiffening of the muscles. He mentioned to me that she regularly used a pressurised chamber, which helped to alleviate her discomfort and to ease her rigidity. Jim felt that I could benefit from sessions in the chamber as well and agreed to make all of the necessary arrangements for me.

I felt a vast improvement after several treatments and when the date for our departure finally arrived, I was walking with only a slight limp. I did not feel any impact from the injury to my lungs, but I continued to worry that this condition might return at altitude, when the lungs are put under great strain. I also worried that the combination of joint problems and breathing difficulties might prevent me from ascending as far as advanced base camp, but I was willing to take the chance.

There were 14 of us from all over Ireland in the second trekking party who set off on the trip from Dublin to Kathmandu, Nepal together. This group comprised men and women who came from all levels of experience in climbing and hill-walking and had a variety of professional backgrounds. I was the youngest in the trekking party, at 25 years of age, with some of the older members in their mid-fifties. Despite the massive difference in age, we all had a common interest and had trained hard to be part of the expedition. There were three trekking parties in all supporting the Irish expedition and all of the groups would ascend to advanced base camp, separated by two-week intervals. This would allow the climbers to maximise the amount of gear and supplies that each group transported. This gear would be stashed at advanced base camp and eventually moved further up the peak to the high camps by the climbers themselves.

From the outset of the trip I was like a child. I was so excited that I couldn't sleep on the long flight over and was restless throughout the entire journey. When we finally touched down in Kathmandu after a short but shaky flight from Delhi, I literally bounded off the plane. At that time passengers disembarked directly onto the tarmac and I will never forget the heat coming up off the ground. It was literally steaming. I could immediately feel the humidity and there was a strong smell of fuel and sweat in the air. We entered the terminal building, which was not much more than a tin shack, and quickly passed through immigration. As we collected our baggage a barrage of people descended upon us in hopes of being paid to carry our things.

Initially I did not know how to react to this. It was my first time in Asia or travelling in the developing world and I did not want to seem rude. However, we were eventually forced to literally push our way past these men as they continued to harass us all the way to the waiting buses. Once we were all on board, we were taken to Thamel, a section of the city where most of the tourists and climbers stay. Our hotel was centrally located and very clean. Everyone on the expedition shared a room and I bunked in with Séamus Brady, a radiologist who was originally from Hilltown but was now living in Nutts Corner. Séamus was a great person for me to be paired with as he was really easygoing and enjoyed having a laugh.

On that first day, Séamus and I tried to sleep for a few hours to get over the jetlag and then we headed out with the other trekkers to explore the city. The streets of Kathmandu were as chaotic and dirty as I had imagined they would be. The never-ending hustle and bustle of the market stalls surrounded by beggars and street children was overwhelming. It took us over an hour to move just a few hundred metres, as we were constantly harassed for money or goods. The streets were packed with cars and motorcycles competing to break through the traffic, and the odd cow would wander down the middle of the road as horns blared around it.

As we were walking along, I suddenly noticed the sky growing dark and heard the distant rumble of thunder. Then, before any of us could seek shelter, the skies opened up and a massive storm dropped inches of rain down within moments. We had arrived just on the cusp of monsoon season. This deluge caused the narrow, filthy streets to flood. We were left literally wading through the water as we made our way to a nearby restaurant. Then, just as we reached the doors of this café, the electricity in the city went out and we were forced to eat by candlelight. It was an interesting introduction to life in Kathmandu and gave me a full appreciation of the hardships faced in the developing world.

Over the following two days we remained in Kathmandu and went sightseeing in the surrounding areas. Finally, on the third day, we departed for our six-day acclimatising trip to the hills beyond the city, known as the Lang Tang Hamal trek. We were collected by bus and taken to the base of the mountains, where we began our journey on foot. It was a pleasant hike, but myself and some other members of the expedition were already beginning to experience the downside of altitude and Third World cooking: headaches and diarrhoea! However, we were all working well together as a team and the scenery on the trek was fantastic.

The lush, green, terraced landscape rose up around us with magnificent precision. We passed Nepali women working in the fields with their babies tied in papooses on their backs. They were so unbelievably friendly and would go out of their way to greet us as we passed. The children would also chase alongside of us, shouting the Nepali greeting of 'Namaste', until they tired of this game and ran back home. In the villages the children were so innocent, they would come to inspect our belongings and ask us to give them pens. This was in total contrast to the children in the cities who were hardened by life on the streets and begged only for money and food to survive.

At night we would camp at pre-arranged sites along the route and all of our gear would be organised and set up by our Sherpas and porters. This was really strange for me. I had never been on a climbing trip where I had not carried all of my own gear and couldn't believe the level of service that these men provided. Once we were all in our tents, there were cooks who would prepare our nightly meals. After dinner we would stay up by a campfire, telling stories and singing songs. The weather was excellent on the trek and all of us finished the six days feeling strong and upbeat. We were now eager to set off on the week-long journey to the base camp of Mount Everest and looked forward to the challenges that lay ahead.

When we arrived back into the valley below the hills where we had trekked, we took a crowded bus back into Kathmandu. Many of the locals ride on the roof of the bus when it is full and myself and some of the other expedition members ended up riding there as well. I will never forget leaning over the side to take in the scenery when some Nepali men held my legs, allowing me to 'surf' against the wind. It was a fantastic experience and thankfully the bus driver kept the vehicle steady whilst it was happening, because the narrow roads climb and fall along sheer vertical drops in the landscape; and cars and buses have been known to plunge over the edge.

Once we arrived back in Kathmandu I went for a walk on my own around the city and began to explore the shops and stalls. It was a stiflingly hot day and I bought myself an ice cream from one of the local vendors to cool down. Within an hour of eating the ice cream I began to experience severe abdominal cramps and immediately knew that I needed to find a toilet quickly. I looked around everywhere for a place that might have a bathroom but could not find a restaurant or hotel in sight. Unfortunately, what followed was not one of my finer moments: I was forced to duck into a doorway in a back alley and relieve myself, with Nepali people walking past. I was mortified, but had no other option. An old woman stopped to check on me and was speaking to me in Nepali as I desperately tried to hide my face from her. By the time I made it back to my hotel, all I could do was crawl into bed. Luckily my roommate, Séamus, gave me medication that night and by the next morning my stomach had settled and I was ready to set off again.

We left Kathmandu in an old bus, which brought us to the border with Tibet, known as the Friendship Bridge. We spent one night here in a small guesthouse before heading across the border into Tibet. At this stage we were driven in a convoy of Land Cruisers along with the Chinese Liaison Officer who had been assigned to our expedition at the border. He was a very stern man who spoke only broken English and immediately appeared to be short-tempered and lacking in humour. He explained to us the rules of visiting Tibet and informed us that we were strictly prohibited from bringing in images of the Dalai Lama (the exiled Buddhist leader) or speaking publicly about him. In fact, when he welcomed us, he actually announced that we were entering China and told us that Tibet was not really an independent state at all. I immediately challenged him on this but he quickly dismissed me. He later advised me that we would have problems with each other on the journey if I continued to speak out about the Chinese occupation.

Once we progressed beyond the Nepali border regions, we entered the dry, barren passes of lower Tibet. It was then that I began to see how remote Tibet really is. Many of the villages that we passed were separated by several hours of driving over rocky, dry terrain where the land seemed completely inhospitable. I could not imagine how they procured water or harvested crops, but somehow these people managed to survive. We also passed convoys of nomadic tribes and yak-herders along the route, but they could only be seen on the horizon in the distance.

We stayed in several small villages along the route to Everest and would visit local monasteries and religious sites. I tried to speak to the Tibetan people in these areas because they seemed so friendly and receptive to foreign visitors. However, no one spoke English in these distant outposts and our Liaison Officer kept us all under a strict watch, so this prevented many of the Tibetans from approaching us. Despite the lack of communication they seemed to be a warm and beautiful people. They have very round faces with scarlet cheeks and bright white teeth. Their jet-black hair is long and thick and they wear brightly coloured robes and scarves over their heavy coats. They even adorn their yaks with brightly dyed silk and many of these animals would pass us with red material woven through their manes.

Once we finally reached the high, snowy passes that cross through the Himalayan peaks, we were given our first views of what was to come. I thought I had seen majestic mountains during my previous climbs, but I was totally awestruck by the sheer size and beauty of the Himalayas. And the first views of these mountains paled in comparison to the moment that I set eyes on Mount Everest, the massive giant towering above its surrounding peaks. This sight left me breathless. I felt so overcome with emotion, I nearly cried. I remembered my first hike up Slieve Donard as a young boy and my dreams of climbing far and wide. I had come from so little and had travelled so far.

I wanted to capture that moment for my mother and my friends and to share with them the sense of pride and achievement that I felt. From the first moment that Mount Everest came into my view until the day we arrived at the Rombuk Glacier to begin our trek, I could not take my eyes off the towering peak. I felt humbled by the sheer size of Everest and wanted nothing more than to be a member of the summit team and to have a chance at seeing the mountain in all of its glory.

On the two-day trek to the base camp, we underwent a serious rise in altitude and all of us began to suffer from various degrees of altitude sickness. I was still experiencing pain in my knee and was afraid that the others would notice my injury if I limped or favoured that leg too much. I could also feel a strain in my chest when I was breathing. We were at nearly 17,000 feet above sea level and at that time, the highest mountain that I had ever climbed was below 16,000 feet at the summit.

I will never forget trying to sleep the first night along the glacier. It was well below zero and I felt like I was suffocating in the tent. Despite the freezing temperatures, I had to keep unzipping the flaps to take in gulps of air. I hoped that my lungs would withstand the low pressure. I knew that the altitude would pose a serious obstacle to many of the trekkers and climbers alike and prayed that the injury I had suffered to my lungs would not make me more vulnerable to the life-threatening condition of pulmonary oedema: where the lungs fill with fluid, causing a person to drown in their own bodily fluids.

I didn't sleep at all that first night, but the high of the experience kept me going the next day and I never felt fatigued. When we finally reached the last stop on the glacier below Mount Everest, where Rombuk Monastery is located, I was nearly giddy with excitement. Rombuk is an amazing landmark along the route. The old concrete building has stood the test of time and, despite the unimaginably harsh environment and a bombing during the Cultural Revolution of the 1950s, it has remained intact for nearly 100 years. I was awestruck by the basic but solid composition of the structure and by its lonely occupants. We met local monks and nuns who reside year-round in this incredibly isolated small community at an altitude of over 17,000 feet!

Many of them were elderly and none showed any sign of strain under the burden of the altitude. They lived and practised Buddhism beneath the stark, white beauty of Mount Everest and apart from the climbers and Sherpas who stop in on their way to the mountain each year, they remain almost entirely cut off from the outside world. I was really taken aback by their isolated lifestyle and could not fathom the sacrifices that they make in the name of their religion. They were so devout and strong, I felt humbled by them.

The monks gave our climb their blessing that afternoon and we set up our camp outside the monastery that night. I am not sure why, but I suddenly felt calm and content and slept very well. I was breathing more easily and had begun to adapt to the cold. The following morning we set off on the one-hour hike to the base camp and arrived on the dusty plateau just before noon. I had not expected the base camp to be so barren and rocky. It was below the snow line of the glacier and was not even really on the mountain itself. However, despite the rather dismal camp, the views around us were breathtaking. Everest loomed over us and the surrounding Himalayan peaks were dwarfed by its presence. There were only a few other expeditions at the base camp when we arrived and the vast glacier made it all seem very remote.

There was a small glacial stream that ran through the camp and this is where we got all of our water for cooking, cleaning and drinking. Despite the fact that this water came directly from runoff of snow and ice on the mountain, it was not very clean. The long history of climbing expeditions on the peak had taken its toll on the glacier and we were careful to boil and treat the water before use. We were all very conscious of the need to maintain good hygiene and health as altitude slows the body's ability to heal. Even a small cut or graze can become infected quite quickly at elevation and it is very easy to pick up germs and bugs whilst living in cramped quarters. Despite all of the precautions we took, many of the expedition's trekkers became ill during those first days at the base camp and were thus unable to progress further up the mountain.

Luckily, I felt very strong and well despite my recent injuries and the excessive weight of my pack. As I had not wanted to draw any attention to my bad leg, I had volunteered to carry a substantial load. I was carrying all of my essential gear along with extra high-altitude gear (in hopes of being allowed to progress to the North Col) as well as a satellite dish with connecting hand-held radios for the climbers to use during the latter half of the ascent. At that time there were no portable satellite phones and this bulky and cumbersome apparatus was their only option for making phone calls home.

After a few days at the base camp those who were feeling well enough began the ascent to advanced base camp. This 21-mile trek across the lower glacier on the peak was completed in two stages. After walking roughly half of the distance, we slept at an intermediate camp before progressing the final 10 miles to advanced base camp the following day. The route consisted of scree slopes and moraine and was technically straightforward, but physically challenging. There were many crevasses and steep hills and the altitude rose by over 3,000 feet as we made the ascent. Despite the challenges, I enjoyed every minute of the experience and was awestruck by the fantastic scenery. There

My mother with me; Eamon in the background.

Myself in primary school, wearing the Christian Brothers school uniform.

The Bosses Ridge just below the summit of Mount Blanc, with winds of 60+ mph, 1990.

The Ben Nevis climbers, taken on departure day, 1993: (*from left to right*) Stephen Ferris, Kevin Quinn, Jim Milligan, myself, Paul Clerkin, and Kevin's daughter at the front.

Paul Clerkin on the rogue pitch, 'point five', Ben Nevis, Scotland.

The epic ascent up 'point five', Ben Nevis.

Mum and I outside the family home, Barcroft Park, upon return from Everest in 1993.

Kevin Quinn, along the river in Talkeetna, Alaska, with Denali in the background, at the outset of our climb in 1995.

Ascending from 14,000 ft to 17,000 ft on Denali, 1995.

Kevin Quinn and I at 17,000 ft camp on Denali, 1995. We are wearing gear from the 1975 Irish Afghanistan expedition.

Kevin Quinn and I on the summit of Denali, 1995.

Myself on the north-east ridge on Mount Logan, 1997.

The view of the north-east ridge of Mount Logan from the plane.

Myself climbing Angels Crest on Squamish, British Columbia, 1997.

Rock climbing, Angels Crest.

Climbing in Yosemite National Park, California, 1999, with the Half Dome in the background.

Myself crossing Lost Arrow Direct by Tyrolean traverse, Yosemite National Park.

Beneath a waterfall outside Cairns in Queensland, Australia, during my around-the-world adventure, 2000.

Rock climbing in Krabi Bay, Thailand, 2000.

The Irish Everest expedition, 2003. (*From left to right*) David Sharp, Martin Duggan, Stephen Synott, myself, Richard Dougan, Jamie McGuinness.

Equipment on route to Everest base camp.

Everest base camp.

A view of Everest through the
prayer flags at base camp.

A yak transporting gear to advanced base camp, Mount Everest.

The Ice Nuns on the East Rombuk Glacier, Mount Everest.

Traversing the Ice Nuns on Mount Everest.

Ascending the north col on
Mount Everest.

David Sharp at camp two on Everest.

Self-portrait on the summit of Mount Everest, taken at 8 a.m., 31 May 2003.

Another self-portrait, summit of Mount Everest, same day.

Looking down from the summit of Mount Everest on the north-east ridge.

were large, white pinnacles of ice, known as the 'white nuns', that rose up from the ground to a height of several storeys. As we passed among these unusual features, I stopped for several moments to reflect on how amazing the journey was.

After passing the 'white nuns', we met a group of nomadic herdsmen who were crossing over the route. These small, weathered old men led their caravans of yaks down through the steep passes and over the rocky scree slopes as they made their way across the glacier to far-off lands. I will never forget the potent smell of yak dung in the midday heat as the animals stopped to rest along the path. None of the men spoke a word of English but we communicated with them through hand signals and head nods. We showed them our climbing gear and cameras and even traded our socks for their traditional knives and other souvenirs. Many of the nomads had fossils from the lower glacier in which the outlines of insects and sea creatures had been set into stone over 60 million years ago, when Everest was submerged under water. The glacier was littered with these remains and the men would dig through the rock and ice to collect them in hopes of trading or selling them on to Western climbers.

The trek between the two camps was a fantastic experience. I was so excited by everything we saw and each encounter with the Tibetan people endeared them more to me. By the time we reached advanced base camp many of the other trekkers were feeling ill, and several were even forced to turn back, but I was feeling great. Thankfully David Irwin, a dentist from Belfast, Frank O'Reilly, a solicitor from Wicklow, and my roommate Séamus Brady were all still feeling well and made it into the camp alongside me. As the four of us arrived at ABC, we celebrated our success. That night we had a little party and split a bar of Dairy Milk chocolate that I had packed for this special occasion. All of the Irish expedition's climbers were based at this camp and we discussed the logistics for the next stage of the climb with them. I wanted more than ever to be able to progress further up the peak, but I was told by Dawson Stelfox that he did not have the insurance to allow trekkers to continue on. Although I had known in my heart that I would not be allowed beyond advanced base camp, I was still very disappointed by this news. I was the only trekker who felt fit enough to continue and was certain that I could reach the North Col without difficulty. Although Dawson could empathise with my desire to progress, in the end he could not allow it as an accident would have jeopardised his reputation and the entire expedition.

Myself and the other trekkers spent only two nights at advanced base camp before we were forced to head back down to reunite with the others for our return journey through Tibet. It was a very difficult time for me emotionally. I felt so strong and confident in my abilities as a climber and yet I was only able to complete the basic trekking route. At the time I did not realise how important it was to build experience and felt as if I could have left them all behind and ascended to the summit on my own. In reality, however, this would have been a far greater challenge than I could ever have imagined and my inexperience would have proven life-threatening.

On the last night at advanced base camp, I got out of my tent and looked up at the stars above me for over an hour. The air was freezing but I could not feel the cold. All I could feel was the mountain beckoning me on. There was something almost magnetic about Everest for me. It had haunted my dreams since I was only a boy and I knew that I would not feel complete until I had stood on its summit. As we set off the following morning and bade our farewells to the climbers who would go on for the top, I knew that one day I would return and follow in their footsteps.

Despite the conflict in my heart and head, I went back down to base camp and prayed that the team would successfully complete a first Irish summit. I felt privileged to have been a part of the team and hoped that all of the men would make a safe return.

Once I arrived back at base camp we stayed a further night before beginning the journey through Tibet. I remember taking one last photograph as the Land Cruisers arrived at the camp to collect us. I stood below the towering peak and looked hard against the white horizon for signs of life above. I imagined the Irish team ascending towards the North Col and setting their high-altitude camps for the summit push. I dreamt of the sights they would see from this towering height and felt a pang of jealousy as I loaded my gear into the vehicle.

We set off that morning in a convoy of vehicles for a tour of Tibet that would take us to the capital city of Lhasa after a five-day journey. From here we would fly back to Nepal and then on to our return flights home. The journey was spectacular. We crossed the high glacial passes on the Tibetan plains and saw yak herds being led through the hills above. There were turquoise-blue glacial lakes that reflected the sun's light like jewels in the ground; the panoramic views of the sweeping Himalayan range sparkled white. The vehicles travelled slowly over the rocky dirt roads and I never rested as we bumped along for fear I would miss even a single moment of the spectacular journey.

As we passed through one of the incredibly dry and dusty low areas, I noticed a speck on the horizon, which seemed to be moving closer to us. As our convoy progressed, the speck took the shape of a person and after a few more moments, I could see a young boy running down the hill towards our vehicles. Our driver was a Chinese man who spoke little English so when I first asked him to stop, he was not aware of what I was saying. However, once he realised what I wanted, he protested in Chinese. I persisted in commanding him to stop the vehicle and he finally relented. Just then the child made his final strides towards the Jeep and I jumped out to shake his hand. He had run all the way from one of the high passes down through the fields and snow to this narrow stretch of road to meet our convoy, and I was not going to let us pass him by. He must have been about 13 years old but he looked far younger. I would guess that his family were nomadic herdsmen and he had most likely never seen Westerners before. He was so eager to meet these strange people travelling in vehicles through his native lands that he ran with all of his might to greet us. When I shook his hand he stared up at me in awe. I had a thick ginger beard at this stage and he seemed incredulous about the hair growing on my face. I was wearing headphones for my cassette player and I gave him a listen. He had a broad smile on his face as I put them on his ears and he jumped with a start when I turned the music on. I will never forget how Pink Floyd's 'Dark Side of the Moon' blared through the speakers as a shocked expression spread across his face. It was a moment that was worthy of a thousand words.

We only spent a few minutes with this young man but my encounter with him will remain with me forever. That chance meeting epitomised everything that I envisioned my trip would be. It was a faraway adventure in a distant land and it was all encapsulated in a matter of seconds. Once we left him, I could see his silhouette waving in the distance as our vehicles continued on and I imagined him standing there until we were only a shadow in the dusky sky. Our journey took us through many of the small villages and isolated monasteries that dot the Tibetan landscape. I could see how important the Buddhist religion was to the people as we passed prayer flags blowing in the wind alongside mountain passes. I was saddened to see the effects of the Chinese occupation in all of the destroyed Buddhist temples throughout the country and found the atmosphere and physical environment in the capital city the most depressing.

The day that we arrived into Lhasa, we passed through several Chinese military checkpoints and drove by the newly established prison on the outskirts of town that had been created especially for political prisoners. There were Chinese soldiers and secret police marching throughout the streets and the Tibetan people did not appear to be at ease in their own country. There was a definite sense of hesitation in the local people we met and none seemed comfortable speaking with us in public. We stayed in a small guesthouse in the centre of the town and visited the important religious sites in the area that had not been destroyed or closed down. Most importantly, we travelled to the Potala Palace, the former home of the Dalai Llama.

The Potala Palace remains an imposing fortress set on a hill high above Lhasa and the many rooms inside are still occupied by traditional Buddhist monks studying their religion. However, even this sanctuary is not without Chinese occupation. The monks are not trusted to study and practise their religion alone, so there are Chinese monks within the building who act as spies for the occupying force. As we walked through the dark, narrow corridors of this building, I got a feeling for the deep history embedded in this nation and had a true appreciation for the peaceful mountain people who live in these harsh lands. I also empathised with their struggles and could relate to their despair at having their native land forcefully taken by a foreign power.

Séamus, Frank and I spent many hours wandering around the vast palace and its small, hidden chambers. Many of the rooms have doors which open onto small outdoor verandas, and we took time to stand in the sunlight and view the city streets below. As we stood on one of these perches we witnessed the violence to which the Tibetan people are subjected by the soldiers. We saw several Chinese officers with canes whipping three Tibetan boys for some minor infraction and we were all sickened by the harsh punishment that they were receiving. Just as I began to comment to Frank and Séamus about how horrible this was to witness, Frank hurled an apple down hard upon one soldier's head. The three of us immediately ducked and ran through the corridors of the palace as the soldiers ceased the beating and began to look for the culprit. We could hear angry shouting and pandemonium from below as we made our escape. There were doors slamming and the sounds of rooms being checked but we had quickly disappeared into a crowd of tourists viewing the palace grounds. I was delighted with Frank and although we had to watch our backs all day, it was well worth it!

Despite the initial warnings that we had received from our Liaison Officer about possession of contraband images of the Dalai Llama, I had imported quite a few from Kathmandu to disperse amongst the Tibetan people. I had about 100 small images of the holy leader's face and spent the trip secretly handing them out to older men and women who I prayed were not Chinese spies. In the end I gave them all out successfully and hoped very much that this small gesture had eased the suffering of the kind and generous people who had welcomed us to their land.

In the end, all of the second trekking party departed Lhasa together on a flight to Kathmandu. Once we arrived there, everyone stayed a further night in the hotel together before setting off for home. I, however, had decided to remain in Nepal on my own for a few more weeks to do some climbing in the Himalayas. I knew that this was a once-in-a-lifetime opportunity and I decided to make the most of it. I had discussed the possibility of making an ascent with one of the Irish climbers at advanced base camp and with his guidance I put together an itinerary.

I met Mick Murphy on my first night at advanced base camp and he told me about his previous climbs throughout Nepal. Mick was a small but very solid man with a strong climbing background and a great deal of ambition. We talked about the expeditions that he had staged in Nepal, including a solo summit of Ama Dablan, and I was immediately impressed. He was impassioned when it came to the mountains and greatly enjoyed his Himalayan experiences. I knew from speaking with him that these remote peaks were the perfect place for me to climb and once he told me about Island Peak, I was confident that this was the ascent I should make.

The climb was accessible through the same gateway used to reach Mount Everest on the south side and could be completed within three days if the weather was good and there were no issues with acclimatisation. I knew that I was strong enough after my trek to advanced base camp and had already made the arrangements to stay off work for several months, so I decided to seize the opportunity and complete a solo ascent of Island Peak.

I set off from Kathmandu by plane to Lukla in Northern Nepal and from here I hired a porter and made the trek to the base of Island Peak within three days. This trek usually takes one week, but I was feeling very strong and my porter was an incredibly fit young Nepali man who had no difficulty keeping up with me. He spoke excellent English and was great company for me along the way. I hired one tent and some cooking gear for us to share and we purchased a supply of local food as well. I did not have the necessary permits for making a summit ascent on Island Peak and did not have the money or time to acquire them, so I told the Ministry for Tourism and the porter himself that I was only intending to trek to the base camp. However, as we made our way towards the glacier, he noticed my ice axes, rope and high-altitude gear and was immediately suspicious of my intentions.

Once we began to trek along the glacier and had passed all of the government checkpoints, I advised him of my true intentions. He was initially quite nervous and reluctant to continue on with me as my planned ascent took us off the normal trail and onto the vast glacier, which was unfamiliar territory to him. However, I had a solid topographical map and was confident in my navigating abilities, and I finally convinced him to go along with me with the help of some extra money. Although he agreed to stay with me throughout the ascent, I worried that he might try to rob me or leave me out on the glacier whilst I was going for the summit. I decided not to pay him until the climb was complete, and hid my money carefully in with my gear in hopes that he would stay with the plan for the monetary reward at the end. I also used guilt to keep him on my side and told him I could die from exposure after the descent if he left me. Thankfully, he was a very genuine man and was somewhat appalled that I would even think he could do such a thing.

Once I knew that the porter was trustworthy, I felt more confident about the climb and we began the difficult work of ascending the moraine below Island Peak together. It took us a full day to trek in and after a brief rest that night, I set off in the early hours of the morning for my attempt on the summit. Before I left, my porter wished me well and said that he would pray for my safe return. I was grateful for his honesty and support and knew that he was brave to have accompanied me this far. If something happened to me on my ascent it would have jeopardised the porter's life as well as my own. He would have been in serious trouble for accompanying a Western climber outside the restricted areas and onto Island Peak without the proper permits and would have been forced to account for his involvement. I was very conscious of this as I climbed and vowed to make a safe and fast ascent to get us both off the mountain quickly.

The climb was fairly straightforward. I followed the slope up to the ridge and then stayed along the ridgeline directly to the summit. It was steep in places but entirely manageable and once I was on the ridge, there was no navigation necessary. I made it to the summit with extreme speed and ease and felt so confident in my climbing that I stopped to celebrate my success for longer than normal. I sat on the summit point with the sun shining off the white-capped mountains all around me. It was not Mount Everest, but Island Peak was a challenging Himalayan mountain and I knew that my experience here would prove vital to a future ascent on the world's highest peak.

I descended quickly and without incident and luckily found the porter and my tent in place at the base camp. We decided not to make the return journey until the following morning, as I was exhausted from the climb. That day the glacier creaked and groaned beneath us as avalanches struck the upper slopes of the surrounding peaks. I could tell that the porter was very afraid of becoming trapped on the glacier if an avalanche blocked our path or if poor weather came in. That night thick clouds enveloped the sky overhead and by early morning it had begun to snow. We knew then that we needed to move quickly, so we set off with the heavy flakes accumulating around us. We made it all the way back to Namche Bizarre in one full day and the following morning we trekked to Lukla and back into the mountain villages.

When we reached civilisation again, I paid the porter well for his loyalty and services and was grateful that I had met such a kind and honest man. We parted ways wishing each other the best of luck in the future and I promised to find him again if I ever returned to climb in the area. When I arrived back in Kathmandu, I returned to the hotel where we had all originally stayed. Whilst I was here, I met up with Mick Murphy again and he informed me that there had been a successful Irish summit. Dawson Stelfox had become the first Irishman to stand on the summit of Mount Everest, on 27 May 1993. Although Mick was disappointed that he had not been able to make it to the top himself, he was also quite proud of Dawson's achievement and had learned a great deal during the ascent. I knew at that moment that Mick would be back to climb Everest again in the future because, like myself, he seemed to be drawn towards the top.

I spent a few more days in Kathmandu, waiting for Dawson and Frank Nugent (another Irish climber, who nearly made the summit) to return from the mountain. When they finally arrived, myself and the other Irish men who remained in the city celebrated their tremendous success at a local restaurant. Within a few days of that celebration, the men set off for home and I decided once again to remain and travel some more through southern Nepal and India.

I flew into New Delhi alone in the midst of a stifling heat wave. The day that I arrived it was over 45°C and there were reports of people throughout the region dying from heat stroke. I could not believe how paralysing the heat was. There was 100% humidity on top of the already rocketing temperatures and my body felt smothered by the heavy air. I did not breathe properly from the moment that I stepped off the plane until the day that I departed.

I went straight from the airport to Connaught Circus in the heart of the city, where there was a YMCA hostel for young travellers. When I arrived at the hostel I was hopeful about getting an air-conditioned room but this hope was quickly dispelled as I learned that the only remaining rooms had basic ceiling fans. I had no choice but to take one and dreaded the long, sweaty night ahead. The man working in reception advised me that the heat was a serious hazard and not to leave the hostel at all until after sunset. He reported that foreign travellers often become severely dehydrated during the heat waves and some have even died as a result of heat stroke.

When I finally got into my small room it was like a sauna. The windows were all wide open and the ceiling fan was turning at its highest speed and yet there was not even a trace of relief in the air. I immediately soaked a sheet from the bed with cool water and stacked together items in the room to prop the bed up closer to the fan. I lay in the room for hours until I could no longer bear staring at the four walls around me. I decided to explore the city and hired a taxi outside the hostel to take me around the local sites. For the first time since I had arrived, I felt a small rush of cool air as the wind blew in through the open car windows.

I was amazed by the crowded streets and bazaars in the city and by the strong smells of the Indian food and spices. I wandered through the small, winding streets and stopped to watch a snake-charmer delicately blowing through his wooden flute. I had seen this done on television and in movies but had never imagined I would see it in person. There were camels being led through the heart of the markets on their way to the outlying areas of the city and children and limbless beggars sat around the streets corners, waiting for charitable donations. I was very conscious of the risk of being robbed and kept a close watch around me at all times. I could not believe how crowded it was and was constantly bumped into and knocked about by the vast crowd of people around me.

After a few days sightseeing in the city I decided to visit the Taj Mahal. I arranged for a taxi to collect me at the hostel in the early morning so that I could make the three-hour train journey and arrive at the site before the midday heat set in. However, as luck would have it my taxi was very late collecting me and by the time we made it to the streets near the train station, it appeared that I would miss my train. Then suddenly, I heard a loud rumble. Initially, I thought that we were in for a serious thunder and lightning storm, but the traffic came to a standstill around us and my taxi driver seemed concerned. We sat for about 10 minutes and by then soldiers and police had begun to stream past us. I realised that the sound I had heard was not a storm but rather some type of explosion. I was still not sure what was happening and kept urging my driver to try a different route. Thankfully he spoke excellent English and after speaking with a passing police officer he told me that neither of us were going anywhere. There had been a bomb at the train station and many people had been killed. The city was shutting down and I was advised to walk back to my hostel and to remain inside until I received further news about the situation.

In hindsight, I would probably have been more concerned about the security situation if I had not grown up in Northern Ireland during the height of the Troubles. I wasn't worried about safety at all and decided to sightsee along the outskirts of the city despite the warnings, but I was smart enough to stay away from government and tourist buildings. In the end I spent a further day in the city before getting a bus north to Darjeeling. A Kashmiri separatist group had taken responsibility for the bomb and the city remained under tight security, so I decided it was best to head elsewhere. When I arrived into Darjeeling, I felt an immediate sense of relief. This mountainous region was significantly cooler than the low-lying city of Delhi and the beautiful scenery and tea plantations delighted me. There were massive colonial estates with a mixture of Indian and British architecture and the marks of the British Empire remained everywhere. I walked through the lush gardens and hills and visited some of the temples in the region before I made my way back to Delhi, where I finally began the long journey home.

My visit to India was the perfect conclusion to my Asian adventure. I felt a great sense of achievement after my successful summit on Island Peak and had learned so much through my travels in Nepal, Tibet and India. I had always struggled academically in school but I discovered a real thirst for knowledge when I travelled. I revelled in the historical significance of the places I visited and was already planning further journeys and adventures as I boarded the plane for home.

When I finally arrived back into Dublin I was exhausted from my time away but excited to share my stories with friends and family. When I got off the plane and collected my gear, I was shocked to see my girlfriend, Lisa, my entire family and many friends waiting for me in the airport terminal. They had travelled down by bus from Newry and had large banners and signs celebrating my journey to Mount Everest. We returned to Barcroft as a large group and there was a party arranged at my mother's house. It was a fantastic night that continued on until the early hours of the morning. Although I was honoured by the festivities that my mother had arranged, I was also disappointed that I had not been on the summit team. I knew that I had a lot of training and climbing to do before I could return to Everest but I vowed that day that the next celebration would be in honour of the ultimate success: I would stand on the summit of the world's highest peak.

Chapter 7 ∿

| DENALI

'It is not the mountain that we conquer, but ourselves.'
SIR EDMUND HILLARY

After I returned home from Asia in 1993, I once again returned to climbing in the mountains of Ireland and spent a great deal of time tackling technical routes with Kevin Quinn. I remained in my job as a welder and fabricator at PWS, but I was spending more time working with Shannaghmore, leading groups in the evenings and on the weekends. I was also more involved with canoeing and was now doing a lot of voluntary youth work with Barcroft Community Centre, where we would take the young people out on trips to the rivers and mountains. Dermie Russell was still working as the warden for the club and he and I enrolled in canoeing courses and competed together in local competitions. We completed the Liffey Descent that year, a national competition in white water canoeing that takes place in Dublin. We were in the open Canadian Canoe category and we placed well in the event.

My desire to work with young people in outdoor pursuits was stronger than ever and I did not mind that voluntary work consumed most of my free time, because it gave me the opportunity to share my experiences with adolescents from the area where I grew up. I felt tremendously proud when I told them about my travels in Asia and climbing in Europe and hoped to encourage them to expand their horizons as well. I was also still involved with boxing and many of the young lads I worked with admired my achievements. Boxing was a great asset for me because the young men were often keen to learn the sport and relished gaining skills within the ring. It was great for me to see them achieving positive things and harnessing their energy in a way that had proven so beneficial for me.

During this time, Kevin Quinn and I began discussing the possibility of staging an expedition during the summer of 1995. I had gained the vital high-altitude experience that I had lacked in previous years and I was now ready to tackle one of the more challenging mountains in the world. Kevin had always had a desire to climb in Alaska and once he mentioned this to me, I knew that Denali was the mountain for us.

Kevin and I were both conscious that Denali would prove a challenging feat. It is the highest peak in North America and stands at an altitude of 20,320 feet (6,194 metres). The name Denali actually means 'the high one' in the local Native American language. It is located deep within the Alaskan range and is situated at latitude 63°N, making it the highest peak near the Arctic Circle. The mountain is clobbered by storms from both the Bering Sea and the Gulf of Alaska and its proximity to the Arctic means that the temperatures are intensely cold. The only other mountains on earth that experience such freezing temperatures are in Antarctica. Denali's average temperature at the high camps is -40°C, even in the middle of summer. The mountain also experiences lower barometric pressure than most of the other peaks in the world. This means that there is less oxygen in the air and each breath on the mountain requires greater effort and provides less relief.

The south summit of Denali was first reached on 7 June 1913 by a group of climbers called Stuck Harper, Karstens and Tatum. There are several routes on the mountain that climbers can ascend to reach the summit, but most use the standard route on the west buttress. This route was not summitted until 1951, when Dr Bradford Washburn reached the top. Although this route is not technically difficult, it still has a high fatality rate due to the intense cold, altitude and volatile weather conditions. The mountain is only truly climbable between May and July; although some ascents have taken place in other months, very few have been successful. The incredibly cold temperatures make winter ascents virtually impossible. In the past, temperatures of below -50°C have been recorded at the high camps in early May, so temperatures at these camps in February or March would be off the charts.

Despite the immense challenges that lay ahead, Kevin and I were eagerly looking forward to the climb and in May 1995 we set out on the long journey from Ireland to Alaska. We flew to London first and then on to St Paul, Minnesota, where we stayed for one night before making the final leg of the journey to Anchorage. By the time we arrived into the hustle and bustle of downtown Anchorage, we were both shattered. We decided to spend as little time as possible in the city, so after two days stocking up on supplies, we set out for the last stop on the long road to Denali, the northern outpost of Talkeetna.

Kevin and I hitched a lift from a guy who was staying in the same hostel as us in Anchorage and made the five-hour journey north in the open back of a 4x4. The scenery along the road was unbelievable. The warm summer air was blowing around us as we passed through the lush forests and endless fields of wildflowers. From the outset of the journey the vast Alaskan mountain ranges were visible in the distance and I could feel my excitement growing as I looked out at their white-capped summits.

When we got into Talkeetna we checked into our accommodation in an old wooden bunkhouse which was nothing more than a shack. The floor downstairs was covered in woodchips, and upstairs, climbers bunked down in only their sleeping bags on the bare wooden floor. Once we had organised our gear and laid out our beds for the night, Kevin and I decided to take a walk around the town. We headed down the single tarmac road, and went into the first bar we saw. As we entered the 'Fairview Inn', it was like walking into an old goldminers' bar in the 1800s. The entrance had two wooden saloon doors and the bar was an L shape with a paining of Denali at one end and a massive moose head at the other. The bar went quiet as we entered but Creedence Clearwater Revival's song 'Rolling on a River' continued to blast from the jukebox. There were mostly men in the bar and nearly everyone was wearing some type of lumberjack shirt.

Kevin and I looked at each other in disbelief. We were both jetlagged and exhausted and the whole scene before us was entirely surreal. I noticed then that several of the men sitting at the bar wore holsters and were carrying six-shooter guns. There was also a big woman sitting at a table towards the back of the room surrounded by men with long grey beards. Once Kevin and I sat down with a drink, some of the men began to speak with us. They introduced themselves and told us a bit about the other locals in the bar. The one who stood out the most was 'Chainsaw Annie', the rather large woman at the back with the zz Top lookalikes. Annie had a massive scar around her upper arm from a chainsaw accident and they told us that she could 'out-drink and out-fight' almost any man in the bar.

Across from Kevin and me, an old man was sitting on a barstool. His legs were quite short and as a result he had been struggling throughout the night to put his feet down onto the ground below him. One of the local men noticed this and as Kevin and I sat talking this man walked outside the bar. When the doors closed behind him we suddenly heard the loud sawing noise of an angle grinder. The next thing I knew, the man returned inside with a large piece of steel from the railway tracks that ran behind the bar. He slammed the metal down and the old man laughed as he rested his feet. No one else really seemed to notice what had happened, but Kevin and I were in shock.

As the night progressed I decided to take a walk on my own further down the road to buy some chocolate and ice cream. I left the bar and headed along the main street to see if any of the shops were open. It was very bright outside, but there did not appear to be anyone else around. When I came to the general store, I found the door unlocked. I went in and had a look around. I called out for the shopkeeper but no one responded so I took an ice cream and left some money on the counter. As I walked out I caught a glimpse of the time on my watch and realised it was after 2 a.m. I had to check my watch several times before I believed what I was seeing. The sky was still so bright that there were no lights on and it appeared to be early evening. I later found out that it never gets dark in Talkeetna during the summer months. It is so far north that they get 24-hour sunlight in the summer and virtually no light at all in the winter.

When I got back into the bar, I told the men Kevin was speaking with that the shop was unlocked. I thought it was bizarre that it was left open and unattended at night but the men informed me that crime is not a problem in Talkeetna. They went on to say that the last time anything was stolen in the town, the guy who did it was found several months later floating in the river once the spring thaw had begun. There had not been another theft in the town since that day.

When Kevin and I finally retired to the bunkhouse it took us ages to fall asleep. We couldn't stop laughing and joking about our experience in the bar. There were Japanese and Russian climbers staying in the bunkhouse as well and I am sure we kept them up all night! The next morning, Kevin and I set out to explore the area and we went for a run. As we passed through the town, 'Chainsaw Annie' raced past us on a quad bike with a rifle strapped to her back. Talkeetna was like something out of an American movie about the Wild West! The local people were as hard and untamed as the Alaskan land itself. However, the scenery around the town was magnificent. Talkeetna actually means 'the meeting of rivers' and there are three rivers that converge and run into this small town.

Kevin and I jogged past the town, through the forest and down to the banks of the river, where our first views of the towering Denali came into sight. The weather wasn't great but as we stood with the massive mountain in front of us the clouds cleared and we had uninterrupted views of the towering peak.

We spent quite a while by the river, talking through our plans for the ascent and working out the logistics for the remaining part of our journey. For many climbers, travelling from Talkeetna to the glacier is the most treacherous part of the trip. From the town, mountaineers have to be flown onto the glacier on a small aircraft capable of manoeuvring in the difficult and changeable weather conditions that are common in this area. Kevin and I had made the arrangements for this flight prior to our arrival and our pilot, Doug Keatings, was also the owner of the bunkhouse.

Doug was a renowned pilot in this area and had an excellent success rate at getting climbers onto the mountain. The weather and air conditions above the glacier are infamous all over the world and the small propeller planes that fly climbers in have been known to crash; thus Kevin and I were very happy to be taken in by the best. Actually, Kevin was especially pleased that Doug was our pilot as he hates flying and the thought of a treacherous flight on a small light aircraft was his greatest fear realised!

After our time on the riverbank we headed back up to the bunkhouse, where we met several of the other climbers who would be attempting Denali that summer. Most of the men did not speak English very well, but they were all friendly. After our introductions we returned to the Fairview Inn for a few drinks and some more interesting conversations. Most of the people we had met the previous night were there again but there were some new faces as well. As I was standing at the bar, I noticed a large black woman pointing to me and motioning for me to come over to her. I looked at Kevin in disbelief. This woman was twice my size in height and weight and I was scared just looking at her. I pretended not to see her but she was very persistent and I eventually conceded. When I finally went over to speak with her, I dragged Kevin along for support. Lou actually turned out to be a very nice woman but her size and personality were quite intimidating!

Kevin and I spoke with Lou about our plans to climb Denali and told her of our first sight of the peak from the river's edge. She looked at us with a shocked expression. At first I thought she was surprised that we would be attempting the climb, but then she proceeded to ask if we had gone through the woods and down to the river unarmed. We thought that she was joking, but she was deadly serious. She could not believe that Kevin and I had gone outside the main street of the town without a gun. Lou went on to tell us that Talkeetna has the highest concentration of grizzly bears in all of Alaska. She told us how none of the locals go across the railway tracks or to the river without a rifle or handgun. She went on to say that the grizzly bear is one of the most deadly predators in the Alaskan wild. At this stage Kevin and I were staring at each other in disbelief as she continued on, saying that 'you can't outrun, out-swim, or out-climb a grizzly'.

Kevin and I were slightly embarrassed by our ignorance and I tried to distract Lou from scolding us by asking her what she would do if she came across a bear. She responded by leaping up from the table and, in the process, knocking her chair back and her drink over. She flexed her enormous muscles and shouted, 'No bear fucks with me.' Kevin and I just burst out laughing. This place was mad!

After a long night drinking with Lou and avoiding her countless advances, Kevin and I again returned to the bunkhouse for what we hoped would be our final night. Our flight was set to depart the following day. However, when the next morning arrived the weather was poor and we were not able to fly. From the day of our arrival there had been storms and cloud over the glacier and Doug warned us that the conditions might not improve for several more days. We later learned that there were a few planes stranded out on the glacier after attempts to drop climbers off earlier in the week and that poor weather conditions had been the main cause of crashes in the past.

Although we were not thrilled about being stuck in Talkeetna any longer, we made the most of our time there. We met up with Lou again the next day and she took us out to meet a friend of hers who lived in the woods. The woman's house was an old, decrepit cabin deep in the forest. When we arrived there everything was literally caked in mud from the spring thaw. The cabin was way off on its own, but next to it was an old bus where the woman kept Alaskan husky dogs. She also kept wild wolves, which were used to breed with the huskies.

The woman was very nice but Kevin and I could not believe how isolated and poor she and her family were. The cabin was more like a child's fort than a house and she told us that their only real source of income was winter sled dog tours. In the spring and summer months she and her husband survived on the money that they made working odd-jobs. They kept the dogs around them at all times and their place was very intimidating. From the moment we arrived at the cabin the pups were all going crazy. She took some of them out to show us and whilst she was carrying one of the dogs, it bit her finger. To my horror she immediately bit the pup back on the ear. She bit so hard that she drew blood and the pup whimpered as it scampered away. She quickly turned to Kevin and me and told us that the pup would be fit to kill her in a few months if she didn't teach it who was the master. Kevin and I just looked at each other with wide eyes but didn't say a word. We stayed for a while longer, speaking with this woman and playing with the dogs. I guess she got a sense of my true personality because before we left she told me that she would name the pup that bit her Banjo after me.

Just when I thought that the experience could not get any stranger, all of the dogs began jumping and howling like crazy. They were leaping hard against their pen in the bus and I thought they were all going to break free at any moment. However, the woman and Lou did not look at all concerned. They casually told us that a grizzly was passing somewhere close by and that the dogs could sense its presence. Kevin and I decided then that it was time to go and Lou brought us back into the town.

When we returned to the bunkhouse we noticed it was becoming pretty cramped. The poor weather conditions had caused a backlog of climbers. The Russian and Japanese teams were scheduled to be on the mountain several days ahead of us but they, along with several other expeditions, were still holed up on the floor of the bunkhouse. There was a sense of boredom and anxiousness amongst the men. We were all beginning to go a bit stir crazy. The local pilots were becoming fidgety as well. Some had tried to make the flight onto the glacier in recent days, but all had failed. When the weather finally began to clear, Doug asked which team wanted to head out first and Kevin and I decided to hold back and let some of the others go on ahead of us. We were both nervous about the dangers of flying onto the glacier and decided to wait and see how the first flights fared before departing ourselves.

Once the initial flights made successful landings, Kevin and I made our arrangements to depart. Doug had once flown as a stunt pilot and we were both quite happy about this when we boarded the small propeller plane on the airstrip just outside Talkeetna. Doug warned us that the turbulence would be pretty rough and Kevin and I strapped in and waited for the excitement to begin. In order to get onto the glacier, the plane had to pass through a narrow gap between two of the towering peaks in Denali National Park and we had been told that the wind and air pressure in this section of the flight are the most dangerous on the journey. As we flew closer to the gap, Doug pulled the plane in very tight against one of the mountains and Kevin and I sat with our teeth and fists clenched. The plane shook like crazy as we made the manoeuvre, but thankfully it was all quickly over and we touched down safely on the glacier. After unloading our gear, Kevin and I moved further down the glacier to set camp and Doug bunked down beside the plane for the night. The weather was poor again and he was waiting for the freezing night temperatures to harden the snow for takeoff.

The Russian climbers came in on a flight directly behind us and we watched the plane closely as it touched down on the glacier. We saw the Russian climbers unload their gear and then, as we were setting up our camp, we noticed that the plane appeared to be preparing for takeoff. This confused Kevin and me. Doug had told us the conditions were too dangerous to fly back out off the glacier. However, we watched the pilot turn the aircraft towards the runway hill and slowly begin to pick up speed. The small plane began to roll down the hill of ice and just as the nose began to lift off the ground, it hit against soft snow and flipped over. The plane was upside down and continued to slide until it finally came to a halt after smashing into soft snow that had accumulated in a gully. Kevin and I stood frozen but we could see a crowd of people on the lower glacier running towards the wreckage.

I was convinced that the pilot would be seriously injured or even killed, but miraculously he climbed out of the damaged aircraft unharmed. He may not have been wounded, but I am sure his pride was. The plane was now unfit for flying and all of the other pilots on the glacier were too frightened to make an attempt to leave, so they all camped in together. The weather that summer had proved troublesome for everyone. Denali has claimed the lives of many climbers over the past century but during the 1995 season the death toll was considerably higher than most. Five climbers died in their pursuits of the summit. The day after we arrived we saw the bodies of three of them being taken out in body bags which were hanging from the bottoms of the rescue helicopters. It was a grim reminder of the risks that this climb posed.

Many other climbers had made attempts on the summit prior to our arrival that season but almost all of them were unable to reach the top due to the inclement weather. Quite a few of these climbers had been caught up in serious storms. In fact, there were several men who spent 28 days on the mountain in their attempt, which is nearly twice as long as most stay. In the end, deep snows and poor weather finally caused them to turn back without ever reaching the top. Kevin and I passed these men in their retreat down the glacier, just as we were beginning our ascent. Their faces looked weathered and tired and they all had an air of defeat about them.

Denali is different to many of the other mountains over 8,000 metres in the world. There are no Sherpas or porters here and there are no pack animals to carry your gear. All of the supplies that climbers require for the journey are carried in on their backs or pulled in by sleigh. With no roads and only air access to the glacier, climbers try to pack light and move fast. The usual amount of time spent on the mountain is two to three weeks and many climbers attempt to reach the relative safety of the plateau at 14,000 feet within the first four or five days. However, Kevin and I decided to take it slower. We did not set any permanent camps until we reached this altitude, but we spent nearly eight days getting there. Most climbers traverse the lower parts of the glacier on cross-country skis, making the journey quite easy. But neither Kevin nor I could ski at that time, so we used old and highly inefficient snowshoes that we had borrowed before the trip. Unfortunately, tennis rackets would probably have been more effective and with the 30 pounds we were each carrying on our backs and the nearly 40 pounds that we were towing in our sleds, it was a slow and cumbersome journey for us both.

We had only packed the essential gear and supplies that we required for the journey but the weight of our provisions was still substantial as we also brought in excess food for emergencies. Although we intended to spend three weeks on the mountain, we had enough food to last us over 30 days as we feared that we could become trapped on the glacier if bad weather came in. In hindsight, we brought far too much with us and many of the items we were using were not suitable for the harsh terrain on Denali.

The temperatures on Denali are extreme. During the day it is unbearably hot. We were both conscious of the dangers of sunburn and we found the glare off the glacier so harsh that it was not possible to take off our sunglasses during the afternoon at all or we would have risked snow-blindness. As a result of the heat, we spent most days in our light, long-sleeved base layer shirts and our thin climbing tights. However, we always kept our warm down gear within easy reach in our packs as Denali is littered with crevasses and a fall into one of these endlessly deep cracks would send the temperature plunging from over 20°C on top of the ice to -20°C beneath it. The risk of falling into a crevasse on Denali is so serious that Kevin and I remained roped together throughout almost the entire climb. There was a climber the year before us who unclipped from the rope to pee and was never seen again, and we were not taking any chances.

Another unusual feature on the mountain is the continuous sunlight. With the perpetual brightness we did not have to use head-torches at all on the climb. However, despite the 24-hour brightness, the temperatures still plummet at night. The cold on Denali is unrelenting. Kevin and I had both spent a great deal of time in the Alps and I had been on Everest but never in our lives had we experienced such extreme cold. I remember looking over at Kevin one night when we were in our tent and his nostrils, eyebrows and eyelashes had all frozen solid with the condensation. Even within the tent we were at risk of freezing.

Defrosting was a slow and painful process. We would have to strip off our gloves every few hours and use our own body heat to thaw the exposed and frozen parts of our faces. We both put on as many layers of gear as possible when we went to bed, but the cold never went away. The risk of frostbite was very serious here. Kevin and I had friends who had climbed Denali in previous years and several had lost fingers and toes. We were careful not to allow this to happen to us and kept a nightly routine to ensure our feet were warm and dry. We changed socks each evening before getting into bed and used mint powder to dry any perspiration. Despite our efforts, our feet were chronically cold and we often woke to massage our toes in the night to keep the blood flowing.

We dug our camps waist-deep into the snow each day to protect the tent from the elements. We would choose an area on the glacier that was secure and relatively flat and would saw out blocks of snow and ice to create a wall around our camp. It was like building an igloo. The snow was so hard that it would take us several hours to complete the process but it was worth it in the end, as our tent was sheltered from the wind. Outside our tent we would also carve out a snow pit for cooking and one for our toilet. During the warmth of the midday sun we would bathe in the melting snow and would prepare our drinking water for the night.

Toileting on Denali is a difficult affair. The park service requires all mountaineers to use plastic bags for removing faeces. All human waste must be carried out at the end of the climb or disposed of in one of the vast crevasses. It is very unpleasant to carry waste during the day with the intense heat, but bagging all excrement keeps the glacier clean and the snow safe for melting drinking water.

Although Kevin and I were moving very slowly throughout the climb, we were both feeling exhausted. Many of the other climbers on the mountain passed us early on and we worried that we might not be fit enough to make it to the summit. On one of the days that we were trekking up the glacier there were whiteout conditions and we both felt particularly poor. The snow underfoot was soft, we were traversing steep ground and we barely had the energy to continue. It was exhausting work but we eventually made it to the area which was safe to set camp. As we were putting up our tent the wind was blowing in violent gusts around us. Then suddenly this half-dead little bird landed right next us. It was a red-breasted robin and the wind from the valleys below the glacier must have somehow blown it all the way up the mountain. We couldn't imagine how the bird had survived the journey, but there it was beside us. We put some crumbs out for it to eat and before it could finish pecking away, the wind blew it off the mountain again. As we retired into our tent that night I couldn't help feeling a bit like the little bird, exhausted and out of my depth.

The following morning the skies had cleared and the sun was shining down upon us. We both felt slightly renewed and set off early to progress up the slope. However, a short time into our ascent the soft snow that had fallen during the night became very deep and our progress slowed to a crawl. We were still using our inefficient snowshoes at this stage and we cursed them the entire day. The difficult physical labour of breaking trail again left us exhausted but as we set camp that night we had to face the reality that the worst was yet to come.

The next day we set off for Motorcycle Hill, a steep and challenging part of the climb that sits just below the infamous Windy Corner. At this stage we switched to crampons and we were now using our ice axes whilst towing our sleighs. The week before our climb, three well-experienced mountaineers had sought refuge from the relentless elements in a crevasse just above this section. Whilst they were in the crack a tremor or small earthquake shook the entire area, causing them all to become trapped by snow and ice. The men froze to death and it was their bodies that we had seen being taken out on the helicopters when we first arrived. Climbing in the same place where they had been killed just days earlier was psychologically challenging but our fear kept us both very alert.

The wind speeds in Windy Corner are often in excess of 100 miles per hour. The terrain is steep and the ice underfoot is a thick and impenetrable blue and green layer. Our crampons only scratched the surface of this vast ice precipice and we were lucky that there was a dusting of snow over the top to give us some traction. If a climber were to fall in this section they would plummet to the bottom of the glacier, several thousand feet below. Kevin and I moved slowly and with great precision as we passed through this area. I remember the biting wind causing my goggles to freeze solid and I was forced to take them off, leaving me with a touch of snow-blindness. I was also beginning to develop diarrhoea and I could feel the strain of altitude with every breath. However we pushed on and after five hours we finally reached 14,000 feet.

As we set camp that night my head was pounding. I could feel the blood pulsing through my veins and there was a sharp, throbbing pain in my temples. Kevin was wrecked as well. He was nearly 45 years of age but incredibly strong and fit. Although I was almost 20 years younger there was no difference in our physical ability. We were both in top condition and yet we felt weak and tired. We crawled into our sleeping bags that night and felt the pain of altitude throughout our bodies. It was unusual for us to be feeling so poor at 14,000 feet, as we had spent quite a bit of time at higher altitudes in previous climbs and had not felt any ill-effects. However, this night was bitterly cold and our discomfort was profound. Psychologically this was very damaging for us both. We worried about our physical condition and the quality of our gear. In addition to our aches and pains, our down jackets were very old and did not feel warm enough. Kevin's jacket was a hand-me-down from the Irish Afghanistan expedition in 1972 and mine came from the Irish Peruvian expedition in 1980.

In the morning we decided to rest until afternoon to regain some of our strength. The sun was very strong and as we lay in the tent it became unbearably hot. We were both dehydrated and still feeling poorly but we decided to organise our gear and move further up the mountain. We left a spare tent at this camp with all of our luxury items, including our books and music and most of our light gear. We packed enough food for nine days and took a gallon of fuel and all of our high-altitude clothing with us. Kevin and I then ascended up to 15,000 feet, where we hooked onto the fixed ropes for our ascent to 16,000 feet. At this point in the climb we were on the west buttress ridge, or the normal route, as it is known to climbers. When we arrived here we could see some other climbers camping along the ledge. The views were stunning. I could see for miles without obstruction and suddenly felt very at ease. There were ice caves above us that had been carved out by climbers in previous years for protection from the wind and I could see the white maze of the glacier below. We set our camp here and rested again for the long journey ahead.

Whilst we were staying at this camp several other expeditions arrived. We spent time eating and socialising with the climbers and we discussed our plans for the final stages of the ascent. When the unrelenting cold set in we all retired to our tents and the following morning we set out for 17,500 feet. To reach this altitude we had to cross over a knife-edge ridge with a several-thousand-foot drop on either side. We took this section very slowly and as we were making the traverse, Kevin began to feel ill. He was too tired and weak to move on. Thus we were forced to set camp right in the middle of the ridge. It was very windy and frightening. We kept all of our gear and boots on throughout the night in case we had to jump out and abandon the tent quickly. We were later told that a team of men were killed here years before when they were blown off the ridge in their tent. We secured our tent as well as possible with ice-screws and criss-crossed ropes which were slung around rocks. I could feel the tent shake with each gust of wind and neither of us slept at all as our minds and bodies were literally on edge.

In the morning Kevin's condition had not improved entirely but he was feeling slightly stronger. We knew that we could not stay at this location another night so we moved on towards the camp at 17,500 feet. This would prove to be the most difficult day of our climb. We set off around 1 p.m. as the weather was unsettled in the morning hours. I led for most of the afternoon and the soft, deep snow meant that the climb was very labour intensive. We passed an Italian team as we made our way up the ridge. A few hours into the climb the clouds began to thicken and we were quickly engulfed in a storm. Normally we would have used a barometer to measure the air pressure and this would have prevented us from becoming caught out in a storm. However, on this particular day we were too exposed to stop or retreat so we knew there was no point in measuring the pressure and continued on directly into the inclement weather.

It was intensely cold. My beard had frozen solid and the sharp air was burning my lungs with each breath. Kevin was wearing a face mask with pinholes for breathing but these holes had frozen solid. I was still leading the climb at this stage and just as I was about to make a leap across an exposed part of the ridge, I felt the rope tighten and was pulled backwards. I looked behind me to see Kevin slumped over in the snow. He was clawing at the face mask but his large outer gloves hindered his attempts to free himself. I did not immediately understand what was happening but as I backtracked towards Kevin I could clearly see the problem. The ice crystals that had formed around the holes on his mask were preventing him from taking in air and as I finally reached him he managed to free himself and took a giant breath.

The weather was ferocious at this stage and we did not have long to rest before moving on again towards the camp. The wind was so strong in sections that I was convinced we would both be blown off the cliff face. Finally, after an exhausting and dangerous climb, we reached the 17,500 camp and bunked down for the night. Kevin was still wrecked and I was numb from head to toe. As soon as we got into our sleeping bags we both passed out with exhaustion. The following morning the weather was still poor and we decided to rest all day. We did absolutely nothing but sleep and eat and by the following morning we were both feeling strong again. However, the weather continued to be overcast and stormy and the temperature dropped to -40°C. Although we were freezing and restless, we were forced to wait another day before we could make our bid for the summit.

On 9 June the weather finally relented and the conditions improved, allowing us a shot at the top. We woke early and could see snow blowing off the summit. Kevin and I loaded up on fluids and carbohydrates and finally set off at 10:30 a.m. We quickly reached a steep slope where an American marine had been killed a few weeks earlier. I was leading at this stage of the climb and was careful to move slowly and with cautious placements. Once we passed this section, Kevin took over the lead and the wind became more intense. We could really feel the altitude at this point and each laboured breath brought a cold blast into our lungs. We eventually reached the 'football field' at 19,200 feet, where we had a clear view of the summit ridge. As we were gazing at the route ahead of us we could hear a helicopter in the distance but could not see where it was.

We progressed further up the ridge and Kevin was now feeling strong, whilst I struggled to keep up. However we both finally made it to the summit after a long and tedious journey and met the two Japanese climbers celebrating on the top. Kevin and I were thrilled. We were standing on the summit of the highest peak in North America and on the coldest mountain in the world. We had made it to the top despite all of the setbacks and I reflected on how far I had come in my life. I had surpassed injury and pain to reach this summit and all of my sweat and tears had paid off.

I stood with Kevin and gazed out at the ridges of Denali National Park. I could see for what felt like hundreds of miles into the Alaskan tundra and the sea of swirling snow below us gleamed up from the glacier that we had crossed. I felt an immense sense of achievement and pride and I was completely confident in our ability to descend safely. The adrenalin from our successful ascent gave us renewed strength and after a short time standing on the summit dome, we began the return journey.

As Kevin, the Japanese climbers and I made our way down the ridge we came across a solo American climber who was struggling to make his way up. We spoke with him briefly before deciding to clip him onto our ropes and help him descend to safety. On the way down we could hear the helicopters again and when they finally passed into sight we saw a large military Chinook overhead. As we reached the camp at 17,500 feet we met up with other climbers, who informed us that the Spanish team were in trouble and the helicopters were on a rescue mission. Whilst we were staying in the camp the climbers got a radio update that one of the Spanish climbers was dead and two others were suffering from severe frostbite. Kevin and I were both saddened by the news but we were also conscious of the dangers that we still faced in our descent and did our best to remain focused.

After one night's rest we descended to the camp we had left behind at 14,000 feet. We dug out our tent from beneath the fresh snow and spent a further night resting before making the final descent back down to the base of the glacier. This was a long and slow journey for Kevin and me. Most climbers ski down this section in a few hours but it took us the whole day and into the middle of the night to complete it. Although for many climbers this would have been a tiring and frustrating conclusion to the journey, it was the opposite for us. The strange twilight glow on the mountain peaks and the beautiful majestic scenery around us was perfect for reflection. We said very little along the way but we both quietly acknowledged our triumphs and felt a total sense of contentment and satisfaction.

We were lucky to have good weather throughout the descent and when we finally reached the base of the glacier we set up our final camp and waited for Doug to return and fly us out. When the plane arrived, Kevin and I boarded without the initial trepidation we had felt upon departure. I remember the engine sputtering along as we passed gracefully through the gap and suddenly on the horizon we could see the green foliage of the lowlands once again. We had been on the mountain for over two weeks and had seen nothing but white the entire time.

When we landed in Talkeetna the air was soft and warm and we both felt rejuvenated. We took hot showers and stood beneath the running water for ages. It was strange to strip off all of our gear and find that in our short period of time on the mountain we had both lost over a stone in weight. Our stomach muscles were completely defined and we both looked tired but fit.

That night we went out for pizza and ice cream and nearly ate ourselves sick. We still had a few days until our return flight home to Ireland and we decided to visit the forest in Denali National Park. The Japanese climbers remained with us and we all went hiking and sightseeing. We could see Denali's stark, white summit towering above the trees as we hiked and I was overcome with satisfaction at our success. We enjoyed every minute of our remaining time in Alaska, kayaking and touring around. When it was finally time to return, we left knowing that our Alaskan journey would remain with us forever and Kevin and I were already planning our next big adventure.

Chapter 8 ∾

FROM MANCHESTER TO MOUNT LOGAN

'Two roads diverged in a wood, and I— / I took the one less traveled by, / and that has made all the difference.'
ROBERT FROST

After we returned home from Denali in 1995, I spent the remainder of the year training hard in the gym and working at PWS, but I was growing disillusioned with my role in the factory. I wanted to progress into full-time paid youth work but I knew that the only way to gain a position in this field was to obtain higher academic qualifications. Unfortunately this would be a very daunting task for me as I had educational difficulties. I considered applying to university as a mature student, but I worried that the work would prove too challenging. I also knew that I would have to give up my job to study full-time, and this would severely limit my finances and consequently my climbing excursions. It never seemed like the right time to make this commitment until one day, whilst I was working on the factory floor, an older man at the facility said something to me that changed my life forever.

Anthony Poacher was a middle-aged man who had been working in welding for many years. He and I met each other at Mor Play Steel, where he worked as my foreman. Once Mor Play closed down, Anthony came over to PWS, where I had already been for several years. Anthony and I always got along well. Every Monday he would ask where I had been that weekend and what adventures I had gotten up to. He loved to hear about my climbs and travels and seemed to relish every detail that I told him. On this particular day, Anthony and I were speaking about my recent climbs when he said something very important to me. He told me not to waste my life working in a factory; he said I would never earn enough and would spend every day working too hard for too little, just like he did. His words were meant with the utmost sincerity and for some reason they really struck me. I thought long and hard about what he said and over the following weeks I decided to apply to the University of Ulster at Jordanstown.

In order to apply as a mature student without my o levels or A levels, I was required to take a competency exam. I arranged to take the exam in early September 1995 and within a week I found out that I had failed. I was discouraged and pissed off and had no idea what to do next. However, my girlfriend, Lisa, was very supportive and advised me to apply to other universities that might have less stringent application procedures. With her support and the encouragement of two of my good friends, Dermie Russell and Sean 'Boo' McStay, I decided to apply to Manchester Metropolitan University in England.

The application required me to write a short bio about myself and this inspired me to put all of my life experiences down on paper for the first time. It was a very useful exercise and I knew that it would prove valuable in my future, even if I were not accepted into university. However, within a few weeks of submitting the forms, I was given a date for an interview. I was very nervous as I set off for Manchester to meet the panel of academics who would decide my future, but once the time finally arrived for my interview, I was calm and collected. I had decided that I would continue to pursue my dreams of further education no matter how many times I was rejected and this relieved any pressure I felt.

In the end, the interview went very well. I spoke candidly about my life thus far and the panel members seemed very impressed with my experiences. Before I left the room they asked me if I was truly prepared to make such a big commitment for my education. I would have to come to England for two full years and leave behind my only source of income as well as my family and my girlfriend. But I did not think twice about it; I was more than prepared to leave it all behind for the chance of a better life and was very excited when they offered me a place.

Once I knew that I would be starting university the following year, I returned to Ireland a satisfied man. I was apprehensive about the work, but was very much looking forward to the challenge. Kevin and I were still discussing our plans for an ascent on Mount Logan and we decided it would be best to leave the climb for a year until we could accumulate enough money and time off work to leave again for several months. Fortunately, the climb was arranged for the summer months, so it would not disrupt my studies.

I spent almost all of 1996 and 1997 working hard to save up as much money as possible before I began my studies in England. Kevin and I also continued climbing and were training hard for our ascent on Mount Logan. We returned to Scotland in the end of February 1997 and set about a full week of technical ice-climbing. Kevin had timed the trip to coincide with the full moon and I remember that the weather was perfect when we arrived. The clear, cold nights gave us longer climbing days and after two ascents, one on Tower Ridge and the other on Comb Gully, we set out to tackle point five. Although most people would never dream of returning to a place where they had taken such a massive fall and come so close to losing everything, I felt drawn towards the route. I knew that I could make it to the top, because I had done so to survive in 1993, but I also wanted to prove that I could climb the route with skill. The day we set about the ascent, the sky was clear and the sun was shining brightly. I felt strong and confident. I was very surprised by how quickly Kevin and I progressed up the pitches and by the time we were half way up the route, I knew that we were well able for the challenge ahead.

This time, I had prepared well for the long climb and Kevin and I were wearing the full winter kit and carrying two 9-mm ropes. The ice was solid throughout the gully and we were able to make sturdy placements along the entire chute without difficulty. After a long afternoon of climbing, the day progressed into night and Kevin and I made it to the summit of Ben Nevis without difficulty after a near-perfect climb. It was such an enjoyable experience, in total contrast to my previous ascent. I completed the climb with speed and accuracy. One of the most stunning parts of the climb was our descent. Kevin and I were the only climbers visible on the peak and the moon lit up the sky brightly overhead. The northern lights were visible in the distance and the stars covered every inch of the darkness. When we finally made it down to our camp by the CIC hut, it was after midnight and freezing but we sat outside beneath the moon and ate our remaining food whilst admiring the majestic mountains around us. It was a fantastic climb; we both felt strong and fit and were now ready for our journey to Mount Logan.

As the winter passed into spring, I made all my final arrangements for attending university and Lisa and I stopped dating but remained good friends. During the summer I met another girl, who was also from Camlough. Her name was Bernadine and she was an outdoor enthusiast who really enjoyed rock-climbing. The two of us spent many weekends away together in the mountains and we climbed as often as possible.

In October 1997 I set off for Manchester to begin my studies in Youth and Community Work and moved into a small bedsit in the Wally Range area of Manchester. My accommodation was a bit dismal, but there were lots of other people staying in the house and we all got along well. I made quite a few friends at the university and found my courses fascinating. I was shocked by how liberal the academics at the university were and could not believe the level of cultural diversity throughout the city. There were lots of African students who had escaped horrible poverty and war in their home countries. There were Indian, Pakistani and Kashmiri students all studying together despite their national conflicts, as well as many other students from around the world. At that time there were so few minorities in the north of Ireland that I had no experience of living around people from such different backgrounds. I learned a lot from the African students in particular and their stories from home really put the conflict in Ireland into perspective for me. Some of these young men and women had fled regions where hundreds of thousands were killed in civil wars and genocides and it suddenly made our problems seem very minor in comparison.

There were also many gay, lesbian and transgendered students in my classes and this was something that I had never encountered before. I will never forget one of my lecturers introducing herself as a left-wing socialist and a lesbian. I came from a very repressed Catholic background and was so shocked when she said the word 'lesbian' that I laughed out loud. I was given dirty looks by the entire class and the teacher even stopped the lecture to ask if I 'had a problem with that', to which I quickly responded, 'No, not at all, as long as you don't.' She half laughed at my response and the class continued on. I knew then that I would learn more than I had ever imagined in my time at university.

Whilst I was in Manchester, I joined the Red Rope rock-climbing club. At the time I did not realise that it was a socialist climbing club, but I soon learned quite a bit about their politics. Every week we would all get together to pick climbing routes for our outdoor climbs and when the weather was poor we would practise our techniques at the indoor climbing wall. After our meetings there would always be political discussions and debate in the local bars. There were a lot of interesting people in the club and I met some gifted climbing partners. One woman in particular, Jo Farrington, and I ended up doing a lot of climbing together on routes in England and in the French Alps. She was a very strong technical climber and taught me quite a bit by leading most of the routes that we tackled. Initially I was a little concerned about climbing with a female partner because at the time I couldn't imagine that she could be as physically strong as I was, but Jo quickly proved me wrong.

The first year at university passed in no time and before I knew it, Kevin and I were preparing to set off for the Yukon in Canada to ascend Mount Logan. We planned to climb the northeast ridge, which is a challenging alpine route. In May 1997 we began the long journey to this remote region of Canada. We flew from Dublin to Vancouver and once we arrived in Vancouver, we made our way to White Horse, where we spent a few days stocking up on supplies before hitching up to Haines Junction. Kevin and I were dropped off at a roundabout on the outskirts of White Horse with a sign that said, 'Irish Climbers for Mount Logan'. We stood with our thumbs out on the side of the road whilst waiting for a lift.

To our delight, only a short while after we were dropped off, a pickup truck went past us and then veered round the circle and headed back in our direction. Kevin and I reached down to grab our packs so that we would be ready to hop in when the driver pulled up. However, when the truck came to a stop, the driver rolled down his window and said, 'Hey Irish, you're heading in the wrong direction for Haines Junction.' He then directed us to the right place before driving off. Kevin and I laughed as he drove away; we were establishing quite a reputation for the Irish over in Canada! Luckily, only a short while later, another driver pulled in and this time we were taken all the way up to our destination.

Once we arrived in Haines Junction, we signed in with the park rangers and prepared to make the next leg of our journey to Klaune Lake. The park rangers were really friendly and showed us slides and photos of the mountain so that we could prepare for the climb. They also advised us how to keep safe in the camp and how to avoid surprise encounters with bears. Kevin and I were startled when they told us that one year earlier a honeymoon couple had been out for a walk along the lake when they encountered a grizzly. They tried to escape but the bear attacked and killed the woman. They told us that there was a high concentration of grizzlies in the area and they advised us to rig up our tent with noisy items so that we would have warning if a bear were to approach. They also told us to hang our food away from our tent and to be careful not to walk alone.

With that in mind, Kevin and I departed and hitched a further lift up to Klaune Lake. When we arrived, we put our tent into a lean-to structure and rigged it with ropes and climbing gear just as we had been instructed. We also decided to sleep with our ice axes out in the tent so that we could fight back in the event of an attack and kept pots and pans at hand to make as much noise as possible. We hung our food near a latrine that was about 50 metres from our camp and hoped very much that we would not encounter one of Canada's top predators. Despite our concerns about the bears, we were both overcome by the natural beauty at the lake and took every opportunity to sit outside and breathe in the fresh mountain air. After a night camping in our tent, two Canadian women arrived and set their sleeping bags out on the sands above the lake. Kevin and I were amazed and felt a bit meek when we saw that these women had not even brought a tent and would spend the night sleeping out under the stars whilst we had fortified ourselves for protection.

However, the next morning we were grateful that we had played it safe. The pilot who was flying us the remaining distance to the mountain arrived at our camp. As we were speaking, he noticed something in the sand by the women's sleeping bags. He took us over and showed us giant grizzly-bear tracks that went directly past where the women had slept. The bear must have come along the beach in the night but thankfully had not bothered with the two sleeping women.

The pilot was a Welshman who had lived over in Canada and been flying out to Mount Logan for many years. As the weather on the glacier was very poor that day we could not set off, but he made plans to fly us out the following morning. Since we were stuck at the lake for a further night, the pilot took us out on a hike. He was very informative and told us a lot about the history of the area. He told Kevin and me that the lake was used in the wintertime as an ice road to reach the gold mines in the far north territories. He said that the area was famous during the gold rush and that the surrounding mountains still had gold deposits.

Whilst we were out on the hike, he introduced us to a Native Canadian man who lived locally in a cabin. Kevin and I spoke with the man for a while and asked him how the locals cope with the bear population. He told us that a bear has never killed a Native because they connect to the animals spiritually. He went on to tell us that when he encounters a bear he talks to it, saying that 'he is only travelling past and means the bear no harm'. He felt that the bears are able to understand the Natives and therefore do not see them as prey or an enemy, and this ensures their safety. Kevin and I were quite impressed until we left and our pilot pointed out that the man was carrying a gun. He went on to say that a Native has never been killed by a bear because they are all armed and would 'shoot first, talk later'!

With that in mind, Kevin and I retreated again to our little fort and tried our best to sleep despite our growing bear concerns! Thankfully, the next morning the weather on the glacier had cleared and our pilot returned to collect us for the one-hour flight. Kevin was dreading the journey; he remembered the rough ride that we had on the way in to Denali and had even considered making the 100-mile trek on foot to the mountain to avoid this trip. However, the trek was not practical and in the end he came aboard the small plane with a white face and sweaty palms. The beginning of the flight was magnificent. We could see deep into the forests below and the mountains in the distance lined the horizon, but this passed quickly and soon we found ourselves in thick cloud cover and storms. I listened intently as the plane's engines buzzed loudly around us. It sounded like the small plane was struggling with its heavy cargo, but I could not let myself worry.

I eventually closed my eyes, put on my Walkman and hoped for the best. When we finally reached the glistening, white snow of the glacier, the pilot warned us that the landing could be a bit rough. With that, Kevin ducked his head between his knees and stared at the floor below him. He had barely spoken a word on the flight and when the pilot made his first attempt towards the ice beneath us, I could hear Kevin murmuring to himself. As the plane moved quickly towards the snow I could see the pilot looking a bit concerned and then suddenly he pulled the nose up hard. The wind was quite strong at this stage and I could feel the small plane rock with each gust. After this aborted attempt, the pilot circled for a few moments before he went for it again. Thankfully this time we bumped down into the fresh snow and the engines rolled to a stop. Kevin seemed to brighten up immediately once we were safely on the glacier and after quickly unloading our gear we made arrangements to radio the pilot again in roughly 16 days to arrange our pickup. He wished us well and we set off up the ice to establish camp.

Except for a few empty tents on the glacier, we were alone with the stark, white snow and ice. Four Canadian climbers were further up the peak along the same route that we intended to use, but apart from their empty nylon shells, there were no other signs of life on the mountain. It was a beautiful place and Kevin and I were really impressed by how remote it was. We had seen pictures of this majestic peak in books but had no idea how vast and spectacular it truly was until we stood beneath its shadow. We were towing sleighs like we had on Denali and were also wearing snowshoes, but this time we had better models and were more adept at using them. After travelling closer to the foot of the mountain we established a base camp. We dug out blocks of hard snow and ice and tucked our tent into the sheltered retreat.

On our first night we both slept well and the following day we began the difficult task of navigating the ice-fall. The glacier is completely littered with crevasses and many of them have vast, impassable widths, so Kevin and I were roped together from the moment we set off. It was a very frustrating task to find our way to the ridge and we hit many dead ends along the ice. The route would simply come to an abrupt end at the mouth of a crevasse and we would then be forced to backtrack, sometimes for hours, as we made our way towards the next camp. In the end we found the correct route after a long day of trekking and navigating and we marked it out with bamboo visibility wands, which we would later use to find our way back down.

At this point, Kevin and I established a food cache at the base of the ridge. We were forced to dig deep into the snow to protect the supply from the ravens that nest in the area. The pilot had warned us that these birds will cut right through a tent to get at your food and we knew that we did not have enough supplies to let anything go to waste. Once our cache was safely in place, we made our way back to base camp for the night. The following day we set out on the marked route and this time we carried heavy loads of climbing equipment to the base of the ridge to establish an advanced base camp. This involved ascending a steep 1,000 foot slope that was very avalanche-prone and exposed. In the middle of this slope there was a massive crevasse that split the ice-fall in two. Kevin and I knew that this slope could be dangerous and we were conscious that the temperature was fairly high and this enhanced the risk of a rock-fall or avalanche. This section was so dangerous that two Czech climbers who had been killed the previous year in this area were still buried deep within the crevasse.

Once we arrived at this break in the slope, our only option was to descend directly into the crevasse and ice-climb up the back face of it. It was a difficult task because we were both carrying such heavy loads and growing increasingly tired. It did not take us long to realise that we weren't going to make any progress with our heavy packs. With that in mind we decided one of us should run out about 600 feet of fixed rope without his pack, whilst the other belayed. This would allow us to easily traverse the slope the following day using the fixed lines, and we would then be able to cache our heavy gear at the top.

Kevin elected to run the rope out and just as he was hauling his first reel I could hear him groan with pain. He injured his back lifting the heavy load, but seemed to be moving fine after only a short break. I was concerned about Kevin's back but figured that it could not be too seriously injured or he would not continue on. Once Kevin began the ascent he started to fix the rope into the snow using aluminium snow stakes. Whilst he was completing this task, the four Canadian climbers who had been on the route above us descended to our location. They said to us that they had made it to the summit after 12 straight days of good weather with low temperatures. They spoke about the route to the top and gave us some pointers and advice before continuing their descent on the glacier.

When they set off, Kevin and I both looked at each other with disappointment. We knew that 12 straight days of good weather meant that a break would be coming soon and we would most likely have poor conditions for our ascent. However, at this stage we had no choice but to continue on. By 2 a.m., the tedious work of fixing the lines was complete and Kevin abseiled back down to me. We then returned to advanced base camp together to rest for the night.

During the night, Kevin appeared to be suffering with his back, but by morning he seemed fit again and we set off to jumar up the slope and cache our gear. The jumar, or mechanical device, would allow us to ascend the rope with metal 'teeth' which grip tightly, making it easy to pull ourselves up. At this stage the weather was beginning to break and Kevin and I both realised that our prediction had been accurate. The temperature was far too high and the snow and ice were beginning to run down the mountain around us. Despite the poor conditions, we continued on and eventually traversed the ridge and cut out a platform for our tent. We were at roughly 11,000 feet and both of us were feeling strong. Once we established our camp for the night, we retired to bed, looking out at the magnificent views of the glacier below. As we finally zipped the tent flaps shut for the night we could see snowflakes beginning to fall and by morning we realised that our view the night before would be the last clear visibility for quite a while.

When I unzipped the tent flaps that morning, the snow was so heavy and deep around us that parts of the tent were beginning to collapse. I got out with a shovel and tried to shift the wet snow, but the flakes were still falling at high speed around me, and eventually I was forced to give up and retreat into the tent. Kevin and I spent the whole day alternating between resting and shovelling and we bunked down for another night. The next day we finally got a break in the weather and we ascended above the ridge on a mixed route of rock and ice. It was Scottish grade three climbing and Kevin and I made it to the gap between the ridges without difficulty. We left a cache of gear at this point and marked our dumpsite with visibility wands before descending back to the tent along the lower ridge for the night.

Little did we know, we would end up stuck in this tent for over four days as bad weather was setting in. The snow fell heavy and fast around us and was so constant that neither of us imagined another break would come. Kevin and I had prepared well for the climb and had all of the essential food and gear that we required, but we had not planned for long periods of rest and had only one book between us. I had packed a book on the Troubles in Ireland and in the end we were forced to tear it in half so that each of us had something to read. I also had a Walkman with me, but we had only one tape with us on the ridge. It was U2, and by the end of the four days, neither of us ever wanted to hear them again. At this point Kevin's back was really beginning to bother him and I could tell he was finding it difficult to get comfortable. Kevin had injured his back on many occasions previously and would often end up immobile from the pain. I worried that this might happen to him on the ridge and wondered what we would do if his pain got any worse.

After the four miserable days, we got a small break in the weather and decided to move up to our cache site above. We made it halfway up the ridge when Kevin slowed to a stop. His back was causing him great pain and every step put him under additional strain. I knew in my heart that we would not be able to continue on, as the route gets progressively narrower and very technical closer to the top. I worried that Kevin's condition would get worse, but also felt torn as I wanted to achieve our summit ambitions. I encouraged Kevin to continue on for a little while longer but within a rope length, I realised that there was no way he could make it to the top.

This proved to be a difficult situation for me emotionally because I felt strong and wanted to continue on, but I also knew that Kevin's safety was paramount and in the end giving up the summit was an easy choice. The two of us began to descend towards our ridge camp but Kevin was now moving very slowly and seemed to be gritting his teeth with every step. Once we finally arrived back at the tent, he could just barely crawl in as he was in such pain. The two of us bunked down for what we thought would be one further night but we ended up being stuck again for over two more days. The snow was incredible. It never seemed to stop. As Kevin was in such pain, I did most of the shovelling and it was a constant job to keep the tent cleared. At this point we could hear avalanches happening all over the mountain but we could not see where they were falling because the visibility was so poor. It was frightening, but we had to stay put and wait for a clearing before attempting to descend.

Finally, the snow let up a little and we began to realise that it was not going to stop entirely, so we set off again. We decided to ditch a portion of our gear at the camp so that we could move fast and travel light down the mountain. We left two coils of rope, with food and fuel, and set off quickly before we really became stuck. I took all of Kevin's gear and led us on an abseil down to advanced base camp. When I reached the crevasse along the slope between the two camps, I was again forced to descend directly into it before climbing back out the other side. Whilst I was in the open ice pit, I noticed old, frozen rope beside me that I had not seen on the ascent. I followed the rope all the way down until I saw a face looking directly up at me. To my horror, I realised it was one of the dead Czech climbers. He was jammed in between the two walls of ice and was looking straight up at the sky above. He appeared exactly as he would have one year earlier as the ice had preserved him perfectly. It was eerie and frightening because the heavy cloud cover cast shadows in the crevasse and I knew that only one rock-fall or avalanche could land Kevin and me in the same position. I immediately began to ascend the ice wall and said nothing to Kevin about the corpse that I had seen.

Once we reached the tent that we had left at ABC, we rested for the remainder of the night. It was then that I told Kevin about the frozen climber and the two of us acknowledged how dangerous the remaining section could be. I couldn't get the Czech climber's expression out of my mind and even as I slept his face flashed through my dreams. Kevin's back was still very bad but he was mentally strong and I was very grateful that he was so fit. Most other men would not have been able to continue on in the same circumstances. In the morning we awoke to a total whiteout. There were regular avalanches happening on the slopes around us and we could not see more than an inch or two in front of our tent. It was very frightening and we were both exhausted from climbing the entire previous day in soft, deep snow but we knew that we must keep descending. I led again for quite a while after we set off, but the work was very physically demanding. We were breaking trail through snow that was up to our thighs. After a while Kevin realised how tired I was and volunteered to take over. However, he had only made it one rope length in front of me when suddenly he disappeared from view and I was violently jerked to the ground. I did not have much time to react but I instinctively dug my crampons hard into the snow below me to prevent myself from sliding. I looked out towards Kevin but all I could see was his hands and poles. He had broken directly through the top of a hidden crevasse and had been saved from a serious fall by his poles. He had quickly thrown his arms out to either side of him and caught himself before he plummeted below. Kevin was cursing loudly and I could see him beginning to struggle up as I tried to right myself. I was unable to move with Kevin's dead weight at the end of the rope and was thus forced to remain where I was until Kevin managed to jumar up. As soon as the weight at the end of the rope was freed, I made my way towards Kevin. He was lying in the snow beside the crevasse and I could tell that the fall had put his back entirely out of commission.

Although Kevin was in agony, I knew that we could not stop to rest for long or camp for another night on the mountain as we had arranged to radio the pilot after 16 days and it had already been 18 days since we set out. We had left the radio at base camp as it was very large and heavy and I was conscious we would not be able to contact him until we reached it. I also realised that once the pilot received our contact, he might not be able to fly out to the glacier straight away as the weather conditions were poor.

Kevin and I continued to move down in a total whiteout. It became impossible to gauge where we were going and what had begun as a straightforward climb was turning into an epic fight for survival. We were forced to make frequent stops where we would construct snowballs to roll in an effort to ascertain which direction was up and which was down. The marker wands that we had left along the route were no longer visible and we were now forced to re-navigate through the treacherous crevasse fields. After several long hours fighting against the wind and snow, we were devastated to find ourselves at a crevasse that blocked the entire path. It was over 30 feet wide and too long to traverse on either side. Despite our exhaustion, we had to double back and try to find our original route. We ended up having to backtrack nearly the entire way to the base of the ridge, where we came upon a gully covered in fresh avalanche debris. We knew that we were in a very hazardous position but had no other option than to continue on. At this point we were both psychologically and physically exhausted and neither of us wanted to move another step.

Despite our need to rest, we continued on and finally, after a 14-hour day, we arrived at the safety of our base camp. We were ready to collapse when we saw the tent but we knew that we desperately needed to rehydrate and dry ourselves off before sleeping. The temperature was beginning to drop and the snow was freezing solid all around us. Once we drank some water and warmed ourselves up, we both got into our sleeping bags and passed out with the exhaustion. First thing the next morning Kevin and I attempted to radio the pilot for our pickup, but were devastated to find that the radio would not work. There were no other climbers on this side of the mountain and we knew that the pilot would not worry until we had been there for up to 30 days as it sometimes takes this long to make a successful summit bid. For over two days, Kevin and I tried everything to fix the radio and finally on the third day, after sleeping with the batteries in our sleeping bags, the radio began to work.

However, we could only get one channel to come in and it was not the pilot's frequency. Thankfully, we did reach some Canadian climbers on the other side of the mountain and they agreed to relay the message to the pilot and get back to us to confirm our pickup. We sat and waited for feedback all day long but never heard a thing. Eventually we were forced to turn the radio off to save the battery and Kevin and I could only hope and pray that they had gotten through to the pilot. We were running low on food and only had rice, granola and three Mars bars left at this point. I worried that we could run out of supplies entirely whilst waiting to be picked up and became very angry with myself for leaving food behind further up the peak.

Thankfully, on the fourth day, we got the radio to work again and this time got through to the pilot directly. We were overjoyed to hear his voice at the other end of the line until he told us to 'hold tight' as the weather was too poor to fly and that he would get out to us in a few days. I knew that our supplies would never last us that long and I was conscious that we both needed to refuel after all of the hard physical work that we had done in the previous weeks. Just then I remembered that the Canadians had mentioned a cache of food that they left about three miles up the glacier. I knew that Kevin was not fit to trek back up, so I set out alone. I was worried about the crevasses but also knew that I could not last without food for a few more days. I am very good with pain and can cope well with extreme cold and snow but I am terrible when it comes to being hungry!

After a long trek back up to the Canadians' cache, I found their buried supplies beneath a marker wand. I dug down through the deep, icy snow and finally pulled out a small bag with M&Ms and muesli. I was so disappointed I wanted to cry. I was starving and had been hoping for something a bit more substantial but I knew that it was our only option so I began the return trek to base camp with what little I had found.

I made it back to camp without incident and Kevin and I spent another two days waiting in total boredom before we heard the distant sound of an engine. I was the first one out of the tent and was so overjoyed when I could see a plane in the distance. I watched as it attempted to touch down but soon realised the conditions might still be too poor for a landing. Kevin was dreading the flight and did not seem as anxious as me when the plane looked like it might leave. He had begun talking about trekking out the 100 miles again. I knew he was insane to even consider it with his back injury, but that is how badly he hates flying! Finally the plane touched down and the pilot kept the engines running as he shouted out to us to 'hurry up and hop in'. He did not want to get stuck in the soft, deep snow that had accumulated. It did not take long for Kevin and me to pack our things and before we knew it, we were off. The glacier soon became a white speck below as we flew closer to the green trees in the distance. We flew back to Klaune Lake, where we had begun our journey. Although we had not made it to the summit, we had endured quite a bit and I was proud of our achievement.

Kevin spent several days stretching and resting and eventually his back returned to normal. Once he was feeling better we headed back to Vancouver and did a bit of rock-climbing in Squamish. There were fantastic granite free-climbing routes. It was similar to the climbs in Yosemite and we enjoyed every minute of it. The weather was great and it was nice to be out in the sun and warmth after our time on the mountain. Once our time in Canada drew to an end, I returned to Ireland to complete a placement with a juvenile justice project in Dundalk. Upon the completion of this placement, I headed back to Manchester for the final year of my course.

In 1998 I completed several major climbs in Scotland and Wales and I again returned to the Alps. I continued with my studies and also joined the university canoeing club, which helped to enhance my canoeing abilities. We spent one night a week practising techniques in the swimming pool and travelled to rivers throughout England, Scotland and Wales on the weekends. I made a lot of good friends in the club and after all of the training I completed my level two canoeing qualification, which allowed me to take people out on the rivers.

Socially and politically there was a great deal of change taking place in the north of Ireland. I returned home as often as possible and I was beginning to see a slow revolution on the streets. The IRA agreed a ceasefire with the government and as a component of this peace treaty the army watchtowers and patrols began to be removed. Although a lot of people were hesitant to sign up to the peace accord, I knew that many more were happy to have an end to the violence. As life at home began to improve I decided to apply to University of Ulster at Jordanstown again. I had completed my two years at Manchester Metropolitan and now had a Diploma in Higher Education but I was still keen to secure a degree. I knew that I could have stayed on in England, but I missed life at home and wanted the prestige of a degree from Jordanstown to enhance my future career potential. I submitted my application in the spring for enrolment the following autumn and waited anxiously to hear back from them.

Fortunately, this time I was accepted and I spent one year at Jordanstown studying full-time before graduating with a Bachelor of Science in Youth and Community Work in May 1999. Although I found the coursework very difficult, I somehow managed to pass and in the end I achieved my goal of securing a degree. Throughout the duration of my studies and after graduation I worked very hard at

Shannaghmore, taking groups out on adventure activities. I also spent time working as a labourer and landscaper and saved every penny I earned to fund an around-the-world trip after graduation. My thirst for adventure and love for travelling were insatiable and I knew that I needed a bit more experience before I could return to the mountain of my dreams.

Chapter 9 ∾

CLIMBING AROUND THE CONTINENTS

'The world is a book and those who do not travel read
only one page.'
ST AUGUSTINE

In August 1999 I set off on a 12-month journey which would lead me
from Ireland to America, Australia, New Zealand and Asia. I knew
that it would be an expensive venture, but fortunately in the weeks
leading up to my departure a good friend requested that I complete
some highly paid specialised work for him. Seán McClelland, the man
who had arranged for me to come to New York in 1989, needed my
assistance back in the States doing technical work on the windows of
high-rise buildings. He knew that I had a good stomach for heights and
there was no one else within his firm who was willing to do this job.
The money that I would be paid during these six weeks was enough to
keep me going for several months on the road and I agreed to set off for
America immediately.

New York had changed a good deal in the decade since my last visit,
but my friends in the city were exactly the same. They all continued to
drink in the Irish bars each night and most were living in the same old
neighbourhood. For the six weeks that I was in town, I worked hard
each day, installing putty around the exterior of windowsills several
storeys off the ground. On the weekends, I travelled to other parts of
New York State, where I could hike and climb. I stayed with Seán's
brother Brian for the entire trip and we had a great laugh heading out
on the town and sightseeing together.

Once my time in New York was complete, I flew to San Francisco,
where I arranged to meet up with Kevin Quinn's brother-in-law to do

some climbing. Eddie had been over in America for several years working as a carpenter and he was a keen rock-climber and outdoorsman. When he lived in Ireland he was a strong fell runner and then he went on to become a top mountain biker, snowboarder and mountaineer. He and his wife had two children and they were living in the Bay area of San Francisco. I planned to spend a few weeks staying in their home before Eddie and I would set off for Yosemite National Park to complete some big wall climbing. When I arrived in San Francisco, Eddie immediately took me sightseeing. I visited the famous Golden Gate Bridge and many of the other tourist destinations and by the end of the day I had a good feel for the city. Eddie and his wife had many connections in the area and before my first week was over Eddie had found me a bit of work. Edwin Drummond was an Englishman who had immigrated to the us many years before and was now running a painting and decorating business in San Francisco. He was looking for a labourer who could assist with erecting high-rise scaffolding for an upcoming job. I immediately agreed to help and spent some time working with him before Eddie and I set off north.

I liked Edwin straight away. He was an old hippie with a really relaxed attitude. Eddie told him that I was a keen rock-climber and Edwin was immediately interested in hearing about the climbing I had done in England and Wales. When I told him about my favourite route, called 'I Dream of White Horses', on the sea cliffs in Gogarath, North Wales, Edwin just laughed and gave me a strange look. It turned out that he had established the route in the 1960s when he was a top rock-climber. He had moved from England to America to be close to Yosemite, where he could practise his skills.

My days with Edwin were enjoyable and he shared a lot of valuable information with me on the ascents in Yosemite. By the time we set off north, I was very excited about the impending climbs. The weather was excellent. There had been nothing but clear skies and warm sun since I arrived. It was late September and the temperatures were just cool enough to make the exposed ascents.

I remember driving into Yosemite for the first time and being awestruck by the sheer size of El Capitan. It is one mile of solid granite rock that juts straight up from the ground into the sky. Eddie and I planned to attempt several routes along this monolith, and I could not believe how vast it appeared. When we arrived at the campsite, we found it packed with other rock-climbers. There was a great atmosphere about the place, with men and women from all over the world descending upon this mecca each year to hone their climbing skills. All of the climbers were really sociable and there was almost a communal feel on the campsite.

Once we were registered with the rangers and completed the standard formalities, including the briefing on bear protection, we established our site. It was fairly late in the day by the time we got ourselves organised so we did a bit of bouldering in the area and scouted out the routes for the following day. When evening came, Eddie and I spent time meeting the other climbers and talking about the routes and conditions that they had encountered. The next day we set out on The Royal Arches, which is a solid multi-pitch route through granite slabs that involves a combination of different rock-climbing techniques. This route was a great warm-up for the more technical ascents that we had planned for later in the week and it got us both used to the height and feel of the rock.

After the first few days, Eddie and I were making excellent progress. We had completed a route on the Half Dome and The Cathedral and we were now ready to tackle some 'aid climbing' on El Capitan. Aid climbing is different to rock-climbing in that you affix slings to bolts or gear within the rock and you stand on these small nooses of rope and pull yourself up to the next placements in order to ascend. It is a slower process than standard rock-climbing but is often the most efficient method when the rock is very technical or has limited placements. It was my first real experience with this type of climbing and I enjoyed it immensely.

Eddie was a top climber and was far more technically advanced than myself, so he led us through all of the difficult pitches. On our last day of climbing together we completed a very high-grade route and it built my confidence for the climbs that I would complete after Eddie departed. It was unfortunate that he was only able to stay for one week as my climbing abilities had improved tenfold in the time that we spent together. However, once Eddie set off, I remained in the campsite and met up with other solo climbers to make ascents with. I even met two Irish men who were looking for a partner to complete Lost Arrow

Direct, an intensely exposed climb along the ridge of Yosemite. Although I knew that this would be a very difficult route, I was keen to test my skills and told them to count me in. We set off the next morning and hiked for over two hours until we reached the top of the ascent, directly beside a waterfall.

Once we reached this point, we abseiled down the route, using a tree alongside the fall as an anchor. For roughly 300 feet we swung off the granite face, until we reached a notch within the rock below. Once we reached the notch, we tailed the rope behind us and made a two-pitch climb up a rock spire that abuts the cliff face. When we reached the top of the spire, we had to pull the rope in tight before making a traverse between the spire and the cliff. In order to do this, we clipped a jumar onto one rope and connected a back-up rope to the person facilitating the belay from the spire. In the end it looked like a tightrope hundreds of feet off the ground connecting to solid points.

Once the system was in place, I went first to test its durability and was frightened to realise that the rope, although pulled completely tight, still maintained a high degree of elasticity. It seemed to bounce up and down and sway in the air as I moved my weight across it. It was a very unnerving feeling because I was flat on my back with the world hundreds of feet below me and I could hear the distinct sound of the rope stretching with each advance. Thankfully, the system held tight and the three of us completed the climb safely. It was a really exciting and challenging ascent and I knew that our success would build the confidence I needed to tackle more advanced routes.

After Lost Arrow Direct, I completed several other climbs, notably Lurking Fear on El Capitan, where I spent the night on the rock ledge in a sleeping bag on a 'porta-ledge' whilst tied into the rock. The route involved aid climbing, and thus we were forced to haul all of our gear, food and water up to our night platform using a pulley system. I found it an exhausting and frightening experience and did not sleep at all that night. It was like being in a metal coffin on the side of the rock and I couldn't help feeling totally vulnerable as we dangled throughout the night. The following day the weather deteriorated and we were unable to reach the top of the climb, but our night on the rock proved to be a valuable learning experience for me.

After my time in Yosemite I returned briefly to San Francisco before renting a car to drive to LA, where I would meet up with one of my cousins. After some surfing and sightseeing in LA, I headed back to Ireland for a week before setting off again for Bangkok.

A good friend of mine from Newry, Marty Patterson, made the journey to Thailand with me and after just three days we continued on to Australia together. I will never forget our first day in Thailand. When we left Ireland the weather was atrocious; it was cold and rainy and completely dismal. When we stepped off the plane in Bangkok the heat, humidity and sunshine completely overwhelmed us. I could not believe how oppressive it was. Despite our difficulties acclimatising to the weather, we visited many of the popular tourist destinations and I immediately developed a sense that Thailand was a place I would return to. The people were very welcoming and the temples and Buddhist sites were breathtaking.

After our brief Thai interlude, Marty and I set off again. We both had cousins in Australia, so we arranged to separate and visit with them before meeting up again in Sydney. When I arrived in Sydney airport my cousin Gerry Hughes was waiting to collect me. He and his wife, Bernadine, had been living over in Australia for quite some time and were very keen to show me around. On the journey to their house, we stopped at Bondi Beach and as soon as I saw the golden sands and crashing waves, I could not resist jumping out of the car for a swim. Gerry and I stripped down to our boxer shorts and dove in and out of the surf for hours.

Gerry and Bernadine took me touring around the local area and into the bush near their house. After about a week with them, I met up with Marty again and we connected with some other friends from the Newry area who were living over in Oz. Whilst we were there we completed the Sydney Harbour Bridge climb and visited all of the tourist sites. Marty was only able to stay for a short while and once he set off for Ireland, I returned to Gerry and Bernadine's house, about 50 kilometres from Sydney centre.

They lived in a fantastic place just out on the edge of the bush and Gerry and I got to spend a lot of time hiking and running. Gerry had taken on side work at a local swimming pool and army barracks and as a result he was able to make use of their facilities. Whilst I was there we did a great deal of physical training and I joined him each morning for runs, swims and bike rides. I soon found myself in fantastic shape and we completed my first half triathlon together. I also joined an indoor rock-climbing gym and met a top-class Australian rock-climber. He and I then went on to complete several climbs in the nearby Blue Mountains.

On one of these ascents, I was just below the top of the route when I put my hand onto a narrow rock ledge above me. Just as my fingers gripped the rock, a large brown snake came out of a crevice and hissed at me. He was only inches from my flesh and I immediately jumped back away from him. Thankfully the gear that I had placed a few feet below held tight and I did not fall. When I told the Aussie climber what had happened, he told me that the brown snake is one of the most deadly in all of Australia and that its venom can easily kill a man! Despite my narrow escape from the snake, I continued to make ascents in the local hills and also began assisting Gerry on long bush runs.

These competitions involved runners racing through the bush for up to 100 kilometres. In the beginning, I assisted in the competitions by driving a Land Rover along the course to provide water and rescue services to the competitors, but eventually I joined in the races myself. The runs were unbelievably difficult, but they left me in great physical condition.

Since I was feeling so fit, I decided to travel to Tread Bow to tackle Australia's highest mountain, known as Kausi Osko. I had prepared myself for a challenging ascent but it turned out to be nothing more than a day-long hill-walk. Despite my disappointment with Kausi Osko, I loved Tread Bow and the surrounding area and decided to look for work as an outdoor instructor. It would have been an ideal place to base myself for a few months but in the end I did not have the necessary visas to obtain employment and thus returned to Sydney.

After my time with Gerry and Bernadine, I bought a car and moved on to Melbourne, where I met up with a friend from Barcroft Park. Justin Hand had been living over in Australia with his wife, Pauline, and working as a chef for a few years. I initially planned to stay with Justin and Pauline for a few weeks but I ended up living with them for nearly two months. They were really good to me and Justin even found me a bit of work as a labourer in the area. I immediately located the local rock-climbing haunts and spent a lot of my free time on the weekends tackling these routes. The most popular area was called the Arapiles. It is about a three-hour drive outside the city right in the middle of the desert. It was a wonderful place to climb and I encountered wild kangaroos and possums during my time out there.

After a few weeks in Melbourne I started seeing a local girl who had an uncle living in the outback near Canberra. She took me out to visit him for a weekend and this was my first experience with a real Aussie 'outbacker'. He was a little bit mad but had a great personality and we got along well straight away. Whilst I was there he brought me around his land and explained to me that he was having a serious problem with overpopulation of rabbits and grey-back kangaroos. They were feeding off his crops and ruining the land and he had even resorted to dynamiting the areas that they frequented. When this was unsuccessful, he took to shooting them. Just as he was telling me this, someone rang to tell him that there was a large group of kangaroos gathered on his vegetable patch. He quickly asked me if I could shoot and before I even had a chance to respond, he threw me a rifle and pushed me into the back of his truck. When we got to the patch there were about 10 kangaroos feeding on his crops and he told me to open fire on the count of three. As soon as we opened fire, killing two of the kangaroos, the rest scattered. I felt terrible about the whole experience. I had only ever seen kangaroos on television and could not stop thinking about the children's show 'Skippy' as I fired the gun. However, I knew that this tough outbacker would not be sympathetic to my concerns and he probably would have laughed me off his land if I had told him!

After my time out in the bush, I returned to Melbourne, where I spent a further few weeks working before setting off on a 'walkabout' around the country. Before I left, I advertised in all the local youth hostels for backpackers to accompany me on the journey. I knew that I would be covering a lot of miles through the middle of the bush and I wanted others to share the expense of petrol and the responsibility of driving with me on this vast journey. In the end I had a great response and picked three people to come along for the trip. They were a German girl, a Welsh fella and an English girl.

The four of us set off together immediately and for the first few days, we travelled around the coast to Adelaide and visited all the notable sights along the way. From here we headed on towards Port Augusta, stopping in many small towns as we drove. In one of these towns we decided to stay the night and ended up going out to a local disco for a bit of fun. When we arrived at the club, we realised that we were the only non-Aborigines but despite the dirty looks and elbows on the dance floor we made our way in for a drink. Not long after we arrived, I went to the bathroom and two Aboriginal men followed me in and grabbed me by the neck. They told me that 'white men' weren't welcome in their disco and just as they were about to hit me, I gave them a quick history lesson about Ireland. I told them all about the English colonising our land and letting my ancestors starve despite the vast supply of food in the sea surrounding the island. I made our plights sound as similar as possible and by the end of my quick and informative plea, they agreed that I could stay and warned their friends not to give us any bother. The rest of the night was a great laugh and we really enjoyed hanging out with the Aborigine people.

From here we drove through the dead centre of Australia, passing the arid bush areas and vast deserts. This trip took us a total of two months and along the way we stopped at famous landmark sites, including Alice Springs, Coober Pedy, the famous opal mines and Uluru (also known as Ayers Rock).

Three days before we arrived at Uluru, we stayed in an Aboriginal camp on the outskirts of the national park. Whilst we were here, we camped amongst the locals and were taught some of their traditional practices. I got to know one of the Aboriginal elders fairly well and I spoke to him a lot about Ireland and the similarities between our cultures. I explained to him the ancient practices of the Celts and told him about my keen interest in the outdoors. I was very excited about the prospect of visiting Uluru, and wanted very much to be able to climb it. However, I knew that the Aboriginals were staunchly against tourists hiking on the rock or taking pictures in the area and I wanted to get this man's approval before I set out. When I asked him for permission to climb, he just laughed. He went on to say that the main Aboriginal objection to tourists climbing the rock did not have to do with the fact that it is a spiritual place but was because they feared tourists would urinate on the hike and contaminate their watering hole.

With that in mind I set off on the hike and was careful to hold my bladder the entire time! Uluru was a wonderful sight; this sandstone monolith juts directly out of the ground in the midst of a vast desert, with no other rock formations in sight. The short hike to the top yielded unbelievable views of the surrounding land, and as far as my eyes could see there were magnificent rolling desert sands. Ironically, in the seven years before our visit a serious drought struck the entire region, but in the days leading up to our arrival, heavy rains had fallen and they created waterfalls, which streamed down the rock when we arrived. It was such an unusual sight that people had travelled from all over the world to see it. We were so fortunate to have been there for this rare occurrence, and to top it off, on the day we departed, a large crescent rainbow formed around the rock, creating a spectacular splash of colour against the desert backdrop.

Once our time at Uluru was complete we headed on to the Devil's Marbles, an unusual grouping of rock formations further out in the desert. It was like driving through a moonscape, the scenery was so barren and unusual. Along the journey we stopped to swim and sightsee in many of the canyons that litter the area and ultimately we drove all the way to Darwin. At this stage in the trip, the four of us had been travelling together for quite a long time in small, cramped quarters and I decided that upon our arrival in Cairns, I would continue on alone.

When we got into Cairns, the Welsh fella and myself kayaked one of the most famous river routes in the area. It was a fantastic and difficult white water experience and I think that it may have put the Welsh lad off kayaking again for the rest of his life! Prior to the trip he told me that he was an experienced kayaker, but it did not take long for this to be exposed as an exaggeration. The water was very rough along the river and not long after beginning to paddle, he capsized his kayak and nearly drowned in a stopper. He was eventually bounced around the river and made it to shore, but the kayak was lost for good! Despite his difficulties, I enjoyed my time on the river and decided that I would spend a bit more time in the area.

After kayaking, I went on to complete a scuba diving course, which would allow me to visit the Great Barrier Reef. Once I was qualified, I set out on the long boat journey to a top diving spot. As a child I had always suffered from seasickness, but I thought that I had outgrown it.

However, only minutes into the journey I began to feel ill. By the time we reached the dive spot, I felt so sick that I was nearly heaving. Despite my poor condition, I decided to continue on with the dive, but when I descended about 15 metres below the surface, my stomach began to heave. Within my group of divers there were several Japanese tourists; they were directly alongside me when I vomited. Once the vomit dispersed into the water, fish emerged from everywhere and began to surround us to feed on it. The Japanese thought that this was great. They were clicking away with their underwater cameras and I was barely able to hold my food down. They were giving me the 'okay' sign and smiling and in return, I was giving them the middle finger sign and scowling from behind my mask!

After my diving experience, I decided to head north for a taste of the Australian rainforest. I went all the way to Cape Tribulation at the north-easternmost point of the island and camped for several days in one of the national parks. It was well after dark on the day that I arrived, so I decided to sleep in the back of the car along the beach. The next morning I awoke to find myself surrounded by beautiful, golden beaches and palm trees lined with coconuts. It was nearly 30°C and the humidity was very intense, so I could not wait to dive into the turquoise waters for a swim. Without hesitation, I ran into the waves and spent about 15 minutes splashing about before I noticed two men waving frantically at me from the beach.

Initially I was not sure what they were shouting about, but after several minutes, I realised that they were waving me into shore. When I swam in, they asked me if I was crazy. They then pointed out the hazard signs that line the beach. I told them that I had arrived after dark and had not seen a thing. They went on to tell me that this beach had the highest concentration of salt-water crocodiles in all of Australia and, in addition to the crocs, sharks and box jellyfish congregate here. Just the previous week another tourist had gone swimming and was killed instantly. From that point on, I did not swim or even sleep near the coast!

After my time in Cape Tribulation, I travelled along the east coast to Fraser Island, where the highest concentration of dingos occurs, and from there I went on to view the tiger sharks. After this, I went to Byron Bay, a surfing mecca, to see the whales, and headed on to Brisbane, where I spent some time surfing and relaxing. Once my journey down the east coast was complete, I headed back towards Sydney and stayed with my cousin Gerry again for a few days before flying to New Zealand, where I planned to travel through the vast wilderness.

I arrived in Auckland in the middle of winter. It was quite a shock having flown over from the warmth of Australia but after a few days I acclimatised to the cold and rainy weather. I spent time touring around North Island and travelled to a place called Lake Taupo. It was a beautiful, vast body of water surrounded by rolling hills and countryside. I spent a few days touring the area and decided to go for a sky dive over the lake. It was an amazing experience but I will never forget how intensely cold it was. The temperatures on the ground were roughly 2°c but hurtling towards the earth at immense speed made it five times colder than that. My face actually froze on the way down and when I finally pulled my chute and came to a stop on the sandy shoreline, I had ice crystals in my nostrils!

After my sky dive experience, I travelled around visiting the thermal pools and traditional Maori sites before moving onto South Island. I took the ferry between the two coasts and whilst I was in transit I met a local man, who advised me to visit the Abel Tasman National Park. He said that there were great opportunities for sea kayaking and you could view orca whales right from your canoe. He turned out to be a very nice fella and in the end he offered to take me there after we stayed at his house along the way.

We travelled west towards his home and passed through an exotic landscape of kiwi forests and rugged sea cliffs. When we finally got to his house, I found that it was more of a hippie commune than a family residence and with all of the rooms taken, I bunked down for the night on the couch. The following morning the two of us set off with five other people to kayak along the coast of Tasman Bay. The scenery was breathtaking as we paddled out into the icy waters and then, not long into the journey, I noticed a dolphin's fin splashing in and out of the waves around us. Within minutes there seemed to be dolphins everywhere. They were swimming directly alongside my kayak and one was even nudging my boat with its nose. I put my hand out into the water, but my Kiwi friend advised me not to play along. He did not want the dolphins becoming too familiar with people and worried that they would accidentally capsize the kayaks in the icy waters. With that in mind I paddled further out but the dolphins stayed so close that I could see their eyes glistening in the sun. At one point they even began to jump and dive and I could not believe our luck as I watched them somersault right alongside us.

After kayaking, I headed further down the west coast to see some of the old gold-mining communities and then onto the Southern Alps glaciers. This is where the highest mountains in New Zealand are located and within my first week in the region I travelled to the Franz Josef Glacier and the Fox Glacier. Along the two treks I did some solo ice-climbing and traversing. The conditions were ideal and the views spectacular. As I completed the ascents the Tasman Sea was at my back and the pure white snow of the mountain was in front of me. I fell in love with the area immediately and decided to visit some of the more challenging peaks. In the end, I completed a solo ascent of Mount Aspiring, which is a small but technical peak just off the coast in Mount Aspiring National Park.

After the climb, I headed on to Queenstown, which is known as the adventure capital of the world. I arrived in this picturesque town to find every outdoor pursuit I could imagine on offer, and the rooms were as cheap as three New Zealand dollars a night. Although I had intended to spend one week in the area, I ended up staying for six! I befriended many of the other backpackers and ski instructors in the hostel and even struck a deal whereby they would teach me to ski and I would teach them ice-climbing techniques.

We hit the slopes immediately and I took to skiing within a few days and then tried my hand at snowboarding. I spent nearly all of my time in the mountains either pursuing my new hobbies or practising and instructing in climbing techniques. I also did a few bungee jumps, some paragliding and more kayaking before I set off on a serious climb. Whilst I was there, I met up with a Dutch soldier and a British soldier who had connected to climb Mount Cook on a winter ascent. Mount Cook is New Zealand's highest peak and can be very technically difficult during the winter months. Despite the challenges that the climb would pose the three of us felt fit for the ascent and agreed to make an attempt together.

We planned to summit Mount Tasman first and then continue over the ridgeline to Mount Cook, where we hoped to achieve a further summit before making our descent. We set off immediately for Cook Village, the small ranger station at the entrance to the national park, and from here we hiked to a climbing hut along the glacier. After one night at the hut, we traversed the moraine to the start of the climb. When we arrived here, I decided that I no longer wanted to attempt the standard route but instead would traverse the Haast Ridge to a hut where I could base myself for the ascent on Mount Tasman. The Dutch and British climbers agreed to this alternative route and accompanied me along the ridge until we reached a snow gully with a 70° slope below the hut. Once you reach that point the only way to the hut is to ice-climb directly up the vertical slope, but when the others saw the gradient of the climb, they decided that they were not ready for the challenge. In the end the other two men decided to turn back and I set off alone.

It was a difficult climb but I completed the gully just before nightfall and arrived at the hut to find it completely deserted. There were no other climbers along this side of the mountain at all and the small wooden hut felt draughty and cold as I bunked down for the night. I could not believe how close the hut was to the edge of the gully. It seemed precariously perched right on the edge of the vertical slope. I found it difficult to sleep as I had constant visions of a strong gust of wind or an avalanche sending the entire structure plummeting off the edge with me inside. I tossed and turned for hours, listening to the wind blow between the wooden beams. Eventually, I managed to drift off to sleep and with the first light of morning I awoke and set off immediately. I made my way further up the peak to the Plateau Hut. From here, the views of Mount Tasman were spectacular. However, with the increased visibility I could now see how technical and exposed the peak was and I knew that I would not be capable of making a solo ascent. It would have taken several days to devise a strategic plan for the climb and I knew that I did not have the supplies or abilities to do that. However, the north-east ridge on Mount Cook appeared to be a very straightforward climb and thus I decided to set off on this route.

In the Plateau Hut there was a two-way radio for weather forecasts to be relayed by the Rangers' Station. I waited that afternoon for a detailed forecast to come through and planned to make my attempt in the early hours of the following day. I spent the afternoon messing around in the deep snow at the camp, where I built snow holes and igloos, before I set out to mark my route with visibility wands and to cache gear for a fast and light ascent. The route was very clear and I figured that the summit attempt would take roughly 10 hours. When the weather forecast finally came in, it detailed perfect conditions for that night. I prepared myself a large meal before retiring to bed just after 7 p.m. and awoke at 1 a.m. to find that the forecast was entirely accurate.

The temperature was well below zero and the sky was completely clear. There was a vast expanse of stars, which spread across the blackness and shone brightly off the snow underfoot. I set off from camp at a good pace and found the trekking easy as the snow was frozen solid. I continued moving well right up the ridge and within a few hours I had passed through the most notorious avalanche-prone section of the route without incident. By 5 a.m. I was well on my way to the top and was still feeling quite strong. Finally, at 9.15 a.m. I reached the summit to find spectacular views of the surrounding area. I could see down to the Fox Glacier and out across to the sea. However, whilst I was there I noticed that thick clouds were forming over the water and I knew that I must descend quickly to avoid being caught in a storm.

Although my time on the summit was brief, the snow along the route had begun to defrost and suddenly the descent became more difficult than I had anticipated. I was now breaking through the upper crust on the trail and would find myself struggling to move as I became trapped in the deep snow. I used my rope to abseil down off sections that were too awkward to climb or looked unstable and within a few hours I was nearly back to the Plateau. Despite my urge to rest, I decided to descend the entire way down the mountain and found that the last section was extremely tedious. I could no longer ignore my exhaustion and finally stopped for a rest. Whilst I was sitting along the route, I heard a massive avalanche roaring down the slope below me and could see the destruction it caused as it tore through everything in its path.

If I had not stopped for a rest just minutes earlier, I would have been directly in the wake of the avalanche. I knew then that the conditions were too unstable to remain on the peak and despite my fatigue I set off again. By this stage there was a heavy mist developing overhead and the visibility had deteriorated severely. The snows were knee-deep and in the final hours of the descent I was soaking wet and very uncomfortable. Finally, by the end of the day, I reached the glacier off the plateau and decided to bivy there for the night. I was freezing the entire time and barely slept at all but with the first signs of light I set off for the bottom of the Tasman glacier. From here I continued on foot all the way to Cook Village. It was nearly a 25-kilometre walk and for much of the journey I was blanketed by heavy snows. When I finally arrived into the village, I was totally drained and exhausted but I had succeeded in my summit attempt and was proud of my accomplishment.

After my ascent of Mount Cook, I headed back to Queensland for a few more weeks before heading up to Christchurch. From here I flew to Auckland and then on to Thailand again, where I spent several weeks rock-climbing on the islands along the south-east coast. The weather was great and I had a fantastic time relaxing in the sun. Once my time in Thailand was complete I returned home to Ireland to return to work again and begin saving up for my next big adventure.

Chapter 10 ∾

RETURN TO MOUNT EVEREST

'All men dream but not equally, those who dream by night, in the dusty recesses of their minds, awake in the day to find that it was vanity. But the dreamers of the day are dangerous men, for they may act their dreams with open eyes to make it reality.'

T.E. LAWRENCE

When I returned home from my travels in 2000, I began to look for a career in youth work and outdoor education. Whilst I was in the process of applying for jobs one of my best friends from Barcroft, Darren Thompson, arranged for me to work with him at a poultry factory in the north. It was a terrible job that involved hanging chickens and cutting them up for processing and it did not take long for me to realise that I was not cut out for factory work. Our shifts involved long hours working on the floor beneath bright neon lights with no natural sun or windows. From my first day at the job, I knew that I would not last long in this facility.

In an effort to make light of the work, Darren and I spent most of our days messing around and having a laugh. He was based on the other side of the factory floor from me and at regular intervals throughout the day I would throw pieces of chicken at him, which would spark small chicken wars. We would go back and forth for ages, throwing the meat and ducking away from pieces flying back and forth in either direction. On one particular day, I threw an especially large piece of chicken at Darren but he ducked just in time to escape the impact and instead it hit the boss square on. With that my career as a poultry worker came to an abrupt end and thankfully within a few weeks another friend of mine, Mark Kimmins, had arranged an interview for me at Glenmona Resource Centre, a boys' home in Belfast.

I was successful in the interview and began my post as a Care Attendant immediately. I worked the night shift and took the young lads out on activities over the weekend. I really enjoyed the work and was finally in a position that I felt comfortable with. Whilst I was employed with Glenmona, I also continued to lead youth groups through Shannaghmore and rock- and ice-climbed at every opportunity. I also returned to Thailand, Spain and the Alps for some technical ascents. All the while I was still intent on returning to Mount Everest but the right opportunity had not yet arisen.

Then one night whilst I was working at Shannagmore with a fellow climber, called Richard Dougan, he informed me that he was planning to stage an Irish expedition on the north ridge of Mount Everest in 2003. I did not think twice about joining. This was the opportunity that I had dreamt about.

Now the only thing that stood between me and my lifelong dream was money. I had very little left in my savings and no other source of finance. I knew that the expedition would cost over £12,000 for each climber and this equalled more than half my total annual income. My only chance at meeting this exceptional cost was to procure sponsorship. I went to everyone I knew, from banks, the credit union, local shops and businesses to my friends, family and employers. It was a strange and humbling experience because once the word got out, taxi drivers on the street would pull up and hand me money. I would pass elderly women in the town and they would reach into their purses and give me what little they had, and I even received funding from a nun who I had been hiking with in 1988 but who was now working as a missionary in El Salvador. The local newspapers all ran stories about my life and my ambitions and the response from South Down, South Armagh and North Louth was greater than I could have ever imagined. In the end, I raised over £8,000 in sponsorship and I worked as many hours as possible to raise the further £4,000 myself. I even went as far as selling my prized motorbike to cover the shortfall.

Once I had the funding in place, Richard and I began training together. Richard was a very solid climber from Markethill in Armagh and he had a lot of valuable experience. The previous year, he had completed a summit on Cho Oyu in Tibet but tragically, his good friend and climbing partner, Adam Cinnamond from Banbridge, died during the ascent. He slipped into a crevasse and was killed, leaving Richard with the unimaginable task of bringing his friend's body home for burial. I am sure that this was a very harrowing experience for Richard and that it had a profound effect on him.

However, despite the tragedy of Adam's death, Richard was still a committed and determined climber and I knew that he had a good shot at making it to the summit of Everest. He was the expedition's organiser and leader and had all the qualities that were required to make a successful ascent. In addition to myself, Richard arranged for two other climbers to join up with the team. He had met these men whilst on Cho Oyu and felt confident that they had the strength and experience needed for an Everest ascent. They were David Sharp from Guisborough in England and Jamie Maginnis from New Zealand. David was a very solid alpinist who had climbed some of the world's 8,000-metre peaks and had a keen interest in adding Everest to his résumé. Jamie worked as a guide and outfitter in Kathmandu, leading climbs and treks through his company Project Himalaya, and was also eager to add a summit on the world's highest peak to his experience.

Logistically, Jamie's involvement with the expedition proved very beneficial. He was on the ground in Nepal and made all of the necessary arrangements for the team, using porters and staff that he knew and trusted. This saved Richard the headache of sourcing staff from Ireland and committing money to companies that he was unfamiliar with.

In addition to David and Jamie, Richard also enlisted two men from the north of Ireland to work as the expedition medics. They were Stephen Synott and Martin Duggan. Stephen worked at Shannaghmore full-time, leading the first aid and rescue emergency courses, and Martin worked as a physical therapist. We planned for the men to accompany us to the base camp, where they would remain as a support team throughout the duration of the expedition.

Whilst we were making the preparations for our climb, a friend told me that there was a job opening with the Garda Special Projects in Muirhevnamor Housing Estate in Dundalk. I had completed a three-month placement with this juvenile justice project whilst I was studying in England and I felt confident that I had a good chance of getting the post. In September 2002 I went for the interview and was thrilled to be hired immediately. I began work in October and savoured the challenges of this post. I had never been as happy with a job before and had a sense that everything was coming together perfectly in the year leading up to the expedition. Fortunately my employer was also very enthusiastic about the climb and allowed me to accumulate a great deal of overtime, thereby ensuring that I had all of the annual leave required to complete the expedition. I figured that the trip would take a total of two and a half months and this left me very busy working nights and weekends until the time of our departure.

When the four of us finally set off from Dublin on 1 April 2008, we could hardly contain our excitement. We were all eager for the challenges that lay ahead and were excited to be pursuing a lifelong dream. We flew to London first, where David joined us, and then on to Kathmandu, where Jamie met us at the airport and took us on to the hotel.

Once we were all rested, we headed out for a tour of the city. I felt comfortable with the chaos of the streets this time and was no longer intimidated by the hustle and bustle around me. After sightseeing we all headed out for dinner and spent time discussing the logistical plans for the season as well as working out the details for the remainder of the journey. This proved to be a valuable task in getting to know each other's personalities and it gave me a chance to see what David and Jamie were really like.

I liked David a lot from the outset; however, I remember being surprised by his appearance. He was so thin and lanky; I could not believe that he was a climber. I was worried that he would have a difficult time withstanding the altitude and cold as he had no body fat to protect him from the elements, and I knew that he could not afford to get sick whilst on the mountain because he did not have an ounce to lose. However, he was exceptionally bright and very enthusiastic and we all got along well with him straight away.

Unlike David, Jamie seemed very business oriented and unable to relax or enjoy a laugh. I immediately noticed a bit of tension between Richard and Jamie in relation to the expedition costs. Although all of

My brother Colum (*right*) and I at the monument erected in my home town of Newry to honour my success on Everest in 2003.

Mount Cotopaxi, Ecuador, 2004.

Lauren and I in Peru, 2004.

A view of к2 from Concordia, 2005.

The Irish K2 expedition, 2005. (*From left to right*) Paul Moran, Salmon, 'The Captain', myself, Turlough Murphy, Pat Christie, Kevin McClelland, Des Murphy, John Fitzgibbon and Lauren O'Malley.

Lauren and I at Concordia with K2 in the background, June 2005.

(*From left to right*) Des Murphy, Pat Christie and Kevin McClelland entering κ2 base camp, June 2005.

Myself outside the tent at camp three on κ2. (*Photo courtesy of John Fitzgibbon*)

Our tent perched precariously at camp two on K2.

Myself at Concordia with K2 in the background, 2006.

Myself trekking up the Austin Goodwin Glacier below advanced base camp, к2, 2006.

Climbing on the ice fall at advanced base camp on K2.

Myself on the Black Pyramid of κ2, 2006. (*Photo courtesy of Jacek*)

(*From left to right*) Myself, Ger McDonald and Mick Murphy at camp three on κ2, 2006.

Jacek resting after the massive rock fall that nearly killed the two of us between camp one and camp two on K2, 2006.

(*From front to back*) Jacek and Wilco, struggling up from camp three to camp four on к2, 2006.

The Russian climber Serguey Bogomolov at the ridge coming up to camp four, к2, 2006.

The Russian expedition leader Yuri Uteshev at camp four the day before he was killed during the summit bid on κ2, 2006.

Abseiling from camp three on K2.

A family photo (minus Colum), 2006.

Proposing to Lauren on the summit of Ben Nevis, Scotland, 17 January 2006.

Myself and Conor on the day he was born.

Conor Bannon, one year old, 2008.

Lauren, Conor and I, Melrose, Massachusetts, 2008. (*Photo courtesy of Josh Riley*)

the expedition finances had been worked out in advance of our arrival, it seemed as if the costs of Jamie's team of staff were constantly rising. In addition to this, Jamie had announced that he did not want to be classified as a member of the expedition but rather would prefer to be seen as a Sherpa instead. This was the most ridiculous thing I had ever heard. Jamie was no more Nepali or Tibetan than I was and I worried that this attitude might cause serious tensions once we were on the mountain. However, despite my impressions of Jamie, I tried my best to get along with him as I knew that conflict amongst climbers can cripple an expedition.

In the end, Richard rectified most of the confusion over the costs and quietly managed any issues with Jamie's attitude. Within days we set off from Kathmandu for the long overland journey to base camp but before we left we met up with a famous local icon. Elizabeth Hawley is an elderly American journalist who travelled to Nepal in the 1960s for a news story and became so enthralled with the place that she never left. Since that time she has taken on the task of recording all of the climbers who attempt Everest each season. Her notes are kept in a comprehensive database, which records every man and woman who has ever tempted fate on the world's highest peak.

Once Elizabeth had taken our details we travelled by bus to the Friendship Bridge border crossing between Nepal and Tibet and met up with our expedition Liaison Officer. From here we continued on the four-day journey to the north side of the mountain. Our Land Rover convoy stopped a two-day walk from the base camp, where we all set off on foot to begin our acclimatisation, whilst our gear was ferried in the vehicles the remainder of the way. In addition to the men in our expedition there were also an independent Polish climber and an independent Romanian climber travelling with our convoy. The Polish climber was very friendly despite his extremely limited English and the Romanian man was also quite sociable, but seemed slightly unstable and behaved a bit erratically.

Despite our rather unusual company, I felt very comfortable on this return journey to the mountain and had a continuous sense of ease as we made our way along the trail. Although I had seen Everest firsthand before, I did not find the sight of the mountain any less emotional the second time around. I was as awe-inspired and moved as I had been 10 years earlier and I could tell that the other men were as humbled by the majestic peak as I was.

I had trained exceptionally hard in the months leading up to this climb and was well prepared for the long trek ahead, but ironically, I could feel the physical strain of the altitude more intensely this time around. I could see that Martin and Stephen were also struggling as we made our way towards the base camp.

After a slow and tiring walk we all finally arrived at the bottom of Mount Everest and set our camp for the season. I was shocked to find so many other expeditions on the peak as it had been virtually deserted in 1993. There was a large South Korean team with tents that seemed to reach beyond the horizon, as well as a British Royal Marine expedition, a Russian and American expedition and a multitude of commercial climbers. There were also now semi-permanent Sherpa tents at the entrance to the camp with a facility for day tourists to stay the night, and food and provisions for sale in the nomadic yak-herders' tents. It was a circus compared to the way it had been a decade before and I was really thrown by the changes. I remembered how remote the mountain had once felt and couldn't hide my disappointment at how commercial it had now become.

Everest had once been a place so remote that the people of the West never even knew it existed. In fact it was not until 1856 that Andrew Scott Waugh relayed measurements and sightings of the world's highest peak via the Great Trigonometrical Survey. Ironically, he elected to name his find after his geographical surveying predecessor, Col George Everest, calling it Mount Everest for short. What Waugh 'discovered' had long been known to the Tibetan and Nepali people as Chomolungma or 'Abode of the Gods', but Westerners were forbidden to travel to these countries so the secret of this mighty mountain had remained intact from the beginning of time.

After Waugh's reports of the mountain the next 'sighting' or reconnaissance did not come until 1904, when Sir Francis Younghusband made his infamous visit to Tibet. However, even this view came from over 60 miles away from the peak itself. A further sighting of the mountain came in 1913, when a rogue Western explorer sneaked into Tibet; but it too was from a distance of over 40 miles away. Despite the sporadic 'sightings' of Everest in the early 1900s there were never any serious attempts to climb it until 1924, when George Mallory and Sandy Irvine set off for the summit.

Although the early stages of their expedition yielded crucial information on routes and conditions throughout the peak area, the final phase of their ascent and possible summit achievement has remained a mystery to this day. What is known for certain is that both men were killed in a tragic fall either on their way towards the summit or on the way back down.

After the tragic deaths of Mallory and Irvine, it was not until 1953 that the first confirmed successful summit on the world's highest peak was achieved. On 29 May 1953, Edmund Hillary, a New Zealander, and Tenzing Norgay, a Nepali Sherpa, reached the top after an epic climb and confirmed to the world for the first time that a summit on the famous Mount Everest was attainable. From that day forward countless attempts have been made on the world's highest peak with expeditions from all over the world. Many of these climbers have achieved the ultimate glory of a successful summit bid but many more have lost their lives in the pursuit.

Once we established our camp, I set out on an acclimatising walk whilst Martin and Stephen lay down for a rest. They were really struggling with the altitude and by the time I returned to the camp, the men appeared to be very unwell. Stephen was pale and complaining of a headache and pains in his stomach. I could tell that he was also struggling to catch his breath and immediately became concerned that he could be suffering from acute mountain sickness or the more serious illness of oedema. The five of us tried to convince him to increase his fluid intake and to minimise his exertion, but it was far too late at this stage to reverse the symptoms. As the night progressed, Stephen's condition deteriorated and it did not take us long to realise how serious the situation was. Stephen was no longer coherent and his movements were becoming uncoordinated and sluggish. We quickly decided that it was time to get him off the mountain. I could not believe how quickly altitude sickness had struck him and I worried that any one of us could be struck next. I had been feeling very poorly all day and hoped that my condition would improve that night.

In the early hours of the morning we radioed for a Jeep to come up to the base camp to evacuate Stephen, and Martin volunteered to accompany him down. In the end Stephen was taken to Kathmandu, where he received medical treatment for altitude-related illness. He was then transferred to the City Hospital in Belfast when he flew home for follow-up care.

After the men departed, I worried that our expedition could be in jeopardy without a medic. I hoped that none of us would become injured or ill and prayed that if we did, one of the other expeditions would be kind enough to offer their services. This fear made me more committed to acclimatising slowly and I planned several small treks in the days leading up to our departure for advanced base camp.

After one of these walks, I returned to camp to be told by Richard and David that a group of American female trekkers had come by the tent whilst I was away. At first I thought that they were teasing me. I had not seen any women at the camp when I set off and now they were claiming that four women had arrived on their way to Nepal and were returning with whiskey and vodka for a celebration that night. Although it was hard to believe, not long after dinner the women arrived as promised with music and alcohol in tow. Three of the women, Lauren, Bridget and Charlotte, had been together for several months, teaching English in Thailand and then backpacking around Asia. They met the fourth woman in Lhasa and were sharing a convoy to Nepal. I was shocked to see such good-looking women on the mountain and couldn't believe how well acclimatised they were. They had been in Tibet for several weeks and were fit enough to drink the night away, whilst myself and the other lads were barely able to walk without losing our breath. We had a great time with the ladies and by the time the night was over I knew that I had met my match!

Although Lauren was American, she was moving to the north of Ireland in a few months to complete a Masters Degree at Queen's University in Belfast and would be living there for the next two years. She had a lot of work experience with young people and was an avid hiker who loved the outdoors. Our chance encounter was brief but it would prove fateful for us both as four years later we would be married! The next day the girls set off for northern Nepal and myself and the lads prepared to move on to advanced base camp, but I never stopped thinking about my night with Lauren and I wondered where things would go between us when I returned home to Ireland.

When we set off for advanced base camp, we decided to take the trek in two stages as I had done a decade earlier, to give our bodies time to adjust to the altitude. We stopped at an intermediate camp along the glacier for a night's rest before departing again the following day to complete the trek. I started the hike off feeling strong but by the time we reached the intermediate camp I could barely walk. I found myself totally overwhelmed with the altitude and was completely sapped of energy. I was also beginning to experience diarrhoea and had a severe and unrelenting headache. I could barely muster the energy to set up my tent and once I had everything in order, I took some aspirin and a load of re-hydration solution and promptly passed out. I slept well throughout the night and awoke in the morning with renewed strength.

We set off as a group for advanced base camp but within a few hours, the others were miles ahead of me. I could no longer see them on the horizon and I became frustrated with my slow progress. I couldn't understand why I felt so drained. Although I no longer felt the strain of the altitude, I still could not make my body move. At this point, there were clouds rolling in overhead and it had begun to snow. After several hours I had not made any real progress. The winds were picking up and I knew that it would be dark soon and this meant I would have to establish a camp somewhere close by to rest. I was nearer to advanced base camp than I was to the intermediate camp but the trek ahead felt daunting. I sat down to consider my options when suddenly I noticed a yak-herder's tent close by. I decided that this would be my best option for shelter and made my way towards it. The sky had become completely dark and the winds and snow were quite strong by the time I reached the old oilcloth tent and due to my exhaustion, I literally stumbled inside. As I came through the flaps I could see three Tibetan men sitting around a small stove and I could immediately smell the pungent odour of their yak butter tea. Luckily, the men were very hospitable and immediately understood my predicament. They took off my pack and sat me down on cushions. The tent was warm and dry and I was so drowsy that I could barely keep my eyes open. They fed me cups of tea and noodles and it wasn't long before I fell asleep. When the first light of morning came, I awoke beneath a yak wool blanket with the three men staring down at me with broad smiles.

Not long after waking, I packed my things, thanked the men and struggled on to advanced base camp. I was still feeling unbelievably tired and weak and could not understand why my body was failing me so badly. I had trained harder than ever before in my life for this expedition and I now felt as if it had all been in vain. Once I arrived at advanced base camp, I met up with the others again and all of us spent the next few days together slowly acclimatising. After our time of rest, I finally felt my strength returning but then a weather front closed in and we were forced to stay put for a further two days.

During this time, all of the romanticism that I had conjured up in my mind about the North Col began to ebb away with each passing day. Ten years ago, I had longed so badly to progress to this camp. I had been crushed when I was not allowed to continue on with the summit team and now I was bored and frustrated and could find little to distract me from my misery. The weather was poor and our days passed by slowly with each mundane minute feeling like an hour. We sat all afternoon in the mess tent and even resorted to playing draughts with corn flakes. It was not long before we had gone through all of our reading material and I had listened to my CDs countless times over.

Fortunately the weather finally broke and we were able to progress to the North Col. Although I was still feeling unwell, moving camps gave me new motivation. We set off early and within an hour I realised that somehow the rest had not improved my condition. I was still the weakest member of the team and I could tell that the others, particularly Jamie, were growing doubtful of my capabilities. We stayed only two nights at the North Col before we all returned to advanced base camp.

From here, the others set off again to make their way towards camp two, but I remained behind, tired and pissed off. After a further few days, I finally progressed to camp two in what I can only describe as one of the most difficult struggles of my life. Every step felt like a marathon and no matter how hard I tried, I could not muster any strength. It was totally devastating for me because mentally and spiritually, I felt stronger than ever, but my body was totally exhausted. I had sacrificed everything to be on this mountain and I was so disappointed with my progress. Before I set off for the mountain, I had imagined that I would summit without even the assistance of oxygen but now I knew that it would take a total rejuvenation to even make it to the high camps. I also felt tremendous loyalty to all of the people who had sacrificed financially to make this opportunity possible and I hoped more than ever that I would not let them down.

Once I made it to camp two, I collapsed with exhaustion. It took me over an hour before I was able to muster the strength to set up my tent and organise my gear. David, Jamie and Richard were still feeling strong and decided to push on to camp three. However, before they departed Richard spoke to me briefly about an issue with the Polish climber from our convoy that had taken place during the night. Apparently the Russian expedition was on the mountain to return home the body of a climber who had died the previous year. His corpse was in a tent just above camp two and they were planning to lower it down and bring him back to Russia. The Polish climber had come to the mountain with few supplies and did not have spare tents to establish camps along the ridge. He most likely spent the first few weeks sleeping in tents that were cached at the various drops along the route, but on this particular night, he could not find a single spare tent. For that reason, he sought refuge in the tent with the frozen Russian climber.

He spent the entire night huddled alongside the icy body in the wind-tattered tent. As horrified as I was to hear this, I knew that the Polish climber must have been desperate and with my exhaustion, I could think little more about it.

It was difficult work to establish camp. I had to dig into the rock and ice to make a platform flat enough for my tent. Once this was done, I rested and refuelled before sleeping for a short while. The weather was growing increasingly poor and I knew that I would have to descend before a total whiteout set in. I established a cache of gear and set off at first light with freezing temperatures and minimal visibility. I worried that some of the other climbers might tap into my cache whilst they were using the camp and hoped very much that I would find my food and fuel in place when I returned.

It was a long journey back down to advanced base camp but I was feeling a slight improvement in my physical condition. Whilst I was at ABC, the others descended as well and we all returned to base camp together to review the weather and our strategy for a summit bid. We had now been on the mountain for about six weeks and were conscious that the weather conditions would deteriorate as the season progressed.

Once we were at base camp, our negotiations about the summit bid began. I begrudgingly admitted that Jamie was the strongest member of the team and accepted that my performance had been the weakest. Jamie argued vehemently that I was a liability for our team and should not be allowed to take part in a summit attempt. This infurited me and I reminded Jamie that he was not the expedition leader. The dispute put a great deal of pressure on Richard but he was an excellent mediator and in an effort to satisfy everyone he agreed to allow two summit attempts. He and David would go on the first attempt and after their bid, Jamie and myself would be allowed a shot at the top if the weather and my physical condition had improved.

I had a lot of respect for Richard and the passive manner in which he conducted his affairs but I could not stand to be around Jamie and was annoyed that I would be left with him. His arrogance and self-righteous attitude angered me constantly and it took all of my restraint not to lash out at him physically when he put me down. I dreaded the thought of making a summit attempt with him, but I knew that it was my only option as I was not fit enough to set off on the first attempt.

During the next few days, whilst we were at base camp, the mountain was battered by high winds and snow and we all lost tents and gear to the storms at the high camps. I worried about the impact that this would have on our summit attempt but I did not have long to dwell on it, as within a few days there was a weather window on the forecast and Richard and David set off on their attempt. Several other expeditions at the base camp also elected to take advantage of the settled weather and on the day that the men departed, the mountain was full of climbers making their way towards the top.

Although Jamie and I were not part of the summit team, we progressed to advanced base camp to wait for word about Richard and David's progress. After a few days, we received radio contact and heard that they made excellent progress to the high camps but were forced to turn back on the top of the second step due to a backlog of climbers and deteriorating weather. As a result of their time on the exposed route they were suffering from frostbite on their fingers and toes and were conscious that if they continued on towards the summit, they might end up facing amputations. I was crushed for them both but felt terribly disappointed for Richard in particular because he had invested so much time, effort and money into this attempt and I knew that it would be very difficult for him to retreat.

After the news about Richard and David came over the radio, we received a further call to say that the Polish climber was missing on the peak and all of the expeditions were being advised to keep a lookout for him. This news immediately worried me because I knew that he had so little in the way of supplies and doubted he had the gear to survive exposure. He had been very kind to all of us and, despite his seriously limited English, he had told about his family and shared photographs of them with us on the way towards the mountain. I could not help feeling sorry for him as we waited for further contact from Richard and David. I knew that if he were lost he would be unlikely to survive and if he had fallen it would not take long for him to succumb to the elements.

Within a few hours Richard and David made contact from the safety of camp three and informed us that they had arrived in extremely poor weather. It appeared that the frostbite on David's toes was quite serious and Richard was also suffering from advanced deterioration on his fingers. At that point Jamie, one of the kitchen porters and myself ascended to the North Col and then Jamie moved on up to camp two to assist the men in their descent. It took several long hours but they all finally made it back to the safety of camp one.

Whilst this was happening, a film crew lower down on the peak used their high definition zoom lenses to scan the mountain for signs of the Polish climber. Within a short while they spotted a body near the Great Couloir. After speaking with the Romanian climber, they confirmed that the clothing matched that of the Polish man and we knew then that he was dead. He had most likely fallen somewhere around the second step.

The news of this fatality struck us all but we had little time to consider the situation because within a few hours we learned that an English climber further up the peak had taken a serious fall and had a broken leg. The news of the accident came in over the radio and we soon learned that the Royal Marine expedition was sending Sherpas to assist in a rescue. Luckily, the Sherpas were able to reach the stricken man fairly quickly and they staged a very daring rescue operation.

Through their unbelievable skill and tenacity they managed to evacuate the man as far as camp two, where there were other climbers waiting to assist.

Prior to this rescue, myself and many other climbers believed that serious injuries in the 'death zone' on Everest were almost always fatal because the prospects of staging a rescue at this extreme altitude were severely limited. However, with the Sherpas' persistence, the myth that an immobilised man is as good as dead was completely dispelled. Once the man reached camp two, the Royal Marines took him as far as the North Col, where I joined in their efforts to lower him down towards advanced base camp.

It was a very daring and time-consuming rescue and the Sherpas and marines gave it 110%. Once the evacuation was complete, I returned to my tent at the North Col and waited for Richard, Jamie and David to return. They rested for a night higher up on the mountain and the following morning they made their way down to me where I assisted them back to base camp. Ironically, for the first time in weeks I was beginning to feel stronger and my confidence was rising. It occurred to me that I might have been suffering from a virus and it was finally clearing. My renewed strength gave me hope and the prospect of making a summit bid became a real possibility again.

Once we arrived back down at base camp, we took special care to treat Richard and David's frostbite. Jamie and I washed their exposed skin with iodine and water and bandaged it to the best of our abilities. I knew that it was important for the men to keep their skin clean as frostbite opens the body up to infection and the conditions in the camp were far from sanitary. Once Richard and David were comfortable, they met with one of the other teams' medics and he advised the two that they must be evacuated immediately. He feared that in the absence of proper medical attention, the men would face amputations. This was devastating news for both Richard and David because it meant that they would not have another shot at the summit.

The following morning, the men were evacuated by Jeep, and Jamie and I retreated to our tents to assess the situation. Ironically, as we discussed our options that night an Indian climber at the base camp informed us that there were forecasts for another window in the next few days with almost completely calm winds on 31 May. This would make for ideal summit conditions. Jamie and I had already been on the mountain for almost eight weeks as this stage and both of us were growing tired of the monotony. In addition to this, the climbing season was drawing to an end and the potential for good weather would soon be over. We knew that this would be our last opportunity to go for the top. Without further hesitation, Jamie and I set off early on the morning of 28 May from the base camp of Mount Everest for the final but most important phase of our journey up the world's highest peak: the push towards the summit.

Chapter 11 ❧

| THE SUMMIT

'It is not those that inflict the most, but those who endure the most who will conquer in the end.'
TERENCE MCSWINEY, LORD MAYOR OF CORK

The morning of 28 May was overcast and cold. Jamie and I awoke early to make our final preparations before returning up the peak. Ironically, I was now feeling very strong and Jamie had begun to slow down, as he was feeling ill. I had reservations about making a summit attempt with Jamie from the outset. We had not gotten along well throughout the climb and I was unsure whether he could be trusted in a pinch; but with little other option, we set off together on the trek towards advanced base camp.

It took us most of the day to reach ABC and when we finally arrived, there was still a thick blanket of cloud overhead. I worried that the forecast might not have been accurate and hoped very much that we would not get any snow or high winds that night as this would impede our summit bid. We both retired to bed quite early and I awoke to find that the sky had cleared, but there was a still a plumage visible at the summit. This white swirl is snow that is blown off the upper slopes by high winds but appears like a cloud to those below. I knew then that the weather remained treacherous on the upper slopes and hoped the Indian forecast was correct and that the winds would settle before our attempt.

Before we set off for camp one, Jamie got an update over the satellite phone from a reliable source informing him that the winds would decrease the following day, confirming that 31 May would be the perfect day for a summit attempt. However, they also warned that these conditions would only last for 24 hours and this weather would be followed by high winds and heavy snows brought in by the monsoon.

We knew then that we must continue to move up the mountain with speed and accuracy in order to reach camp three by 30 May, thus allowing us adequate time for the final push. We set off straight away from ABC and reached camp one without incident.

I was still feeling strong when we reached the North Col and Jamie's condition was well improved, although still not 100%. When we arrived at the camp, many of the other expeditions were heading down after several nights at the high camps waiting for the weather to clear. Unfortunately, like Richard and David, they were beaten by the elements in the end and most no longer had the strength or supplies to make a further attempt. Jamie and I dug out the tents that we had left in place and bunked down for the night after a solid feast. I ate a can of sardines which had been left behind by other climbers, as well as some soup and biscuits, and Jamie ate from freeze-dried supplies which he had packed. I was careful to take in as much fluid as possible and drank a great deal of orange Tang before I fell asleep.

I awoke the following morning to find that the snow around the tent had frozen solid and the temperature was quite low. These conditions were ideal for moving quickly towards camp two. We would no longer have to struggle with the deep slushy snow. Jamie and I began packing up our gear and within an hour we were moving up the steep slope above.

For the first few hours I felt great and was really enjoying the climb. I was awestruck by the scenery as I gazed out at the vast Himalayan range around me. The route consisted of snow and ice, which was followed by rock and scree. The latter half was rather difficult underfoot and as I made my way up to the halfway point between the two camps I began to feel ill. My stomach had severe cramps and before I knew it I was seized by diarrhoea. The sardines from the night before had come back to haunt me. I had no time to unclip from the rope or to move off the trail when it happened—I was forced to stop and relieve myself whilst other climbers moved past in either direction. Jamie had progressed well ahead at this stage, and despite my urge to keep up with him, I knew that I needed to wait for the diarrhoea to cease before setting off again.

After several further episodes, I became increasingly concerned about my potential to make it to the top. I was moving very slowly and

I was also beginning to suffer from a headache. I knew that I was becoming dehydrated, but I had only packed 2 litres of fluid for the journey between the two camps and was now forced to suck on pieces of snow and ice to keep me going. It was a long and painful trek and by the time I reached camp two, Jamie was already well rested in the tent.

As soon as I crawled into the tent I could see Jamie shaking his head at me. His negative and condescending attitude had returned. He had been putting me down from the outset of the expedition and he was again voicing doubts over my abilities. I knew it would be futile to argue with him and I refused to waste energy defending myself, so instead I dismissed him. It was a long and painfully quiet night in the tent next to him. However, once I was rehydrated, I fell into a deep sleep and awoke the following morning feeling far better. Psychologically I prepared myself for the difficult journey ahead and I remember thinking about a quote that I had read years before. It went, 'It is not those that inflict the most, but those who endure the most who will conquer in the end.' The Lord Mayor of Cork spoke these famous words on his deathbed whilst succumbing to starvation through hunger strike in 1920. He had been arrested, detained and sentenced by the English, but they never broke his spirit and this really struck me. Although Jamie thought that he was stronger and fitter than I was, I knew that I had the mental and physical strength to endure the final challenges of this peak and this put my mind at ease.

We set off early for camp three and Jamie moved off quickly again. Within an hour he was well out of my sight, but I slowly persevered up the fixed ropes between the camps. It was not long before I reached a Swiss climber who was sitting on a rock alongside the lines. He had unclipped from the ropes and I could see that he was drinking from a flask. As I moved closer to him, I got a whiff of alcohol off his breath. I was shocked that anyone would be drinking with the technical ascent ahead, but this man had no intention of climbing.

I asked if the man was injured and his response came out sharp and abrupt. He told me that he was fine and to go away. I could tell immediately that there was something wrong with the man so I leant in closer to him to speak with him again, but he pulled back away from me. He repeated his command for me to leave and then stated that he wanted to die. At first I did not know what to say or do. Sitting before me was a perfectly healthy, uninjured man, who for no apparent reason wanted to suffer the harsh and painful death of exposure. Without hesitation, I grabbed the man and began to shake him. I told him to wise up and advised him that I was not going to let him die next to me. He continued to protest and pleaded with me to leave him alone. When I could think of nothing else to say, I slapped him hard across the face. At this, he stared up at me with a mixture of anger and shock. I quickly went on to question him about his family and his friends and demanded to know why he would give up everything he had in his life over a mountain.

The climber then broke down in tears. He told me that he had been at the high camps waiting for the weather to break and he could no longer physically bear the altitude. He was too ashamed to descend without a successful summit bid and would rather die than return home to be disgraced. I advised him that the mountain was not worth a single finger or toe and told him to continue down and make another attempt next year. I went on to say that he would not be the first man to climb Everest and would certainly not be the last, so he should go home and plan another attempt. I was beginning to tire of the situation and could feel myself wasting vital energy speaking with him. With no patience remaining I told the man to fuck off and make his way down or I would throw him down the mountain myself. To that, he stood up and shook my hand as he clipped back onto the rope. He yelled up to me that I was crazier than him and I watched as his silhouette slowly disappeared below me.

It was hard to gauge how long I had been with the man, but I knew that Jamie was so far ahead of me at this stage that I would not see him again until I reached camp three. I slowly traversed the final section and reached the precariously perched tent just after 2 p.m. Jamie was already inside resting as I made my way into the nylon shell along the edge of the rocky slope. It felt as if one strong gust of wind would have blown the tent straight off the north face. The camp was totally exposed to the harsh elements and the gradient of the slope below was quite severe. Despite the dangerous conditions, I knew that I needed to rest well in order to recover sufficient energy for the summit bid. Just as I was making my way into the shelter, Jamie stuck his head out of the tent and I shouted to him before he could speak that I was going to do this.

To that he said nothing, but smiled, and the two of us prepared our things for the task ahead that night.

As we were now at over 27,000 feet, every movement seemed painfully slow and awkward. I felt as if I were on the moon. My gloves and outerwear were cumbersome and my breathing was heavy and ineffective. Jamie was also struggling under the burden of the altitude, but fortunately he found a full, discarded oxygen bottle not far from our tent. He jimmied the bottle open and let it run into the tent as the two of us lay down for a rest. Within minutes I felt the benefits of the oxygen. It was like someone had given me a new lease of life. In addition to this bottle, Jamie then located a further four canisters which were all still full. This discovery proved crucial to our summit bid. Each of us would now have two bottles to support us to the top and back down as far as this camp if we required it. Despite the obvious benefits of this find, I was concerned about using the oxygen. I worried that I would be 'cheating' if I took the assistance of the oxygen and that I might never know my full potential if I used it. However, I had suffered throughout the climb and the summit was now so close it would have been foolish to cast off this added support; thus in the end I took it.

I finally drifted off but slept only intermittently, as my nerves and the excitement of the journey ahead kept me on constant edge. As the night fell, the sky remained clear and the temperature plummeted. I unzipped the tent at regular intervals to check on the weather conditions and found myself in a world so foreign and pristine that it is hard to describe. There was no moon in sight, but there were stars so low overhead that they reflected directly off the snow. There were no other climbers around us, although I could hear their echoes on distant parts of the mountain. I felt so close to the majestic peak that I was nearly a part of it. I imagined how beautiful the world below would look when I finally reached the top and could not stop thinking about how intensely emotional this entire journey had been.

The time passed quickly and before long it was 10 p.m. and Jamie and I were both up packing our gear for the final stage of the climb. I quickly set out to collect snow, which we would melt for drinking water whilst Jamie was organising his gear. I returned to the tent and lit our small gas stove. The process of melting took far longer than I had anticipated it would. The extreme altitude meant that it was taking twice as long to melt and within a few minutes I decided that we would not have time to let it warm. When the snow was finally sufficiently liquidised, I began to fill my water bottles. I had no appetite but knew that I would need food for energy and managed to stomach some chocolate biscuits as well as a Power Gel before I packed up my final things.

Once I had all of my gear in place, I began to pull my crampons on over my outer boots. I was wearing a heavy down suit with many base layers underneath and under the strain of all this clothing, I found the process of putting my crampons on very slow and demanding. It was so consuming that I had not even noticed Jamie leaving the tent. Once I had everything on, I finally emerged out into the dark night to find myself totally alone. It took me a minute or two to realise what had happened, but then I remembered Jamie saying that he had seen four or five head-torches on the route above us a short while before. I knew then that he had left me to follow these climbers. Words cannot adequately describe the rage I felt at this discovery. I could not believe that Jamie would take off without a word and I cursed his cowardice as I set off alone into the darkness.

Thankfully, the anger gave me a rush of adrenalin and with this strength my determination was further cemented. I scanned the horizon above and eventually saw the distant glow of head-torches. I began to move in the direction of the light and scoured the route ahead for fixed lines. Much to my dismay, I could not find a single rope as I progressed upwards. I was conscious of the exposure and used a single axe as I navigated my way up and across the slope above.

It did not take long to discover how dark a moonless night can be. My head-torch did little to light up the route ahead and I could only intermittently see the glow of head-torches above. I finally came across a single rope and although it looked slightly old and battered, I imagined that it must mark the correct route and hooked onto it with a jumar. After progressing a few rope lengths above, I realised that the route was becoming extremely steep. Then suddenly a large slab of rock appeared directly above me right in the middle of the route. By the time I reached the base of this slab, the rope came to an abrupt end. I was confused. I could see some rope slung around a rock above, but I could not tell if it was intentionally hooked on, or if it had just fallen. I had

spoken with Dawson Stelfox and several other Everest climbers about
the summit route before my departure and none of them had described
these conditions. However, I was conscious of time and felt that I had
no other option than to continue on. I reached up above myself in the
darkness and felt a shelf along the rock. I used this for leverage to pull
myself onto the ledge above. Once I was positioned along the ledge, I
realised that there was something drastically wrong.

The route had become far too technical and steep and there was no
visible trace of ropes above. I cursed myself for not checking the route
more carefully and Jamie for leaving me on my own. I began to
carefully lower myself back down off the ledge but found that my foot
was no longer able to reach the rocks below. I stopped for a moment to
take my outer gloves off, giving me a better grip along the shelf. I had a
sick feeling growing in the pit of my stomach as I again attempted to
lower myself off the ledge. I could feel the total weight of my pack
pulling me down and the muscles in my arms shook with the intense
effort that I was making. I had a vision of my body plummeting
backwards off the north face and I knew that nothing would break my
fall if I lost my grip. Sweat began to bead on my brow, despite the fact
that it was nearly thirty below zero, and to my horror it began to drip
directly into my eyes. My right eye burned with the salt of my
perspiration and it began to cloud over, distorting my vision. I
desperately stretched my body until finally one of my toes touched a
narrow rocky ledge below. I used this placement to shimmy across the
shelf above until I reached a wide enough point on the ledge to support
both feet.

When I finally felt the safety of my footing, I stopped to regain my
composure. My goggles were totally steamed over and I had to wipe the
sweat beads that trickled down the glass onto my outer sleeve before
moving on. I was talking to myself out loud and the words rang in my
ears with muffled confusion as they were filtered through my oxygen
mask. I kept trying to reassure myself that I could navigate this final
section no matter how difficult it was, but I knew that I would now
have to retrace my steps to locate the correct route. I backtracked to a
point where the route above looked manageable and again began to
ascend.

This time I came across a fixed line of rope, which looked far stronger and newer than the one that I had previously encountered. I checked the durability of the rope before clipping on, but still did not trust the strength entirely, in case I was again along the wrong route. I moved on carefully and within half an hour, I had made decent progress upwards. However, just as things seemed to be going well for me, my head-torch went out completely. I made several attempts to get it working again, and tried warming the batteries in my hands, but the light would not return. I sat down along the route and began to consider my situation. I did not have another head-torch or extra batteries with me as I was trying to keep the weight of my pack to a minimum and I was beginning to realise that my chances of making it to the top were growing increasingly limited. I could not help thinking that all of this misfortune might be an omen telling me to stop. Jamie had left me, I had gotten lost, and now I was alone on the mountain without light.

As I sat on the cold, exposed slope, I suddenly remembered a small LED light attached to the zipper of my fleece jacket. My mother had given me this cheap torch to use in my tent and it dawned on me that this could be the answer to my prayers. I pulled down the thick outer jacket and freed the small light from beneath. To my delight, when I turned it on, a small but surprisingly bright light shone out before me. My only problem now was that the torch only remained on when there was pressure on the switch. Thankfully, I had duct tape in my pack and I was able to secure the small torch to my head strap in such a manner that it remained on. With that, I immediately pulled my gear together and again began to ascend upwards.

I was very conscious of the time that I had lost since I set out and I knew with total certainty that I would have to make it to the second step before dawn in order to make the summit within a safe turn-around time. I moved as quickly and carefully as possible through the vast darkness above me and within a few hours I had nearly reached the north-east ridge. As I made the final traverse onto the ridge, I encountered a pronounced lump stacked against an outcrop of rock. As I got closer to the lump, I realised that it was a body with tattered and wind-blown clothing, wrapped tightly in reels of rope. This corpse was directly to my right as I continued to ascend upwards and I tried to avert my gaze as I moved past. I could hear the wind howling all around me and eerie shadows began to appear on the mountain, making the situation seem very haunting.

I finally progressed onto the ridge proper and encountered a rock alcove along the route. As I rounded the corner where the rocks jut in, creating a shelter from the elements, I could see a pair of bright neon green boots sticking out. For a second I thought it might be Jamie but as I stepped in closer, I could see the huddled body of an Indian climber who had perished years before during his summit attempt. I was now speaking loudly to myself and coaxing my nerves to settle. My voice sounded dry and foreign from the oxygen pumping through my mask and for the first time since I had gotten the light to work, I knew that I needed to rest for a moment. I felt anxious and excited at the same time. I was very conscious of the dangers around me and could feel butterflies in my stomach as I tried to calm my nerves and refuel before moving along the ridge-line. I was still close to the Indian climber's body and as I began to organise my gear a very strange and frightening thing happened. My mind began to play tricks on me and for a moment I was certain that I could see the corpse moving. I leaned in closer to be sure that the climber was dead and was shocked to find his eyes wide open. They had crystallised a pure white colour that sparkled beneath the glow of my torch. This took me by complete surprise and I immediately pulled back away from the body.

Within seconds I was moving, but I suddenly had images of ghostly apparitions creeping up behind me and I could feel my heart racing in my chest as the wind blew icy gusts at my back. Part of me knew that I was hallucinating from the altitude but I could not shake the frightened feeling as I moved on. Thankfully, as the ridge grew narrower and increasingly exposed, my focus was restored and I was able to concentrate completely on the task ahead. As quickly as night had descended on the mountain the sky suddenly broke into light with the coming of dawn. It was an awesome sight and I made my way safely over the first step as the golden rays broke through the darkness above. I could suddenly see climbers illuminated on the second step and I knew that I needed to move quickly because the cutoff time for a safe summit bid comes when the sun shines directly above this section.

I became very anxious about my pace and pushed on with remarkable speed until I reached the base of the second step. I stopped here and changed my oxygen bottle, leaving the old one jammed between two rocks in case I needed the remainder on my descent. From here I had a clear view of the climbers above and I got my first sight of Jamie since he had left me in the tent. I shouted up to him, calling him a wanker, but he could not hear me. I thought I saw him look down at me briefly as he set off again, but if he saw me at all he did not acknowledge it.

Directly above me I could also see a Japanese woman who was being pushed and pulled by a team of Sherpas. It was completely apparent that this commercial client was totally out of her depth and I decided that I would need to move around the group quickly or risk losing my shot at the summit.

From here, I had to climb hand over hand using the fixed lines that were running down the rock face. At one stage, I even had to push my crampons into a Sherpa's legs to get him to move out of my way. I had little time to think about the ridiculousness of the situation. The Japanese woman seemed barely conscious and it was blatantly obvious that she could not progress. Despite the Sherpas trying to convince her to go down, she was insistent that they pull her up. Once I made it beyond the first section of this route, and the circus act behind me was nearly out of sight, I reached the aluminium ladder on the sheer rock face that the Chinese installed in 1975.

Ironically, this is the same place on the mountain where many believe Mallory and Irvine took their fateful fall. It was easy to imagine how they could have perished on such a steep, exposed rock face whilst free climbing, and thoughts of their tragic demise kept me extremely focused.

The ladder, though once secure, was now precariously perched along the ledge and swung to the side as I moved up each rung. I was trying not to rest my full weight on the aluminium and remained hooked onto the labyrinth of rope that cascaded down the side of the ladder for added protection. Once I finally reached the relative safety of the small plateau at the top of this ascent, the full weight of my exhaustion bore down upon me. By this stage the sun had risen into the sky and it must have been approaching 6.30 a.m. I was no longer cold and had actually begun to sweat with each exertion. I unzipped my heavy down jacket and pulled it down around me as I made my way up the summit ridge. From here all that lay before me was a final stony outcrop and then the summit dome. Initially, I thought that the second step was the last obstacle before the top but only after passing it did I realise that there was one final challenge ahead. My energy was seriously waning but I knew that I was so close to the summit that I could not stop now. I could nearly taste the glory of success.

My body continuously cried out for a rest, but I kept willing myself on because I knew that the men I had passed earlier in the day had also only stopped for a brief reprieve and now they were interred for eternity on the mountain of their dreams. It is strange because no matter how close I got to the summit dome, I still knew that each step could be my last and was very conscious of my mortality. I never felt the reckless abandon that some describe as 'summit fever' and made calculated moves right to the end. It took me a further hour and 15 minutes to overcome the final icy slope and subsequent rocky traverse before the true summit appeared in front of me.

However, just as my excitement was nearly at its peak, I saw Jamie resting on a rock to my left. As much as I would have liked to throttle him, I did not want to ruin this moment. I went closer to him and could see that his nose was bleeding from the altitude, but I did not stop to ask how he was. I instead demanded that he give me the satellite phone. To this he responded that he had already been on the summit and made his calls. I ignored this completely and told him again to give me the phone. When he finally produced it, I continued on my way and never gave him a second thought. At this point the summit was so close to my reach that I wanted to run onto it. I felt as strong as ever and suddenly I became overpowered with joy.

It only took me a further five minutes to reach the true summit and when I finally arrived words cannot describe the sense of total accomplishment, pride and excitement that I felt. All of my dreams, my desires and my hopes were pinned on this single moment and the glory of it all was almost entirely overwhelming. It was 8 a.m. on 31 May 2003 and I was standing on the top of the world. I could see the silhouettes of mountains reaching as far as the horizon. I had a clear view of the Tibetan Plateau to the north and Nepal to the south and the entire Himalayan range stretched east and west as far as the eye could see. I could barely breathe with my happiness and I actually had to stop for a moment to compose myself so that I could take it all in. My oxygen was completely gone at this stage but I felt strong from the adrenalin and decided not to rush my time on the top. I took out my digital camera and attempted to take some shots.

Much to my dismay, the camera would not work. I tried to warm it between my hands and armpits, but nothing helped. Fortunately, I had a disposable camera in my pack and I immediately took panoramic shots of myself and my surroundings. I held the camera out before me and smiled into the lens as I clicked away. I felt like the 14-year-old boy who I had once been on that first trek through the Mourne Mountains. The adventure and excitement of it all was completely surreal. Once I was done taking photographs on the disposable camera, I managed to get the battery of the digital camera warm enough to take a few shots.

I balanced the camera on my rucksack and set the timer to take a self-portrait. This process did not prove easy. The timer was very short and the altitude made my movements very slow. Each time I would back away to get into position for the picture the timer would go off before I was ready. After several failed attempts, I finally got one or two decent shots and then sat down to rest and take it all in. There were Tibetan prayer flags blowing in the wind behind me, with a tattered brass Nepalese flag staked into the summit dome. The summit was so beautiful and remote it nearly felt spiritual. I was the last climber to reach the top that day and would actually be the last summiteer for the entire season. I had the top all to myself and I enjoyed every minute of it. I thought a lot about my family and friends as I sat looking out at the world below me. A slide show of my life flashed through my mind. All of my memories from home and childhood ran through my thoughts. I must have sat there for half an hour when I finally realised that I needed to prepare for my descent.

Just below the summit dome, I made a call to my mother. It was the middle of the night in Ireland, but her phone was engaged. The media had received word from Jamie that we were on the summit and reporters were phoning her for a comment. I left a message to say that I had made it to the top and then phoned David Malone, our expedition's PR coordinator. Once I finished speaking to David, I phoned my mother again. This time she answered and I could tell by the excitement in her voice that she had already heard my news. She told me how proud she was of my achievement and cried with joy as she advised me to get moving and to make my way down safely. Even my mother knew that my journey was far from over. After I hung up, I took a few final looks around and went across to the south side to see what it would look like to summit from that angle and then I made my way back across the top towards the route down.

Almost as quickly as I began my descent, all of my adrenalin, excitement and energy just slipped away. I knew that I was only at the half way point and that the downward journey would be every bit as hard, if not harder than the ascent. I tried to keep myself alert and constantly fought off the exhaustion that was trying to overtake me. It felt like I was driving home late at night and could barely keep my eyes open behind the wheel. I worried that this was what it would feel like just before a crash. I knew that the climbers below me had felt the same urge to rest and their misfortune kept me from giving in. I finally reached the second step and began to abseil down. However, just as I reached the bottom, I unclipped from the rope and as I moved away, I slipped on some rocks. I was not hooked onto a line to break my fall, but thankfully I was able to reach up and grab some of the old rope above just in time.

This slip had a really profound effect on me. I knew that one false step would send me plummeting and I decided that the only way to make it down safely was to rest every fifth step. Counting the steps out loud gave me focus and after a few hours I could see camp three in the distance. I stopped along a jagged rock for a rest when suddenly I could see small, white feathers blowing around me. I felt totally confused and again thought that the altitude must be playing tricks on me. No matter how hard I tried, I could not figure out where all the feathers were coming from. However, later on in the descent, I noticed them again and only then did I realise that I had torn my outer gear on the rock and the down feathers were coming through the tear.

By the time I made it to camp three, I was so exhausted I could barely walk. Jamie was in the tent and when I came in he congratulated me on making it to the summit and handed me a drink. I had no fight left in me. I congratulated him back, took the drink and told him that I could not stay the night. I felt confused and tired with the altitude and worried that if I went to sleep I might never wake up. Jamie was tired too, and agreed that we would be better off outside the 'death zone'. The two of us set off a short while later with the tent in tow.

I have no idea where we found the energy to make it down to camp two, but when we finally arrived, we barely made it into the tent before we collapsed. We slept through the night and with the early light of dawn, I felt excited again. I wanted nothing more than to finish the descent and make my way home to celebrate my success on the mountain. As we set off that morning, the clouds began to roll in and we pushed on all the way to the North Col, where we were met by a member of our kitchen crew. He was a young Nepali lad who had been cooking for our expedition at the base camp throughout the season. He was very enthusiastic about our successful summit bids and carried our tents to lighten the load. Once we were further down the peak we met other members of the kitchen crew, who took on the remainder of our gear, thus allowing Jamie and me to move fast and light.

With the assistance of the Nepali and Tibetan crew, we all made it to ABC within an hour. We spent one further night at ABC, where the crew made us a cake to celebrate our success. It was a great night and Jamie and I got along well despite all of the issues that we had experienced throughout the season. The following morning, it began to snow quite heavily and we were all conscious that bad weather was moving in quickly. We set off as quickly as possible and made it to base camp within a few hours.

When we arrived at base camp, it was nearly deserted. All of the other expeditions and Sherpas had cleared out for the season as the monsoon was rolling in, and our Liaison Officer had already phoned to arrange our transport. He was very worried about heavy snow blocking the passes between the mountain and the border, and did not want to become trapped. That night the Jeeps arrived and we set off on the return journey to Nepal.

It was a quiet trip for both Jamie and me. We were tired from the difficult journey up the mountain and were both reflecting on all that we had achieved. However, at one point Jamie spoke to me about why he had left me at camp four. On reflection I think that he felt bad about what had happened but at that moment he feared I would not have the strength to make it and felt I would hold him back as well. I understood now why he had panicked and in hindsight I might have felt the same about a climber with such a poor performance throughout the season. In actuality Jamie's actions had made me stronger and in making it to the summit alone I had proven to myself how capable I actually was.

Once we got to the border, we were told that there had been a serious outbreak of a respiratory disease throughout China and other parts of Asia and that we might not be allowed to cross into Nepal. Apparently an illness called SARS was rapidly spreading throughout the region and they were quarantining travellers to prevent an epidemic. When we arrived at the immigration post, they took our temperatures and found that mine was slightly raised. I tried to explain that I had just come from the summit of Everest and that this might explain my high temperature, but they were not satisfied with this. They took me into a separate room, where they took my temperature three more times before, thankfully, allowing me to go.

As soon as we crossed into Nepal, Richard met up with us again. He had maintained radio contact with us since his departure and already knew of our successful summits. David had returned to London immediately after leaving the mountain to seek medical attention for the frostbite on his toes. In the end he was forced to have two of them amputated, as the damage to the tissue was so severe. Richard's fingers were still blackened, but they would recover. He was very enthusiastic and supportive of our success, but I could tell that he was also very disappointed that he had not been with us on the top.

That day the three of us set off together for Kathmandu, where we spent a further few days until we could get return flights to Ireland. On the day we left, I said goodbye to Jamie and forgot about all of the anger and ill will that I had harboured throughout the climb. In the days after our summit bid I thought a lot about my resentment towards him and came to understand his rationale a bit more. Despite our clash of personalities, we were both capable climbers who had achieved success and had fulfilled a lifelong dream.

Richard and I set off for Ireland together. The flight seemed to take forever and by the time we touched down at Belfast City Airport, I was totally exhausted, but also excited. As Richard and I stood waiting at the luggage carousel, I could already see a crowd of friends and family gathered in the arrivals terminal. It was the most fantastic feeling to walk through the doors and embrace all of my loved ones. I could not believe how many people had come to the airport to celebrate my success. From here I was taken by bus down to Newry, where a large celebration had been planned. When we got closer to the town, we switched into an open-top bus and drove through the crowded city streets with onlookers cheering from below. I could see massive posters of me throughout the town and everywhere I looked I saw friends, neighbours, old classmates and colleagues. I was so humbled and honoured. I had no idea that any of this had been arranged for me.

The bus finally came to a halt outside the town hall, where a stage was prepared for me. There was also a live band and when I walked up onto the platform, they adorned me with a wreath. The mayor had also arranged for a monument to be constructed in my honour, and it would eventually be placed directly in front of the town hall. The celebration was spectacular and most importantly I had my family alongside me to share in the glory. My mother had been my biggest supporter throughout all of my climbs and expeditions. She had always believed in me and had nurtured my enthusiasm and thirst for adventure. Without her, I never would have achieved the summit on Everest.

In the first few weeks after I returned home from Mount Everest, I found it difficult to rest. I was so excited and full of energy that I just kept moving all the time. I returned to work, but also continued to train and climb each evening and spent a lot of time hiking and camping on the weekends. Lauren and I made contact again by email and that summer, I planned a trip to the USA to see friends in New York and then to visit Boston, Lauren's hometown. Ironically, by the time I arrived there that summer, she had already moved to Belfast to begin her studies at Queen's University. However I did not let this dissuade me from seeing her again and on the day that I returned home from America, I arranged to meet up with her. I was a little anxious as I drove up to Belfast, but as soon as I saw her, I knew that she was going to be an important part of my future.

Chapter 12 ∾

SOUTH AMERICA AND THE
AMAZON CHALLENGE

'A journey of a thousand miles must begin with a single step.'
LAO TZU

After I returned home from Everest in August 2003, Lauren and I began dating. I knew straight away that Lauren was different from the other girls I had gone out with. She was very active and adventurous, and we had a lot in common. Instead of doing the usual things that most new couples do, like going to dinner and the movies, we went hiking, camping and climbing. We spent time in Donegal and the Mourne Mountains and travelled to Spain as well. Although Lauren had done a lot of trekking and some climbing whilst in Asia, she was keen to learn more about mountaineering and rock-climbing and we began to train together as often as possible.

That winter a friend and work colleague, Paul Moran, asked me if I would like to join up with a team that he was putting together to complete an eco-challenge in Brazil. There would be seven members in total and we would have five days to complete a 200-kilometre run through the Amazon basin. From the outset I knew that this race would be immensely challenging but after my Everest success I felt strong and confident and immediately agreed to participate.

Once the plans were in place for the 'Jungle Marathon', Lauren and I decided that we would head over to South America for a few months prior to the race to complete some climbing. We spent the spring hiking and camping as often as possible and in the summer we set off for Ecuador, the first stop on our South American journey.

After a very long flight we arrived in Quito, the capital of Ecuador, and checked into a bunkhouse for the night. We slept most of the first morning and in the afternoon we set off to tour the city. It was a beautiful old town with lots of interesting markets and squares. On the second day, I was having difficulty adjusting to the time difference and found myself wide awake just after dawn. After several failed attempts at falling back to sleep, I decided to set out on a walk. Quito sits on an old volcano and there is still a rim visible at the top of a hill on the outskirts of town. I walked through many residential neighbourhoods and finally reached the top, but found myself in the midst of a slum. There were a lot of stray dogs following me at this stage and after many unfriendly stares from local residents, I realised that it was not customary for tourists to be here.

I walked very quickly on the return journey to the hostel as I was growing concerned about being bitten by one of the strays but also about being robbed by one of the locals! We spent a further few days wandering through the town before we headed north to Otovalo, a quaint village that is renowned for its weekly market. Whilst we were here we stayed in a beautiful old farmhouse on the outskirts of town that has been converted into a backpackers' commune.

We both loved the atmosphere in Otovalo and found the scenery fantastic. The village is completely surrounded by mountains. We spent several days hiking and shopping for local handicrafts before we set off south to climb Mount Cotopaxi, one of Ecuador's highest and most majestic peaks.

To reach Cotopaxi we travelled by bus along the Pan-American Highway until we came to a small village on the outskirts of the national park. By the time we arrived it was already late afternoon so we decide to sleep in one of the many guesthouses along the road. We found a great little place with spectacular views of the mountain. Mount Cotopaxi is a volcano that stands at 5,897 metres, or 19,347 feet, and is centrally located within the Ecuadorian range. The weather at the bottom of the mountain was a comfortable 25°c but we could see from the solid snow-cap around the summit that the temperatures near the top would be well below zero.

In the morning we set off to purchase last-minute supplies for the ascent and then hitched a lift in the back of a pick-up truck to the lower slopes of the mountain. It was incredibly dry and barren as we made our way up the steep dirt path and finally, when the truck could go no further, our driver helped us offload our gear and we set off on foot for the climbing hut at 4,800 metres. It was a long and exhausting walk as Lauren and I were both carrying far too much gear and the sun was incredibly hot. On our first water break we realised that we had purchased the wrong bottles in the local store—we had seltzer water instead of ordinary still water. The carbonation and salty taste did nothing to quench our thirst and both of us were finding it hard to stomach.

Despite our issues with the water, I knew that it was important for us to drink as much as possible during the ascent as we were gaining altitude very rapidly. We stopped for frequent breaks along the path but could not seem to catch our breath. In hindsight, we had not allowed ourselves sufficient time to acclimatise but at the time we were keen to reach the hut and rest.

Towards the mid-afternoon we reached the large wooden structure and were met by large groups of guided climbers who were practising basic glacier trekking techniques for their summit attempts that night. The entire facility was packed but thankfully there were a few bunks left and Lauren and I were able to get in for a rest. After a large dinner and a solid attempt to re-hydrate using water from the glacier that we had boiled and treated, the two of us went to bed so that we would have plenty of rest before our 1 a.m. departure. Originally I had planned to scout out the summit route prior to sunset, but once I saw the vast number of commercial clients on the peak, I knew that would not be necessary. There would be a long line of head-torches to follow to the immense open crater at the top.

I fell to sleep almost immediately, but Lauren tossed and turned for hours. She was feeling unwell from the altitude and had begun to experience a headache. By 10 p.m., the pains in her head had grown quite severe, despite taking aspirin and water at regular intervals. She finally fell asleep just before midnight and then, with just one hour's rest, she rose with me at 1 a.m. to prepare for our departure. We packed our gear quickly and set off at the same time as two very large groups of commercial climbers. We made our way slowly across the glacier and although it was a perfectly clear night, it did not feel that cold. Mount Cotopaxi is a straightforward ascent and does not pose much of a challenge technically, but it does have a few vast crevasses and can be prone to avalanches. In fact, the hut that we were staying in had only been reconstructed after the original one was destroyed, killing eight climbers, in a large avalanche in 1996.

In light of the high temperature, I was concerned that there could be a risk of avalanche on the descent and worried that the sunrise would cause considerable melting. Although Lauren was moving slowly at this stage, she was making steady progress and I was hesitant to push her on too hard as she was still suffering from a headache. We continued until we reached a rock wall at a point referred to as Yanasacha. Once we were here, we stopped for a rest and Lauren told me that she was feeling very ill. Her pulse was rapid and she was struggling to catch her breath. Although she had taken the maximum dose of aspirin, her head was still pounding and she was complaining of dizziness. I too had a heavy throbbing in my temples and was beginning to feel the strain of the altitude but I felt fit enough to continue on. I encouraged Lauren to ascend a bit further and promised her we would stop again to rest soon.

She pushed on for another 20 minutes or so, but our progress was now painfully slow. Although we were more than three quarters of the way to the top, I could tell that she would not make it to the summit with a safe turnaround time and decided then that we should descend. It took us quite a while to reach the hut and when we finally did, Lauren barely had the energy to make it to her bunk. I could tell that she was in the first stages of acute mountain sickness and was conscious that we must descend at first light to prevent the condition from becoming critical.

After a fitful few hours, the sun rose high into the morning sky and Lauren and I again donned our heavy packs for the descent. She looked exhausted and pale but within an hour or so her colour had improved and she was breathing more easily. We were able to move down with astonishing speed and by the end of the afternoon we were at the bottom of the peak, waiting for a vehicle to pass so that we could hitch a lift back to the main road. By this stage, Lauren's condition was almost entirely better but we decided to rest for a few days to allow a full recovery before attempting our next ascent.

We spent a further night at the guesthouse along the road and then set off for the small village of Banos, in the valley beneath Ecuador's most active volcano, Tungurahua. This peak has been in an eruptive phase since 1999, when it spewed out molten lava which destroyed many of the forests and neighbouring villages. As a result of the high risk of further eruption, it remains off limits to climbers, but you are able to hike on the lower slopes and throughout the surrounding valley. When we arrived in this quaint village we checked into a guesthouse on the edge of the thermal springs and relaxed on hammocks in the lush jungle foliage. It was a beautiful and tranquil spot and after a few short hikes, we decided to view the lower slopes of the volcano on horseback.

I am not usually into horseback riding, but it was an amazing if slightly nerve-wracking experience. The narrow trail that edges its way up the peak criss-crosses over the lower slopes until the entire valley is visible below. The rocky dirt path became so narrow and unstable at times that our guide had to lead the horses over first and we would then follow on foot. On some of the passes, the trail seemed barely wide enough for a person, let alone a horse, but somehow these animals maintained a secure footing and by the end of the day, we had toured most of the area.

Although we had only initially planned to stay in Banos for a day or two, we were so comfortable that we decided to stay on longer. We ended up going on a white water rafting trip down one of the nearby rivers and had a great day splashing about in the waves. Once we were sufficiently rested we set off for Mount Chimborazo, our next ascent.

Chimborazo is actually an extinct volcano formed by several peaks, with Whymper (or Ecuador, as it is sometimes called) being the highest point in the country. It is 20,696 feet, or 6,310 metres. We made our way first to the nearby village of Riobamba and then into the valley beneath the mountain. By the time we reached the small village near the entrance to the peak it was nearly dark and we knew that we would not be able to ascend that night. We met a few local people who told us that there was a small community centre in the village where climbers could pay to sleep for the night, so we hiked in and paid for our beds. When we got into the centre we found basic wooden bunks and a shower facility as well as a small kitchen. It was an ideal little place and we were fortunate enough to have it all to ourselves.

We bunked down for the night pretty early but after only a few hours' sleep, we found ourselves freezing cold. The structure had no heat and little protection from the elements and the temperatures had dropped severely after dark. We spent the remainder of the night huddled together in an effort to share body heat. We awoke at first light to find children standing next to our bed!

Apparently the facility had not been open for very long and few climbers had actually stayed there prior to our arrival. The children could not suppress their curiosity about the foreigners who had arrived in the night and had to come in and see us for themselves! It was really funny to wake up with them standing just feet away but they were very friendly and immediately began chatting and playing with our things. Soon after we rose, many of the other villagers came out to greet us and before we had packed to set off, even the elders and village leaders were there. We got some fantastic photographs with our very welcoming hosts and then set off to hitch a lift up the mountain's lower slopes.

A local man picked us up quickly and he took us to a drop-off point two hours from the refuge hut. From here we set off on foot and made our way up to the wooden structure by early afternoon. Whereas we had encountered throngs of climbers on Cotopaxi, the hut on Chimborazo was empty bar two Germans and a Swiss couple. We had plenty of time to rest and prepare for the summit attempt that night so we organised our things and set off on a short acclimatisation hike. We traversed the mouth of the glacier and continued on, using crampons and ice axes, until we had clear views of the summit route. The weather was perfect with clear skies and no wind, but the mid-afternoon sun was very hot and I was concerned about rock-fall or avalanche. We spent a short while scouting out the route and then began to descend back towards the hut.

Just as we started the descent I could hear a creaking noise coming from the upper slopes. Within seconds a small landslide of pebbles and scree began and then a heavy onslaught of rock-fall followed. Lauren was below me on the glacier when the larger rocks began to dislodge and I shouted down to her to take cover quickly. The two of us ducked into small ledges beneath the cascade of ice and waited for the pounding to stop. It went on for nearly 20 minutes and finally, during a lull, I shouted down for Lauren to move towards the hut. At this stage, we had come off the ice and were no longer wearing our crampons, so we were able to run down the slope. It was very steep but the sound of rock smashing overhead kept us moving quickly and after a further five minutes we had reached a sheltered point along the route.

The two of us then sat for ages trying to catch our breath and relax our anxious nerves. Neither of us had been wearing helmets and we realised how dangerous the situation could have been. Once we were able to compose ourselves, we returned to the hut for dinner and a rest before our planned summit push at 1 a.m.

Lauren and I slept for a few hours and then around 11 p.m. she woke me to tell me that she was again feeling ill. This time, however, I noticed that her speech was slurred and she appeared to be struggling to sit up. We had exerted ourselves a lot during the afternoon whilst making the rapid descent and I worried that she had put her body under too much pressure before she was properly acclimatised. I gave her some dexamethasone for acute mountain sickness and advised her to take in more fluids and to try to get more rest. She soon fell back to sleep but by 1 a.m. I knew that she was not going to be able to make a summit attempt. She had begun to vomit and was not responding well to the medication.

Her condition deteriorated very rapidly this time and I was worried that we might need to set off before first light to bivouac somewhere further down the peak where she would have a reprieve from the altitude. However, she felt too sick to move and in the end we decided to wait until dawn to set off. Once the first rays broke through the night sky, the two of us set off down towards the bottom, but Lauren found even the descent tedious and difficult. It took us several hours to reach the lower slopes and even though the altitude had decreased substantially she was still feeling very ill.

We decided it would be best to return to Banos for another period of rest so that Lauren could recover, and then we set off again in a few days. However, even whilst we rested in Banos, Lauren continued to feel poorly and could not seem to shake an overwhelming feeling of fatigue. After a few days we departed and toured around a few other towns and villages but Lauren did not feel well enough to climb again, so in the end we decided to fly over to Lima, Peru, where I had arranged for a friend from home to meet up with us.

We set off early for Lima and although Lauren was still not feeling 100%, her condition had improved slightly. We met my friend, Hugh

Murphy, at the airport and set off to tour the city together. We spent the day in the markets and down by the beach watching the surfers. That evening Hugh and I decided to check out a few of the local bars but Lauren went to bed early as she was still feeling very tired. We ended up having a great time at an Irish bar and stayed out until well after midnight. When we finally returned to the hotel we were met in the lobby by a frantic bell-boy who told us Lauren had been taken to hospital.

At first I could not imagine what had happened. She had seemed fine when we set off and the hotel staff had very limited English so they could not explain to me what was wrong. I thought that maybe she had fallen or cut herself, but before I had too long to consider it, they had arranged a taxi to take us to her. When we arrived at the hospital they took me straight in to see Lauren and I found her asleep and hooked up to an intravenous drip with a member of the hotel staff by her side. One of the nurses spoke excellent English and she advised me that they suspected she was suffering from typhoid fever. When she said it my face must have gone completely white because she quickly attempted to reassure me. She told me that typhoid is a very common condition in Peru and when it is caught early, it is totally curable with antibiotics.

Once Lauren awoke she explained that shortly after Hugh and I set off, she became uncontrollably sick. She was vomiting violently and was unable to stop shaking. At one point she was not even able to lift herself off the bathroom floor. She rang the front desk for help and they arranged for one of their staff to take her straight to the hospital, where they gave her something to make her sleep and took blood tests. A short while later, the doctor confirmed that she was suffering from typhoid and began her antibiotic treatment straight away. Fortunately, they allowed Lauren to be discharged from the hospital the following morning with a course of antibiotics, but they advised that she should not travel for five days as she might require further treatment.

I could not believe how quickly her condition had deteriorated. She seemed fine one minute and then literally looked like a corpse the next. She was so ill when she came back from the hospital that she could not even lift her head off the pillow and for the five days that we had to remain in Lima, she never moved from the bed. Hugh and I still managed to do some sightseeing but we now stayed close by in case

anything else happened. The doctors said that she most likely picked up
the infection from water at the beginning of the trip as it takes several
weeks for typhoid to develop in the body before the potentially deadly
symptoms become apparent. Looking back, it was probably the water
on the glacier that we drank at the climbing hut on Cotopaxi, or water
that she may have accidentally swallowed whilst rafting on our first
visit to Banos.

Once the five days passed and Lauren began to feel stronger, we
decided to take a short flight to the ancient city of Cuzco, where we
could base ourselves to see Machu Picchu. Although she was able to do
some sightseeing in the town and at the surrounding markets and
ruins, she was still feeling very weak and needed to rest each afternoon.
Whilst Lauren rested, Hugh and I visited almost all of the famous local
landmarks and finally, after several days, Lauren felt fit enough to make
a day trip to the renowned Incan ruins of Machu Picchu.

We took a train from Cuzco and then made a short hike to the
ancient city of the gods, where we spent an entire day wandering
through the ruins. It was such a fantastic sight, with the high Andean
peaks surrounding this remarkably hidden jungle city. I was sorry that
we had been unable to make the trek along the Inca Trail as originally
planned but I was thrilled that we had the opportunity to spend time
in this unique place.

After our visit to Machu Picchu, Lauren flew back to Lima before
returning home to Belfast for follow-up medical care. She was feeling
far stronger by the time that she set off, but she was concerned about
the long-term effects of the typhoid and wanted to see a doctor in the
city's Royal Hospital to confirm that she was entirely clear of the
infection. Once she set off, Hugh and I continued on to Southern Peru
to visit the famous 'river islands' and then we continued on by bus to
La Paz, Bolivia.

La Paz is an incredible city, located high within the Andes at just
over 10,000 feet. Although I had just come from the high-altitude peaks
in Ecuador, I could still feel the strain of the altitude as we made our
way through the winding streets. Whilst we were here we decided to
complete a cycling trip along one of the most infamous roads in the
world, which winds around the edges of a cliff as it sharply falls into the
valley below. There have been countless collisions and fatalities along

this route but this has not prevented adventure companies from running mountain bike tours down the harsh vertical incline.

The outfitter transported Hugh and me along with our cycles to the top of the mountain, where we set off at racing speeds for the valley below. It was an amazing and exhilarating ride which yielded unparalleled views of the surrounding countryside. After several days in La Paz, we set off for the jungle to see where the Bolivian Army killed Che Guevara. The journey into the jungle was very rough and when we finally arrived at the site, I was surprised by how remote the outpost was. It was strange to think that Che had been able to operate in such a vast and wild area and both Hugh and I found the tour fascinating. After our time together in Bolivia, Hugh returned to Ireland and I set off for Brazil to begin my preparations for the Amazon Jungle Marathon.

I flew from La Paz to Manaus in northern Brazil, where I spent a few days adapting to the extreme heat and humidity. From there I flew further into the jungle to a place called Santarem, where the race organisers provided transport to a hotel. Once I arrived in my room, I immediately set my air conditioning unit onto high and went out for a walk to stretch my legs. Whilst I was out, I met with many of the local people and several of them advised me that it would be best not to use the air conditioning as it would prevent me from adapting to the jungle environment. Although the room felt so refreshing on my return, I knew that I had been given good advice and I promptly shut off the unit. From that point on, I felt like I was in a sauna, but in the end this preparation for the extreme heat I would encounter proved very beneficial.

On my third day in Santarem the other members of the Irish team arrived. There was Paul Moran, the team's leader, as well as Sarah Moores, John Shields, Pádraig O'Reilly, Maureen Slavin and Jim Gleeson. They were all avid runners who had trained very hard for the challenge ahead. However, no amount of training could have prepared them for the heat and nearly all of them were overwhelmed by the high temperatures and stifling humidity on their arrival. The morning after the team's arrival, all 75 competitors were transported by boat along the Amazon River subsidiary of Tapajós. It was a long journey but the views from the boat were absolutely spectacular. The further we progressed into the jungle, the more lush and colourful the foliage became.

Once we arrived at a small outpost along the river in the state of Para, the boat pulled in towards the river's edge and we all jumped off to wade through the water onto the shore. The race directors met us here and showed us around the camp. There was an open wooden structure which the local people had constructed to house all of the competitors. There was also a kitchen hut, outhouse toilets and a meeting place in the middle of the camp. Behind the wood and canopies, there was nothing but thick foliage as far as the eye could see.

Once we had a chance to organise our gear and set up our hammocks, we were taken into an induction meeting, where all of the competitors and staff were introduced to each other. Before long, the sun had set and in the midst of total darkness, we bunked down for the night in our hanging beds. It was so warm that we did not require blankets or sleeping bags but we did have to sleep beneath thick mosquito netting as the bugs were very active after dusk. I will never forget how once the sounds of human chatter faded into silence, the animals of the jungle began a chorus. I lay for hours listening to all of the foreign sounds until I finally fell to sleep. At dawn all of the competitors rose for breakfast and we began our training for the race.

The first phase of this induction involved each competitor being evaluated by a team of doctors. They checked our heart rates and our overall physical condition as well as taking detailed information on the preparations that we had undergone for the race. After this was completed, members of the Brazilian army and some indigenous people gave us a presentation on the dangers of the jungle. This involved detailed information on health and safety whilst on the course as well as emergency procedures for animal attacks, getting lost and dangerous plants and reptiles. They also issued each of us with an emergency hammock and advised us, if we became lost, never to sleep on the jungle floor.

Once our safety training was complete, we all set about organising our supplies for the race. Each of us was required to carry our own food and clothing as well as any other items needed throughout the duration of the event. I had packed some freeze-dried meals as well as Power Bars and Gels. I kept all of my supplies to a minimum and in the end, my pack weighed less than 8 pounds. I knew that the 200-kilometre run would be very challenging and I wanted to be able to move fast and light. The other Irish team members had also employed the same approach and all of us were ready for the struggle ahead.

On the second night we went to bed early in preparation for the race, which would begin at dawn. I could tell that everyone was excited but also nervous about what was to come. Before light even broke on the camp, there was a flurry of activity as all of the runners packed their things and completed some stretching before the call to the starting line. The race would commence along the riverbank and continue directly into the thick jungle. The course was divided into six stages with distances of 15.7, 23.9, 31, 21.6, 86, and 24.7 kilometres.

Stage one was short but very hilly with steep ascents and descents. We crossed through thick impenetrable bush and over sandy riverside banks. The terrain was very difficult underfoot and I found myself falling up and down the sharp inclines but after a long and hot afternoon of running, I finally reached the finish line, which was based along the riverbank. Miraculously, I had come in fourteenth overall and was the lead Irish runner. Despite the immense challenges of the race conditions, I really enjoyed the first stage and when we set camp that night I found myself feeling very strong. However, seven of the other competitors could not acclimatise to the heat and were forced to drop out with exhaustion.

For stage two of the race the course was not as hilly but the distance was longer, at 23.9 kilometres. This time we went directly into the heart of the jungle and had to cross over rivers and swamps. For many of the runners, the predawn start was slow and a little bit painful but within the first hour they were back into the rhythm of the run. At many points along the route, we were forced to walk, balance on logs and rocks and even climb up riverbanks after wading through dark and murky waters. I could not believe how difficult the afternoon was and I was completely humbled by a fellow competitor who was blind. He was running the course whilst tied to a runner who led him along the route. I cannot imagine how demanding this must have been for him. I was covered in cuts and scrapes and I was able to navigate around most of the obvious branches and leaves, but that poor man must have been absolutely torn to shreds. However, he continued on regardless and I never once heard him complain.

By the middle of the second stage we encountered a massive swamp, where some of the indigenous staff kept an anaconda at bay so that we could cross the murky waters. Several of the men were barefoot and they stood directly on top of this slithering beast as we moved past. Once we were beyond the swamp we passed more of the local wildlife before finally reaching the finish line along the river. Paul and I were together for the latter half of this route and came into the finish together at numbers 39 and 40.

That night I was so exhausted that I could barely make it to my hammock. My leg muscles had begun to cramp and I was now suffering from blisters on my feet but I knew that the worst was yet to come.

The following morning stage three of the race began. It was 31 kilometres through thick jungle foliage, up sharp hills and down through vast swamps. There was little respite from the soaring temperatures and although the route was very difficult, myself and the other Irish team members were enjoying the challenge. Local people came out to greet us along the route and the scenery was fantastic. By the time we reached the finish line, there were several runners suffering from heat stroke and injury and many had been forced to drop out, but myself and the other Irish runners were still going strong. I had, however, suffered countless gashes and cuts along my legs and arms and was really feeling the strain of each exertion in my muscles.

For stage four of the race, we began the 21.6-kilometre run through a wide river where we had to swim and wade until we reached the bank on the other side. The water was extremely dark and murky and I was concerned about what might be lurking beneath us but I continued on with my pack on my head and finally made it to shore. Once we reached the sands, we again ran directly into the jungle, where we crossed between trails and untrod paths. By the afternoon the heat was almost unbearable, but we continued on until reaching the finish line again and all of the Irish team finished strong.

For stage five, the real challenges of the Amazon Jungle Marathon were realised. It was 86 kilometres of extremely harsh terrain which the organisers had dubbed 'the Road to Hell'. I found every minute of the run totally agonising, as I was suffering from terrible blisters, but somehow I managed to complete the course and I made it to the finish line well in advance of the cutoff time. The organisers had been forced to stop some of the slower runners from completing the course, as the surrounding jungle was very dangerous. This area had one of the highest concentrations of jaguars in the country and there were wild boars and wasps as well. In fact, one of the female runners had actually gone directly across a wasps' nest and had been stung over 20 times. Paul and I were passing by the woman just as the wasps began attacking and the two of us assisted her but were both stung as well in the process.

That night, despite the pain from my stings and blisters, I slept well. On the final morning we set off for the final 24.7 kilometres of the race.

The last day's route ran entirely along the riverbank, passing along the sandy shores, and although it was a reprieve from the harsh jungle foliage, it was unbearably hot. The blisters on my feet were excruciating at this stage and I found each step completely agonising. However, with the assistance of Jim, Sarah and Maureen I made it all the way to the finish line and the completion of the race. Pádraig and John were forced to drop out due to the heat and exhaustion but Paul was quite strong and came in ahead of all of us on that final leg. In the end, I finished first in our team and twenty-seventh overall in the race. By the completion of the course, there were only 50 competitors remaining and I was very happy with my results.

Once all of the runners made it to the finish line, the organisers threw a large celebration for everyone. There was music, food and drink and everyone partied the night away along the river's edge. It was an immensely challenging experience but still fantastic—I thoroughly enjoyed it and I knew that it was great preparation training for my next big adventure, an ascent on the world's most difficult peak, K2.

After the celebrations, Paul, John, Pádraig and I set off for a few days of rest and relaxation in Rio de Janeiro. We stayed in the famous Copa Cabana hotel and did a bit of sightseeing before flying home to Ireland. When I returned home, Lauren and I again began to train hard in the mountains. She had been fortunate enough to make a full recovery from the typhoid and was keen to begin preparations for the ascent on K2.

| K2 2005

'The true measure of a man is not how he behaves in moments of comfort and convenience but how he stands at times of controversy and challenges.'
MARTIN LUTHER KING JR

It has always been a dream of mine to climb not only the highest but also the most difficult mountains in the world. Many people expected my mountaineering dreams to be complete once I stood on the summit of Mount Everest but the opposite was true. Reaching the summit only further fuelled my imagination. The vision of becoming the first Irishman to stand on the summit of K2 was already on my mind as my flight from Kathmandu arrived in Belfast City Airport. Before I even faced the crowd of family and friends who had gathered to celebrate my success on Everest, I had decided that within two years I would embark upon a far more difficult journey. An expedition to the northern regions of Pakistan would be both financially and physically daunting but the infamous 'savage mountain' beckoned me on.

K2 stands at a height of 8,611 metres and is only slightly lower than the world's highest peak. However, it is technically superior to Everest in every way. Many mountaineers view Everest as a playground for the rich and inexperienced. Those who are not interested in true mountaineering or the ethos of climbing often attempt Everest for the fame it brings them. Commercial expeditions have hijacked the mountain, with Sherpas paid to drag inexperienced and often unfit climbers to the summit (and sometimes their deaths) just so that they can say they've reached the top. K2 on the other hand is notorious for another reason; it is so steep, technically challenging and vicious that no inexperienced or celebrity-seeking individual has managed to pay their way to the top, and even world-class mountaineers are often forced to turn back from the summit due to the ferocious weather conditions. Nearly 3,000 climbers have made it to the top of Everest since the first summit over 50 years ago, but only roughly 300 people have achieved the same success on K2 within the same time span.

Even by virtue of location, K2 presents a logistical nightmare. It is located deep within the peaks of the Baltoro Glacier and is not accessible by road from any side. It takes almost five days and nearly 80 kilometres on foot through the challenging terrain of the Pakistani border regions just to reach the base camp and this is only after several days travelling by vehicle through the northern tribal areas. This region of Pakistan has long been seen as a distant and dangerous land. The unstable social and political atmosphere throughout the country, coupled with the historically remote and lawless image of the north, has dissuaded many expeditions from the peaks of the Baltoro Glacier.

Despite the daunting task ahead, in 2004 Lauren and I spent a great deal of time bringing together a team of trekkers to accompany me to the base camp and to assist with ferrying gear to the low camps on the mountain. There were Des and Turlough Murphy, two brothers from the village of Camlough, Kevin McClelland, my lifelong friend, Pat Christie, a colleague with the Garda Special Projects, and Paul Moran, the Garda Superintendent who I had completed the Amazon Challenge with. Most of the men had never trekked or climbed and none of them had ever been on an expedition of this nature, but they were determined to challenge themselves and to bring a bit of fun to the trip as well.

As the support team would only be able to accompany me as far as camp one, I hoped for another climber to join up with the expedition. I initially thought that Kevin Quinn might be interested, but he declined due to other commitments and I then decided not to ask anyone else, as I knew that the climb would be inherently dangerous and I could not take on the burden of guilt or responsibility if something went wrong.

Although I was not keen on making the attempt alone, I reassured myself that there would be other solo climbers and teams on the mountain whom I could link in with when I arrived. Then during the winter of 2004 a highly qualified and talented Irish mountaineer named John Fitzgibbon made contact with me. He was living in Boston and had seen information about the expedition on the internet. He too was planning an ascent on K2 and was keen to join forces. Although John was married with a family, he and his wife, Susan, were both devoted mountaineers and they fully understood the risks that a climb like K2 posed. John was a very solid climber with strong ideas about mountaineering. He was a true alpinist who was totally against the use of high-altitude porters, guides or the use of oxygen, and from the start I knew that he would make an excellent climbing partner.

In addition to organising the team, I was also faced with the task of procuring sponsorship. Fortunately a friend and fellow Newry man offered to fund the venture. Gerard O'Hare covered the main expenses for the expedition whilst a longtime friend, Malachy McGuinness, ensured that all of our technology needs were met. As a component of this assistance, he put me in touch with Simon Scott, who went on to manage a webpage for the expedition and sourced all of our vital weather information. In addition to this, Leslie Lawrence and Ken Costigan from Great Outdoors in Dublin provided all of the essential gear for the trekkers and me, and a Belfast solicitor named Michael Flannigan provided funding for incidental costs. Without the vital support and generosity of the sponsors, the expedition would never have happened.

Once all of the final arrangements were made, we set off in June 2005 for Islamabad, where we met John and Adventure Tours Pakistan, our trekking provider. They introduced us to our Liaison Officer, Tiamur Khan. Tiamur was a captain in the Pakistani army who was assigned by the government to accompany us throughout our journey. We were very fortunate: Tiamur, or 'the Captain', had excellent English, a great sense of humour and an enthusiasm for the mountains. This was in total contrast to stories I had heard about expeditions in previous years. There were awful tales of teams who were assigned to army officers with little interest in mountaineering and a poor attitude about completing the assignment.

We spent our first few days in the country with the Captain touring around the myriad of shops and stalls on the busy streets surrounding our hotel in Rawalpindi. We also visited the world's largest mosque, which is located in the heart of Islamabad. It was an impressive and humbling experience. The Shah Faisal Mosque is a massive white structure that looms over the sprawling city streets with a pure and pristine presence. We wandered around the holy site as the scorching heat of the midday sun began to subside and were treated to a crimson sunset over the hills that towered in the distance.

After our brief sightseeing tour, we spent the remainder of our time in the city working out a plan for the ascent and making our final arrangements. We were also waiting for the weather in the northern regions to improve so that we could fly to Skardu, the farthest point accessible by plane in the proximity of the mountain. However the weather never improved and after five days we set out by bus on the infamous Karokoram Highway, or KKH, as it is popularly known.

The KKH is considered a feat of engineering all over the world as the narrow stretch of highway clings to the crumbling walls of the Indus river gorge. It rises and falls with dizzying heights above the ancient carved banks of the flowing river and has since the day it was completed been in various stages of disrepair! In fact, just a few weeks before our expedition arrived in Pakistan, the leader of a Chinese K2 expedition was killed when his Jeep was battered by rock-fall. Several other members of his climbing party were injured and all were eventually forced to return home before they ever even set eyes on the mountain. This was not an uncommon occurrence; many foreign travellers and Pakistanis alike have been killed in accidents and landslides on this perilous route.

In addition to the crater-sized pot-holes that litter the tarmac and the perpetually crumbling, landslide-prone support walls, this stretch of road is also notorious for dangers of a different kind. The wild tribal areas of Pakistan have a well-earned notoriety for being lawless. This region was virtually left alone by British colonists after it became rapidly apparent that neither the people nor the terrain could be tamed. In these distant outposts it is not uncommon to encounter gun-wielding robbers who block portions of the highway in an effort to sabotage passing vehicles. The dangers of this type of attack rapidly increase after sunset and with no lights on this steep and treacherous route, we were forced to make the journey north to Skardu over two days.

The only blessing about the journey towards the towering peaks of the Baltoro Glacier was the distinct improvement in the air and scenery. The landscape began to change several hours north of the 'capital cities', where the brown earthen tones of the arid lowlands were replaced by the lush, green hills of the northern areas. The air was fresher with little industrial pollution and the sinking temperatures provided a welcome feeling of refreshment. However, once we reached the last stop on the road to K2, the northern capital of Skardu, the vast openness of the fields and rivers was replaced again by the grey tin shacks and concrete slabs of human settlement.

When we first arrived into Skardu we checked into the popular K2 Motel on the outskirts of the town and made our way into the central market area to make our final preparations for the climb. We set about purchasing large batteries for our computer and phones and extra food and provisions for the long months that John and I would be on the mountain. It was quickly apparent that the northern tribal people were rather different from those who reside in the capital city and outlying areas. Whilst we were in Islamabad and Rawalpindi, we saw many Pakistani women on the streets and in the shops, but there were no women visible anywhere throughout the town here. The men ran the shops and café and all of their patrons were male as well. Lauren was immediately conscious of the lack of female presence and sensed hostility towards her as we walked throughout the streets. As a result of this, she spent most of her time within the hotel grounds and thankfully after two short days we set out on the long road towards the mountains.

About an hour north of Skardu, the road becomes a barren path and the ancient Land Rovers in our convoy lumbered cumbersomely over the rocky and often wet terrain. After roughly an eight-hour journey the vehicles finally veered up the unimaginably steep and dusty final pass before the first camp of Askole came into view. This final stretch of road is so sharp that after our drivers left us at the camp, one of them rolled his Land Rover over the edge of the narrow pass, but thankfully survived unscathed. However, the vehicle was not as fortunate! It took a team of local men to flip it back over and it was so severely damaged that it was left in a ditch at the bottom of the hill.

The camp of Askole is like a microcosm of Rawalpindi. It is the first camp on the trek to the peaks of the Baltoro Glacier and the last point accessible by vehicle. It is here that expeditions meet their support team of porters, cooks and pack animals and all of the final preparations for the season take place in the midst of total chaos. Thankfully, the Captain and the leader of our trekking party, Salmon, were able to translate for me in all of the negotiations that had to be done in selecting our crew of porters. This is serious business for the men of the Baltoro region. Many families rely entirely upon the wage that the porters earn over the summer months and this season hundreds of men from all over the region had descended upon this camp in the hope of being selected to work. Salmon and the lead porters from our trekking company selected the men they saw fit to ferry our gear over the 80-kilometre trek to the base camp, whilst the others were sent home or waited on the edges of the camp for other expeditions to pass through.

The men who were chosen to accompany us ranged in aged from their late teens right up to their sixties, although they all looked twice as old. The harsh sun and the dry air at altitude had weathered their dark skin and the effects of hard physical labour and poor diet and hygiene left their thin bodies wiry and hunched. But despite their appearance, the strength of the porters was astounding. Loads of gear and food in packs and barrels were carefully weighed by Salmon before being distributed amongst the 100 men who would lead us to base camp. Those known to be strong and fast were given the largest loads and therefore would earn the most for their services, whilst many of the younger men, some of whom were making the trek for the first time, were given lighter loads. All of the men strapped these heaping parcels to their backs and bore the brunt of the weight on straps spread across their foreheads. The weight of the gear caused their necks to pull at an awkward angle, which looked terribly uncomfortable, but none of these men even seemed to notice.

The porters were all clad in totally inadequate clothing for the harsh conditions of the Baltoro Glacier despite the fact that expeditions pay a mandatory supplemental allowance for their clothing and gear to be upgraded. Most of the men use the money from this allowance to cover essential family costs and make the 80-kilometre trek in only a pair of rubber tennis shoes, without even the basic protection of socks. They nearly all wore the typical *shalwar kamiz* and only a few had jackets or sweaters to put over the top of this loose clothing when the night-time temperatures plummeted. The sun on the glacier is extremely harsh and can cause snow blindness without proper eye protection. Very few of our porters had sunglasses, but most had fashioned eyewear out of various other objects. There was even one man who had cut a roll of camera film into makeshift glasses.

At night when our expedition retired to bed in tents and sleeping bags, the porters built fires to sleep around. A few had blankets, which were shared out amongst the men, and they all slept in a close huddle with each other to share body heat. Once we reached the snow line, these men would dig snow holes, which they would then pack full of men to conserve body heat. They would cover the top of the huddle with a tarp to prevent the wind and snow from penetrating their outerwear and all of them appeared to sleep well despite the impossibly uncomfortable conditions.

Several days into the trek we reached an oasis along the glacier. Paiju is a camp that has been erected with the financial support of foreign mountaineers who have embarked upon expeditions throughout this region and the vital physical labour of the Pakistani porters. The site has solar-powered electricity, running water for showers and outhouse toilets as well as magnificent scenery. It is an ideal resting spot for expeditions on the final stage of their trek towards the towering peaks and we decided to camp here for two nights to allow for acclimatisation.

Before we arrived at Paiju our interactions with the porters had been limited. None of the men spoke any English and none of us, including the Captain, could understand their Balti dialect. These men came from the remote mountain tribes of Northern Pakistan and few had ever been schooled beyond early childhood. They maintained a class system unto themselves and seemed to have clear divisions in seniority and rank. Because of these social divides, many of the porters did not even socialise with each other, but once we had all relaxed for a few days at this camp together, they began to interact more. They enjoyed seeing our photos from home and having their pictures taken on digital cameras, where they could then review their image and laugh with disbelief. They came to us with a myriad of illnesses and injuries in the hope of securing Western medicines and they examined our gear with innocent curiosity.

Late in the evening on the second night these men sacrificed a goat as a reward for their hard work and dinner was followed by a celebration of song and dance. The men lined the narrow ridges of the camp and crouched to watch as the young and talented musicians amongst them began to sing in their native tongues. At that point many of the Irish team had retired to their tents but it wasn't long before the laughter and song drew us out for a bit of fun with these men.

Lauren was a big hit with the porters. In Pakistan it is unusual to see Western women and even when they are present it is rarer still for local men to have any interaction with them. However, Lauren had been very sociable with the porters and had gotten to know the men carrying her gear quite well despite the language barriers. When she came out of her tent to see the celebrations that night, she was quickly drawn into the circle for a dance. The porters used our storage barrels for drums and sang and danced in wild off-pitch tones as she was twirled around. It was then that the lads and I decided to show off our purchases from the duty-free shop in Dublin Airport. I went into my tent and came out in a giant green leprechaun hat with an attached beard and entered the circle. The men thought that I was crazy but they really enjoyed having a laugh with us and liked the fact that we could relax and enjoy the journey, as many of the mountaineers who travel to this region are highly conservative and serious.

After our time in Paiju, we trekked for a further two days until we reached the camp at Concordia. It was here that the first views of K2 came into sight and with a mixture of excitement and nervous anticipation we studied the peak before us. I now understood how the Englishman Francis Younghusband must have felt in 1887 when he set eyes upon the peak from the Muztagh Pass. He was the first Westerner to see the mountain and reported back to England that the beauty of the peak and sheer scale of its immensity meant that only the most qualified and talented explorers could even attempt to get near it.

K2 is unlike other mountains in the world as it stands nearly 1,000 metres higher than any of its neighbouring peaks. This creates an interesting and often ferocious weather situation on the mountain. Storms roll in quickly and can blanket the entire upper slopes in deep and unstable snows that are totally blinding. The wind rips through the entire region with hurricane strength at very short notice, leaving the crevasses that litter the mountain hidden from view beneath deep coverings of snow. The composition of snow and ice on the upper slopes combined with the unpredictable weather means that the high camps on this peak are dangerous places which afford little protection from the elements.

The vicious storms on this mountain have claimed many lives. In 1986 alone, which was the worst year on record for loss of life on K2, 13 climbers died trying to reach the top. Seven climbers were trapped for six nights at over 26,000 feet by treacherous storms and high winds and only two survived to tell the tale. A hidden crevasse just moments from the base camp claimed the life of another, whilst an avalanche buried two more on the upper slopes. The other climbers died in accidents or unknown circumstances and many of their bodies have never been found.

K2's history is filled with tales of success and survival as well as death and despair. It was first climbed in 1954 by an Italian expedition led by Ardito Desio under the sponsorship of the Italian Alpine Club. Two men from his team, Lacedelli and Compagnoni, made it to the summit on 31 July 1954 but their triumph came with serious sacrifice and controversy. The two summiteers received vital support from two other expedition members and these men nearly died for their efforts. Bonatti, a young Italian climber, and Mahdi, a Pakistani climber, supplied the oxygen to Lacedelli and Compagnoni at camp four which enabled them to rest before making their summit attempt. However when Bonatti and Mahdi were attempting to deposit the oxygen at the previously agreed location, they found no camp in place. They called out into the darkness for the two Italian climbers and eventually received a response from one of them advising them to deposit the oxygen bottles in the snow and make their way down. The men were incredulous. They were freezing and exhausted and Lacedelli and Compagnoni appeared to be keeping their camp hidden from view. Bonatti and Mahdi were forced to bivouac in the 'death zone' with no tent or protection for the night. They barely survived and at first light they eventually made their way down to safety after what can only be described as a miraculous descent.

Although the two men made it down alive, Mahdi later went on to have all of his fingers and toes amputated due to frostbite and Lacedelli and Compagnoni went on to make the summit. The events of that fateful day have remained in contention to the present date and since that time K2's history has been filled with tales of dissent, injury and death in the pursuit of the summit. The peak is so challenging that after the successful Italian bid, it took 23 years before anyone was able to make it to the top again. Expeditions from all over the world staged countless attempts on the mountain but it was not until 1977 that a Japanese and a Pakistani climber made it to the summit again using the Italian route. Since that time the odds of a successful summit bid have remained low and it estimated that nearly one in six climbers is killed in their attempt.

Despite the risks that this climb posed, I was in total awe of the peak and felt driven by the challenges that lay ahead. John and I had elected to climb along the Abruzzi Ridge, a route named after the Italian Duca Degli Abruzzi Expedition, which reached an altitude of 6,600 metres along the south-east crest of the mountain in 1909. This route has since become known as the classic route or 'normal route' for climbers to use and most of the successful summits have been done this way.

After one night's stay at Concordia, several members of the Irish expedition made their way towards the base camp on K2. The trek was long and slow. We left camp late in the morning as several of the trekkers were feeling ill. All of the men were struggling with the demanding physical schedule and none had anticipated the toll that altitude takes on the body and mind. Worse still, each of the trekkers was experiencing diarrhoea and coping with this in the absence of a toilet or privacy can be very daunting. Two of the men were so unwell that they decided to remain at Concordia for an extra night whilst the rest of us pushed on to establish base camp. The heat on that final day was intense and the unusually deep snow that had fallen that season was going soft beneath our feet. Every few steps my weight would break through the surface crust and I could be hip-deep in slushy snow before I managed to free myself. Finally, after several hours navigating around the foothills of Broad Peak, we crossed the final crevasse field before base camp appeared.

It was a great feeling to arrive and set camp for the season. Once I have unpacked and organised my gear, I am able to focus on the challenges that lie ahead. For a bit of fun we again donned the leprechaun hats as we made our arrival into the camp. I am sure that the Norwegian team and all of those already at the base were very surprised to see men wearing tall green hats and beards on the horizon, but we were not the usual team of mountaineers!

Our first night at the base camp was quiet. The sky was clear and the air was unbelievably cold. The previous night at Concordia the air had been very sharp, but the rise in altitude between the two camps meant that the temperature was now significantly lower. We all ate dinner together in the mess tent and introduced ourselves to the other climbers in the camp. It was then that we met Rolf Bae and his wife, Cecile, from the Norwegian team. Coincidentally, Rolf had spent several months with Irish climbers and explorers in Norway whilst they were training for a trek across Greenland and the North Pole. In the group were two men who I would come to know well over the following years, Pat Falvey and Ger McDonnell. Spending time with the Irish team had left Rolf well versed in the Irish sense of humour and he really enjoyed our company. However, it was not long before the relentless cold forced us all to retire to our tents for the night.

After a chilly night, the two trekkers who had remained behind at Concordia arrived at the base camp and we began to discuss the logistics for moving gear to the low camps. It was agreed that those who were feeling strong enough would move a few loads of supplies to advanced base camp the following day. For the remainder of the day John and I met with the other climbers in the camp and the trekkers explored the area. That night one of the men began to feel very ill and retired to bed early. A short while later his tentmate came to me with concerns that he was suffering from pulmonary oedema. He had grown ill very quickly and was struggling to breathe in the thin air. When I went into see him his colour was poor and it was apparent that he was not acclimatising to the altitude. I was concerned that the situation could deteriorate rapidly and was conscious that, unlike on Everest, there was no vehicle that could be called to stage an evacuation. I immediately contacted Cecile, who was the medic for the Norwegian team. She confirmed that he was suffering from altitude sickness and gave him oxygen. I knew then that we needed to bring him down to a lower camp soon or his condition would continue to deteriorate.

In the early hours of the following morning the trekking team was forced to descend back down the glacier. In addition to the man suffering from altitude sickness, many of the other men were also feeling unwell and none felt strong enough to ascend to advanced base camp. This was unfortunate for Lauren, as she had been feeling well and was very keen to ascend to the higher camps with John and me to ferry ropes and supplies, but she would not have been allowed to hike down alone so she too descended with the men. As the trekking team set off along the glacier, John and I set out upon the tedious task of moving supplies up the mountain. The sky was dark as our two groups departed in separate directions. I looked back across the horizon for quite some time until the faint glow of the trekkers' head-torches disappeared entirely into the night sky.

Once the trekking team was gone, the difficult work began for John and me. Fortunately we were both feeling strong but the extra support the trekkers could have provided was sorely missed. The camp also felt empty once they were gone. It was suddenly very quiet without the Murphy brothers' constant joking and laughter!

John had gotten along very well with everyone and enjoyed having a laugh with the lads but I could tell that he was also very focused and did not mind having solitary time. He was unbelievably strong both physically and psychologically and he had acclimatised well. I knew from the outset that John was the perfect man to be making this ascent with. He and I both worked tirelessly over the following days to ferry supplies up the mountain and to establish our camps for the season. We were fortunate that the Captain had such a keen interest in learning the skills of mountaineering. He volunteered to assist us with taking supplies to advanced base camp and after some training he even came as far as camp one on one of the ascents. Once camp one was in place, John and I fixed ropes up part of the route to camp two.

On the day we set about laying the rope, the weather and visibility were very poor and the weight of our packs took a serious toll on our bodies. We were carrying pitons (steel hooks) to fix the lines into the ice, as well as an assortment of other gear, including tents, sleeping bags, stoves, pots, food and fuel to deposit. Our goal was to fix lines as far as camp two, which is situated above House's Chimney, a notoriously technical but short section of the climb, as this would allow us to move quickly with a safe place to rest on our summit push.

Once the exhausting work of bringing the lines to camp two was complete, we descended to base camp for a period of rest before again returning to camp two to begin our work on camp three. It was on this section of the mountain, between camps two and three, that we reached the dreaded Black Pyramid. This area is composed of an unstable mixture of rock and thin ice. The vertical incline in this section is so intense that even those with a stomach for heights feel a twinge when they look below. If a climber were to fall in this section they would not hit snow until they reached the bottom of the mountain, several thousand metres below, and in fact many of the fatalities in K2's history have taken place in this section of the climb.

When we reached this area, the visibility was poor and we were finding it difficult to see the route ahead. However, we gradually made our way up through this section, using slow and painstakingly careful climbing. When we finally reached the long vertical ice chute below the plateau, which camp three rests upon, we stopped for a rest. At this stage the sky was beginning to darken. The ascent had taken longer than we had anticipated and we were conscious that there was little light remaining and our strength was waning—this would make it very difficult to reach the plateau for camp three. We continued to move further up, but once we reached an area where the snow was stable we decided to cut a platform into the side of the slope and pitch our tent there for the night.

It was a restless night and, in hindsight, we should not have stopped there at all. As we slept there was heavy snowfall and only after we awoke did we realise that the angle of the slope above was an avalanche risk. We dismantled the tent and decided to cache it further up the slope along with our sleeping bags, food, fuel and down suits for the summit. We left the gear in a hole, which we marked with 6-foot-high visibility wands, and made our way back down to advanced base camp for a reprieve from the altitude. Neither John nor myself were using oxygen and long stays above camp two took a toll on the body.

After a time of rest at the base, we again returned to our intermediate camp to collect our gear and move it higher to the safety of the plateau above. However, when we arrived at the location where we had left our things, there was no sign of the visibility wands and the curvature of the slope had changed entirely. It was quickly apparent that an avalanche had buried our gear or moved it further down the slope. Both John and I were totally devastated. We were exhausted from the journey back up and had been looking forward to arriving and establishing camp for a rest.

We were both growing increasingly short of breath in the bitterly cold air and the sky was again beginning to darken. We knew that we had to devise a method of searching for the gear that would not waste precious time or energy. John and I staked out a line and each of us probed three feet in either direction. I had a collapsible metal probe, a tool which is commonly used to search for people after an avalanche, and John had a trekking pole from which he removed the snow basket to immerse into the deep snow below us. We both had aluminium shovels as well, which we used to dig in areas with hard surface crusts. After over an hour of searching in this manner we were beginning to lose all hope of finding the lost gear.

We took a break and the two of us fell back into the snow with exhaustion. I had the satellite phone with me and I rang Lauren. She was at home in Ireland and had been expecting to hear from me. I could not hide the disappointment in my voice. I was too exhausted to be outwardly angry, but inside I was raging at myself for our stupidity. We should not have stashed the gear there. We should have moved it up to the plateau on our last stay. Now all hopes of the summit appeared lost. I spoke to Lauren for a few minutes but I don't remember anything that she said as I was too pissed off to listen. John was quiet, but annoyed. We were both silently acknowledging how devastating this loss was. Without our summit gear it would not be possible to go on towards the top. To ascend without a down suit or a high-altitude camp to rest at would be suicide.

At this point we were both far too tired to descend to base camp so we moved further up the mountain to where a joint Polish/Bulgarian expedition was staying. They were kind enough to allow us to share in with them in their tents. We didn't have sleeping bags, but they fed us and gave us boiled water for the night. It was a miserable night both physically and psychologically. John and I were wearing gear that was still wet from digging and when the night-time temperature plummeted I could feel my outerwear freezing. My feet never warmed and I was worried about the possibility of frostbite. Emotionally I felt drained. I was so angry but I knew that I had only myself to blame.

As soon as dawn broke over the camp, John and I were up and quickly made our way back to the site where our gear was lost. We again commenced the hopeless search. Both of us were too strong-willed to accept defeat and neither of us was willing to turn back without our gear. After again exhausting ourselves, we collapsed into the slope for a rest. It was time to give up, but neither of us wanted to admit it. In bad temper I threw a pole into the snow and began stabbing at the crust of the slope. I was shouting at John that I would not descend without my gear when the pole struck something solid. I heard a thud and John turned to see the shocked expression on my face. I was only about 15 feet from where we had dug all day yesterday and lo and behold: buried several feet below the surface was our cache.

John and I were both ecstatic. I could feel adrenalin pumping through my veins and suddenly I could not feel the cold or exhaustion. It was like a new lease on life. The two of us uncovered our supplies and quickly moved them onto the plateau above, where we established a camp. As it was again late in the day, we bunked down for the night and returned the kindness of the Polish and Bulgarian climbers by sharing our food and fuel with them.

After camp three was safely in place, we returned to base camp and over the following weeks made several more journeys up and down the mountain, acclimatising and waiting for a weather window to break that would allow us a shot at the top. At this stage we had been on K2 for nearly two months. When John set out his wife, Susan, was pregnant and caring for their young daughter alone. He was conscious that she was now moving closer to her due date and would need him home soon. The pressure was on for both of us to make an attempt on the summit. Our permits were set to expire in early August, and Lauren and my family were waiting for my return. Finally decent weather arrived and John and I nearly made it all the way to camp four, but it was an exhausting and very tedious journey. We were breaking trail after storms had deposited heavy snow on the upper slopes and we were often thigh-deep. Despite the good weather, the task was daunting. There were dangerous seracs above every section of the upper slopes and avalanche risks were very high.

In the end, John and I decided that it was too dangerous to go on and we returned to the base camp to wait until the conditions improved. After several days back at base camp John made the decision to return home to Boston. It did not appear that the weather was going to relent any time soon and he had family commitments to attend to. Our last night together was just like any other. The weather was mercilessly cold and shortly after dinner we both retired to the relative warmth of our tents. I knew that it would be difficult to remain on the peak once John left as he was a good friend and a very solid climbing partner, but I wanted to give the summit one more shot.

Once John left, I spent quiet nights at the base camp with the Captain and the cook. We had great times despite the language and cultural barriers and I found solace in their company. I spent several more weeks on the mountain and made countless further attempts to ascend to the high camps, but I was finally forced to call it quits in late August and return home to Ireland without ever reaching the top. I had extended my permits and stayed on as long as possible but the weather had beaten me in the end. Despite the setbacks, I felt satisfied with my persistence and the knowledge that there were no successful summits at all that year on the peak. In the end, I flew home to Ireland on 23 August with a total resolution to return to the 'savage mountain' again the following year to finish my work on K2.

Chapter 14 ꙮ

K2—THE SECOND ATTEMPT

'Only those who risk going too far can possibly find out how far one can go.'
T.S. ELIOT

The months after I returned home from K2 in 2005 passed quickly. I was still very physically fit from my time on the mountain and I continued to work hard training in the hills and at the gym. I also began to work out my strategy for a repeat attempt on the savage mountain and was put in contact with two excellent Irish climbers who were keen to work as a team for an Irish summit. Mick Murphy, who I had met on Everest in 1993, and Ger McDonnell, a Limerick climber based in Alaska, would attempt K2's neighbour, Broad Peak, at the start of the season and then meet me at the base camp of K2 in late June once their climb was complete.

I was excited to have two very solid climbing partners lined up for the attempt and was thrilled to learn that two of the previous year's sponsors would again support the venture. Gerard O'Hare agreed to take on some of the main responsibilities whilst another Newry businessman and close friend, Cathal McCoy, agreed to fund the rest. Malachy McGuinness again met all of my technology needs, whilst Simon Scott resumed the responsibility of managing a webpage and keeping me abreast of the weather forecasts.

Once my arrangements were in place for a return trip to Pakistan I was able to relax and enjoy the winter months. For Christmas, Lauren and I headed over to Boston to be with her family and we arranged a climbing trip to Scotland for early January with her cousin Brian and two brothers, Jim and Neil. It would be the men's first experience ice-climbing and we were all really looking forward to it. Unbeknownst to

Lauren I also had a surprise in store for her. I decided that I would propose to her on the summit of Ben Nevis after our ice-climb. On the afternoon of 17 January we set off on the long trek to the CIC hut. The weather was poor and it was raining on the lower slopes. Once we reached the hut we rested for a short while before beginning our ascent up gully number five. Mid-way through the climb the rain turned to snow and the conditions improved slightly. By evening we reached the top of the route and then ascended the short distance onto the summit. Once we reached the final dome, I dropped down on one knee and unravelled a sign that I had made asking Lauren to marry me. In the midst of heavy snowfall with freezing temperatures and her family by her side, Lauren agreed to be my wife!

After the proposal Lauren and I returned to Ireland and began to make wedding plans. I also accompanied Lauren on a trip to Durban in South Africa, where she was running an exchange programme with a group of four young Irish people and Zulu children in KwaZulu-Natal.

It was an amazing three-week trip. The first two weeks we worked directly with charitable organisations supporting young people in Africa and the final week was spent in the bush with the Wilderness Leadership School. Here we slept out under the stars in a safari park, surrounded by big game animals. We could hear lions roar in the distance and could see crocodiles in the rivers below our camp. I am not usually a spiritual man but I found it very moving being so close to the animals in their native land. The trip gave me the opportunity to reflect and to mentally prepare for the challenges ahead.

Unfortunately, during our time away I received a telephone call from my old climbing mate Richard Dougan. He shared with Lauren and me the tragic news of David Sharp's death on Everest. We both found it really difficult to digest but the gravity of the events surrounding his death were not fully realised until we returned home to the media hailstorm.

Never in the history of Mount Everest has a single death proved so contentious. The events surrounding David's final hours were relayed on television newscasts, internet reports, TV chat shows and radio programmes all over the world. Mountaineers and members of the public cried out for an inquiry into the episode. The climbers who were on the peak when David passed away spoke out in defence of their actions but their explanations were completely inadequate.

David had achieved his dream and reached the summit after a strong solo ascent on 14 May 2006. On this, his third Everest expedition, he was beyond determined to make the final traverse onto the summit; he was resolute. David was a strong alpinist who employed an entirely minimalist approach to climbing. He did not bother with expensive gear or high-tech gadgets. He set about even the most difficult high-altitude climbs with basic but reliable gear and took little in the way of comfort items. He was a dedicated climber who spent all of his free time in the mountains. After we climbed together in 2003, I knew that David was intensely focused on making the summit but I also knew that he was a cautious climber who would not take unnecessary risks.

When I first heard the media reports of David's final hours I was appalled by the callous behaviour of the mountaineers who passed him in their pursuit of the summit. I was further angered by their misguided attempts to disparage David as a climber. It was claimed by several of the 40 climbers who passed directly over him as he lay dying in a rocky outcrop just below the summit that he was ill prepared and had taken dangerous risks in making a solo ascent. I found their allegations ironic. Most of those who passed over David were commercial climbers being led by Sherpas and guides to the summit. These 'climbers' were incapable of making the ascent without the assistance of their high-priced commercial outfitters and most lacked vital experience climbing at such extreme altitude. These men and women epitomised the commercial circus that Everest has become. High-priced guides will take even the weakest climber to the summit if the money is right and none of these individuals was willing to forfeit their opportunity for glory to save the life of a stranger.

David had set out for his third attempt completely alone and was strong throughout the season. He had completed all of the difficult and time-consuming work of establishing camps under his own steam and though he had befriended several fellow climbers that season, he remained almost entirely alone. According to reports he completed the final ascent to the summit without incident and then on the way down he stopped in the rocky outcrop where I had encountered the deceased Indian climber known to many Everest mountaineers as 'Green Boots' in 2003.

Based on the information that the media reported, David was likely in distress at that time. He appeared to be low on oxygen or completely out of it and he was most likely cold and exhausted. I remembered feeling that same deflation after making my summit bid and could relate entirely to him succumbing to the urge to rest. However physically debilitated David was at that stage, one thing is certain in my mind: he was not beyond help. With oxygen and assistance from fellow climbers, David most likely would have been able to descend to the high camp, where he could have been warmed in a sleeping bag and given food and fluids. Although this might not have guaranteed his survival, it certainly would have given him a chance at it.

It was easy for climbers who passed him to claim that he was beyond assistance when they encountered him, as this would justify their ascent to the summit whilst a man lay dying below them. However, that was not the case. Rescues have been successfully executed in equally audacious circumstances. The Royal Marines' Sherpas lowered the English climber with the broken leg to safety in 2003 and he was completely immobile. David was coherent for most of the time that he sat in the outcrop and although he was certainly suffering from the serious effects of altitude sickness, he did not have any broken bones or physical injuries that would have affected his mobility. David survived at an altitude of 27,890 feet, in freezing cold temperatures and without oxygen, for 48 hours before he mercifully passed away. His suffering must have been unimaginable and all the while, only one person, Dowa Sherpa, even remained by his side to provide emotional support to him in his final hours.

I was disgusted by the reports of David's death and the horrible way in which he was abandoned by his fellow mountaineers, and my sentiments were shared by other climbers throughout the world. Even Edmund Hillary took the opportunity to speak out against the commercial chaos on Everest and noted that never should a summit be more important than a man's life.

Despite my feelings of concern and sadness for David and his family and my intense anger at the moral failures of his fellow 'climbers', I did my best not to dwell on the events, as my own departure and climb were imminent. In the final days before again departing for Islamabad, I promised to be safe and not to take any unnecessary risks and said my goodbyes to Lauren and my family, hoping very much that I would return to Ireland to see them all again.

My flight passed quickly and when I arrived in Islamabad I was confronted by the familiar heat and chaos. However, this time a fellow passenger stood out to me as I entered the arrivals terminal at the airport. I had noticed this man at London Heathrow Airport wearing what would normally only be seen on the high slopes of a Himalayan mountain, and here he was again, speaking with Pakistani immigration officials. This was my first introduction to Jacek, a solo Polish climber who would also be making an attempt on K2. Jacek struck me immediately as an unusual character. He had worn his plastic climbing boots and summit gear all the way from Poland to Pakistan to save money on his luggage fees and he didn't even seem to notice the stares from fellow passengers. He was a stocky, solid man with a quick smile and a good sense of humour. He informed me that he worked as an international climbing guide in Russia and seemed to have a great deal of experience. We soon became friends and he agreed to join forces with Mick, Ger and myself.

Once we arrived at our hotel, we met the Adventure Tours Pakistan staff and they advised us that Jacek and I would be listed on a permit with a Russian expedition as well as two other solo climbers. This permit would enable the company to assign all of us with one liaison officer and would mean that we could either choose to join forces or to make solo attempts once we arrived on the mountain. Mick and Ger had used a different trekking company as they were tackling Broad Peak first and thus they were listed on a separate permit.

The Russian climbers were staying in a hotel in central Islamabad, and Jacek and I decided to meet them there to clarify all of the logistical and strategic plans for the season. The leader of the Russian expedition, Yuri, was reluctant to allow the solo climbers onto a permit with his team. He feared potential conflict within the expedition and worried that the Russians could be held accountable if anything were to go wrong on the mountain. Eventually, however, ATP persuaded Yuri to accept us all onto the permits and the terms for the season were agreed. Prior to departing from Islamabad, we were met by the founder of ATP, who is also the first Pakistani man to have summitted K2. Ashraf Aman was very gracious and wished all of us luck and safety in the upcoming climb. We saw this as a good omen for the season ahead.

Fortunately this year the weather in the Northern Regions was good and we were able to fly from Islamabad to Skardu. This saved us from the long and tedious journey overland up the Karokoram Highway. We flew out early in the morning and as the plane passed over the dusty, brown earth below, I could feel the excitement growing inside me. I felt confident about my chances for a summit bid this season and my experience from the previous year had given me a sense of ease and comfort on this return journey. When we arrived into Skardu we checked into the K2 Motel and enjoyed a feast of curries and rice before our convoy set out the following morning for Askole.

The five-day trek to base camp was uneventful. The Russian climbers had varying levels of English but they were all friendly and enjoyed the craic. The doctor, who was called Novosti, and Jacek both acted as translators for me and the Liaison Officer, 'the Commander', who only spoke English. We were very fortunate to have another excellent liaison officer working with us. He was very friendly and keen to participate in the journey. He was not a member of the Pakistani army, which is standard for the post, but rather a commander in the navy. He had requested a stint in the mountains as he had never been to this region before. His enthusiasm and ease with all of the climbers immediately made him very popular with the team.

We were one of the first expeditions to arrive into base camp this season. I noticed on the trek that many of the ice fields along the glacier were lower due to the warmer temperatures this year. The runoff from the glacier that flows through the carved, white banks of the Baltoro River seemed faster and deeper. Water appeared to be running everywhere from the melting ice. Deep snow on the trek in was not an issue this year, but the risk of avalanche was much higher due to the increased temperatures.

I felt stronger than I had on the previous attempt and the altitude did not seem to be affecting me at all. I also felt more prepared for the task ahead and was ready to begin the tedious work of establishing camps sooner than I had the previous year. Prior to departing from Ireland, John Fitzgibbon had given me a book about fast and light mountaineering. This book had a profound effect on my philosophy for ascending K2. I had a habit of packing more than I really needed and often took small comfort items to the higher camps. But this book stressed the benefits of strength and speed through minimalist packing. As a result I employed a new approach this season and brought very little to establish my camps.

In the first few weeks that I was on the mountain I worked primarily with Jacek to stash gear at camps one, two and three. We also all took turns fixing lines along the summit route, which was very labour intensive. It involved carrying heavy reels of rope along with supplies through unbroken trail, which we fixed into the slope using pitons. It was on one of these journeys between camps two and three, on the Black Pyramid, as it is commonly known, that I encountered my first serious setback of the season. I was abseiling down a section of the route on my own with a heavy rucksack, which contained a sleeping bag, food and rope. Suddenly, as I made my way down, the rope I was using snapped. Since I was abseiling, my axes were clipped onto my pack and therefore I had no means of arresting my fall. This sent my mind into a wild panic. As I plummeted down the vertical incline of snow and rock I worried that the weight of my pack would pull me down off the edge of the peak. I was moving very fast and it felt like I was falling for a long time, but in reality it was probably only seconds. Fortunately, I was able to turn on my side as I fell and tucked into a protective position. I slid along the rocky outcrop until I hit against a solid line of stone, which slowed my fall. I knew that I was getting closer to the edge of the route when finally I hit hard against a large rock. I felt as if my ribs cracked with the force of impact but I was alive and safe.

When I caught my breath and began to right myself I noticed how perilously close I had come to being another casualty of K2. I was less than five feet from the edge and although slightly battered, I was overjoyed to have survived without major injury. However, I was soaked in sweat and my mouth was completely dry. I had to stop for several minutes to regain a normal rate of breath and to relax my nerves. Despite the pain in my ribs and my urge to stop, I was conscious that it would not be safe to rest at this altitude with even a minor injury.

I continued to descend but at a much slower and more prudent pace. I no longer trusted the ropes and feared that in another similar fall I would not have the strength to survive. My ribs were aching on both sides and there were shooting pains in my back but I somehow managed to make my way down to base camp without further incident. However, once I arrived at camp I quickly realised the psychological toll that the fall had had on me. I felt really anxious and couldn't settle into my tent to rest. I thought a lot about David Sharp and all that he had lost in his pursuit of Everest, and I promised myself that I would be more cautious in future. I was also physically exhausted and battered so I decided to rest here for a week before re-ascending to the higher camps.

During that time Mick and Ger made their way over to k2 following Mick's successful summit on Broad Peak. He became the first Irishman to make the ascent; Ger had been with him throughout most of the climb but was forced to turn back due to a combination of weather and illness. When the men arrived I was greatly relieved. Although Jacek and I had become quite close and I was friendly with the Russian climbers, it was great to have Irish men in the camp and to relax and have the craic with them without the language and cultural barriers.

Ger had a small stereo with him and was a great fan of traditional Irish music and dance. He entertained us most evenings with songs and stories from home and it was apparent that he and Mick had become close friends. Jacek and the Russian climbers also enjoyed their company and their arrival was a boost to all those at the base camp. Their presence also distracted me from memories of the fall and helped me to prepare again to ascend the peak.

After a short time at base camp Mick, Ger and Wilco (a Dutch climber) established their camp three. Jacek and I already had our supplies in place at this camp so we met the men there to make a group effort at establishing camp four. Unfortunately we were unable to do so because the trail was laden with heavy, soft snow and the forecast predicted poor weather conditions. We all returned to base camp, where we were forced to wait for nearly another week before again setting out for the high camps and a chance at the summit.

With the receipt of a positive weather forecast predicting a solid weather window of nearly three days, we set out again as a group for the high camps and a push for the summit. We were determined not to waste precious time by sleeping at the low camps so instead planned to continue until reaching camp two. Upon arrival at camp one, the five of us stopped to eat and drink before moving up. Whilst several of us were resting, Ger and Wilco pushed on ahead towards camp two. Shortly after they departed I heard a loud smashing sound come down the side of the mountain and move directly past us. This sound was quickly followed by several more loud bangs and then the sound of rock breaking echoed throughout the mountain and we all rushed to take cover. It was as if someone was shooting directly at us from above. We ducked into whatever tiny spaces would afford protection from the falling rock. Those of us who remained at camp one were spread out along the ledge in protective huddles as rocks hurled down upon us at speeds that could kill a man instantly.

I managed to tuck myself into the small snow pit where our tents had been. I covered my head with my arms and lay tightly into the snow and ice. I could feel the sharp cold running through me as I lay flat against the frozen mass. I waited for the rock fall to pass and could hear the other men in their hiding spots shouting back and forth. I was conscious that Ger and Wilco could have been directly in the line of fire and worried that they might be thrown down the mountain with the impact of the rocks upon them.

After roughly a minute of intense rock fall, the sounds became fewer and further between. Large rocks were still breaking free from the ledges above but it was now mostly showers of small pebbles and scree. It was then that I heard a shout from Ger and could see him abseiling down in my direction. Wilco had been above Ger at the time the rock fall began and was unaware of what was happening below so he continued on towards camp two. When Ger reached us in camp one he shouted that he had been hit. I immediately went to him and although he was only requesting a plaster, I knew his injuries were far more serious. I could see blood running down his face and there was a visible dent and crack in his helmet. It was ironic because Ger was wearing a carbon Kevlar helmet, which is the strongest on the market and far superior to the ones worn by the rest of us. I couldn't help thinking that the stone that had hit him would have killed me instantly.

I took Ger into the sheltered ledge that I had tucked into and sat him down. His speech was slow and slurred and I was afraid he had a serious head injury. I took his pack off and made sure he was warm whilst I scoured through my pack for items that could be used to stop the bleeding. I found a pair of socks along with my bandana and some duct tape. I took Ger's helmet off and saw a gaping wound in his head. It appeared to go all the way down to the skull. I quickly applied the socks with pressure to the wound and then tied the bandana around his head to keep the socks in place. I took the duct tape and brought it around his jaw to secure the bandaging in place and finally I put his helmet back on and taped it up as well.

Once the wounds were bound, Mick, who had gone to scout the route ahead, returned and the two of us decided that Ger should be taken down immediately. At this stage Ger seemed confused about the incident and was quite pale. We worried that his condition would deteriorate rapidly at this altitude or that he could go into shock from the bleeding. As luck would have it I had a pre-arranged radio contact to make with my Liaison Officer at the very time the accident had occurred so when I radioed him from my walkie-talkie he was waiting on the line. He immediately notified the Russian team as well as the other climbers and support crew at base camp of the accident and advised them to make their way towards advanced base camp to assist in a rescue. He also notified our trekking company that Ger would need a helicopter to meet him at the base camp to evacuate him to a hospital.

Although Ger was conscious and still able to walk, we worried that his judgment and coordination were affected and determined that the best way to get him down was through an assisted abseil. To facilitate this, I took his pack and hooked him onto a sling, which would allow him to descend on the rope below me whilst I controlled the speed and he held on for balance. As there was still some rock-fall coming from above, Mick was on a rope above us, shouting down warnings. The descent was slow and tedious because we were forced to stop and duck into the ledge for safety as large rocks whizzed past. Ger was having difficulty holding on and keeping himself upright and his strength was quickly fading.

On certain parts of the route, the lines looked worn and battered and I feared that they would not be strong enough to support our combined weight. As a result, I was forced to go ahead of Ger and assist him from below as he slowly abseiled himself down towards me. This was time-consuming and difficult, but after nearly four hours we finally met the rescue party at advanced base camp. There were a Japanese and a Russian doctor waiting to attend to Ger when we arrived. They examined the wound and cleaned it thoroughly before they lifted Ger onto a makeshift stretcher and took him to base camp. Mick caught up with us at this point and decided that he would descend with Ger for support. He encouraged me to go back up the mountain as the weather window was still open for a summit bid. He said that he would go out on the helicopter with Ger to ensure that he received all of the proper medical treatment that he required and he would provide Ger's family with vital contact details.

Although I was exhausted after the laborious descent I was pleased that Ger was safe and knew that he would be well looked after with Mick at his side. I also knew that despite my exhaustion I was still strong and had a chance at making it to the top in good weather. I decided to climb up again, but recognised that I would not have the strength to make it to camp two, so I instead opted to return to camp one, where I met Jacek.

Jacek had remained at camp one after the rock-fall, waiting with several other climbers who were fearful of moving in case further falls occurred. They moved their camp from the original site, which was in the direct line of the rock-fall, towards another small section of the ledge. The tents were precariously perched on the edge of the cliff but the men were safer there than in the line of fire. I decided to bunk in with them for the night before again setting off for camp two with Jacek and several others the following day.

In the early hours before the dawn, Jacek and I left camp one and finally made our way to camp two, where we only stopped briefly for a rest before pushing on towards camp three. It was here that we saw the rescue helicopter coming into base camp for Ger. I radioed down our support and let the base camp know that we were heading up to camp three. When we arrived at camp three we again met Wilco, the Dutch climber. We were the only men at the camp and thus the three of us bunked in together. I explained to Wilco the events surrounding Ger's injury and evacuation. He was shocked at the news. He had thought Ger had turned back to wait out the rock-fall and would re-ascend with myself and Mick. Despite our concerns for Ger and the fact that we were behind schedule we remained enthusiastic about our chances for a summit bid and were optimistic that the weather window would last.

After a short and fitful sleep the three of us set out at dawn for camp four. It was a tiring and difficult journey. The snow was soft beneath us and was nearly thigh-deep. Each of us took turns breaking trail but we could not gain any speed. Eventually a heavy mist set in and we were unable to see around us. It was like being on the inside of a ping-pong ball; everything was pure white. It was very frustrating work and we finally decided that it would not be possible to make it to camp four without an improvement in the visibility. We begrudgingly returned to camp three, where Wilco decided to continue his descent back to base camp. Jacek and I remained at camp three for the night and again tried for camp four the following day. Much to our dismay, the conditions remained the same and Jacek too decided to return to base camp.

I have always been a very stubborn man and have never easily accepted defeat. I was utterly frustrated with K2. It was my second attempt and the setbacks were unrelenting. I refused to concede and instead stayed on alone. I set my camp in a whiteout and waited for the weather to clear. It was after this foolish decision that I again nearly succumbed to the mountain. Whilst scouting the trail ahead, I broke through the snow into a crevasse and was only able to arrest my fall after the entire lower half of my body was submerged in the crack. Crevasses in this part of the world can run to immeasurable depths and I was conscious that the wrong move could send me plummeting into the abyss. Luckily I found strength in my fear and was able to pull myself back out. I lay down briefly beside the crevasse to regain my composure before I made a slow retreat. Now I was shaken and alone.

When I returned to the relative safety of camp three, I spent a long and lonely night on my own. In the morning I awoke to the same poor weather conditions and prepared to climb down to camp two. However, prior to departing, I received a weather forecast from Simon Scott over the satellite phone that predicted a break in the weather over the next few days. This news lightened my mood considerably.

I returned to camp two late that morning for rest and a reprieve from the altitude. It was after a night here that I reconnected with Jacek and the Russian expedition. They were re-ascending from base camp after also receiving news of the upcoming weather window. We were all delighted with the possibility of clear skies and low winds and hoped very much for one final shot at the summit.

That afternoon we set out together towards camp three knowing

that the climb ahead would be difficult, but we were all feeling strong
and optimistic. This would be my final shot at the summit. I had been
on the mountain for over two months and my permits would be
expiring soon. All of my efforts were focused on the task ahead and I
was determined to commit 110% to the summit push.

Chapter 15 ∾

| THE AVALANCHE

'Great love and great achievements involve great risks.'
HIS HOLINESS THE FOURTEENTH DALAI LAMA

It was around three o'clock when we arrived at camp four. The climb from camp three had proven a long and arduous journey. There are large seracs that hang over this section of the climb like window-washers' scaffolding clinging to the sides of a skyscraper. These large crusts of snow teetered dangerously above us as we carefully navigated the crevasses littering the pass between the two camps. I was very conscious of the risks these crevasses posed and we all took turns scouting the route ahead for safety. The temperatures had varied considerably as we progressed from one camp to the next. The radiation from the mountain was reflecting off the clouds above, causing the ice on the top layer of snow to melt. We were thigh-deep at times and our progress was painfully slow. After seven long hours of this tempered climbing, we were all exhausted.

They were now nine of us in total, seven Russian climbers, Jacek and me. When we had set out from Islamabad we were all distinct representatives of our own countries and expeditions; however, at this stage we were more like a single team, with a single goal. For the past two months we had worked together and alongside each other in establishing all of the low camps and even when we were keeping different schedules or working with different men, we passed each other on the ascents and descents knowing that we had a single aspiration.

I had learned through broken English the stories of their lives. The wives and children they had at home, the work they did to pay the bills, the mountains they had climbed and the dreams they had for the future. Their family photos and souvenirs from home lined the narrow corners of their tents and, like myself, they were keen to share these little comforts with their fellow climbers. I understood little of what they said but could relate to them entirely. I felt their drive and shared their passion for the mountains, for this mountain.

I too spent time alone in my tent at night looking at pictures of family and myself and Lauren, tanned on a beach somewhere warm, the dim bulb of my head-torch illuminating just enough of our faces for me to see the happiness in our expressions. There was a strange sense of comfort and warmth in this nightly ritual. Like the reassurance I get from the cool touch of the miraculous medal my mother gave me against the skin of my chest, the little things from home keep us sane.

This miraculous medal had travelled with me on many of the mountains I undertook in my lifetime. My mother, a staunchly religious woman, believed that it would provide me with protection when I was away from home. She took great care to remind me before departing for every expedition to tuck the medal into my pocket or to drape it around my neck so that it would always be there, reminding me that God was looking out for me.

Many of the men I was with on this mountain were religious as well, although not all in a conventional sense. Some were more religious about mountaineering than they were about any church and they placed their utmost faith in the mountain and its elements. They had trained for this climb with great passion and were deadly serious when it came to mountaineering. Many of them had summitted Everest and the other Himalayan giants. They trained in the far corners of their native Siberia and had an unimaginable capacity to endure the cold. In fact, they seemed to thrive in the subzero temperatures that froze the condensation from our breath to our beards within seconds. They enjoyed Russian vodka and even a smoke at the end of the day, but when it came to climbing they had an intensity about them that told me they were willing to risk it all to reach the top. These men became my companions and without Mick and Ger by my side they were the only teammates I had.

After nine long days above camp two at an altitude of over 6,700 metres our bodies were beginning to break down. As we set up our tents at camp four, my fingers and toes were permanently cold. No matter how often I stopped to warm them, it felt as if nothing could restore the normal sensation to the ends of my limbs. The pink colouring had long since drained from my right foot and the tips of my toes were beginning to blacken. I have known many climbers during my years in the mountains who have witnessed this same phenomenon, and I am acutely aware that many of them now have small stubs where their fingers and toes should be. In fact, many of the Russian climbers smoked with rolled cigarettes between the bumps that remained where their fingers had once been. The strange pink shine on the skin that is stretched to cover these amputations made me reflect on a promise I made to Lauren that this mountain was not worth a single finger or toe, and I hoped more than ever that I could keep my promise to her.

My lungs burned with each strained breath and the cramps I had begun to experience in my abdomen at the lower camps were now getting worse. My ribs still ached from my injury earlier in the summer and I had nagging pains in my lower back. I was exhausted and yet alert at the same time. My heart rate was fast and even at rest I was anxious. I was so consumed by excitement that I couldn't slow my thoughts down. I had moments of clarity where the summit seemed so close to my grasp that I could feel it in my hand, and cloudy moments where I had trouble focusing on all the preparations that lie ahead. In the back of my mind I worried about my health and whether or not I had acclimatised properly for the strain which I was about to undergo.

The sky was beginning to darken and it must have been approaching 4 p.m., but we were all so focused on bedding down for the night that we no longer noticed the hours passing. The clock that dominated the world existing so far away from us was no longer relevant. Jacek and I had run out of food and gas. We had no way to refuel before sleeping and were forced to share in with the Russian climbers on their dwindling supplies. We used a small stove fired by a gas canister to boil cups of soup and noodles. Dehydration was a real danger and we were all aware that every sip of water we could muster would help us in our ascent. None of us ate well. The appetite disappears at altitude and even though the body demands food as fuel, we had to force our stomachs to accept it.

It was not long before we were all too tired and cold to speak. Jacek and I bedded down together in our tent with no sleeping bags or blankets for warmth. We had lost all these vital supplies to an avalanche at a lower camp and now we had only our down suits to keep us warm for the summit. The cold of this night was unrelenting. I tried desperately to make my body warm. I lay in the smallest position I could manage and Jacek and I were directly against each other in an effort to share heat, but nothing worked.

I shook and shivered as the wind blew through the seams of our tent. Nothing is airtight in these conditions. The cold from the snow and ice below me was permeating all of my layers of gear and it felt prickly against my skin. I tried to imagine warm places, the beach in the photo with Lauren, the sweat and humidity of Islamabad, sunburns and rock-climbing in Thailand, but I was still cold. Jacek and I were too tired to communicate but neither of us was sleeping. The summit was close and we were anxious to begin our final ascent. Both of us made silent checklists of the supplies we would need for this last leg of the journey. We both knew that the next 24 hours would be the most dangerous and that preparation would mean everything.

The hours passed by slowly. I checked my watch frequently as sleep would not come and the seconds ticked by like hours. A Christy Moore song was in my head; 'an endless night without dawning' repeated over and over as I tried to remember the rest of Bobby Sands' lyrics to 'Back Home in Derry'. I distracted myself with thoughts of home. I wondered about Lauren and my mother. I thought of all the beauty of an Irish summer: the wind bush blooming yellow behind my house and the heather in the low light of dusk on the hills of Slieve Gullion. These thoughts calmed my anxious nerves.

At 11 p.m. we arose and made the final preparations for the summit bid. We all looked tired and I imagined the others had not slept either. Jacek and I packed our gear into our bags and I checked a 6-mm rope which I carried for use on the bottleneck above us. We decided to undertake this remaining section unroped. The plan was to make use of old ropes at the bottleneck and to employ the rope I carried only as a backup.

It was unbelievably cold. The sky was clear and the stars shone down upon us so low it felt as if I could reach up and touch them. It was 1 a.m. and the crust beneath our feet was now solid, allowing us to depart with ease. Our tents and what remained of the Russian supplies were left anchored at camp four to provide a resting spot for our descent. We had estimated this final push would take 16 hours, maybe more. We knew that the descent would be the most dangerous part of our climb and that the elation of the summit would have faded and all that would remain was our exhaustion. I again thought of David Sharp and promised myself that I would not rest until I reached the safety of the low camps.

As we made our way higher into the sky my toes were again on my mind. They had become numb and I worried that I was progressing from frost-nip to frostbite. I was anxious to stop and check the skin to see if they had worsened. I let the others pass and kicked out a platform in the snow to sit. I removed my boot and found the skin turning black. The blood in my foot did not seem to be reaching the tips of my toes at all. I warmed them with my hands and tried to massage the feeling back into my foot. After a moment or two I knew that I must begin again. The others were moving at a good pace and I needed to catch up to them.

After half an hour I caught up to Serguey, one of the older Russian climbers, who had already summitted nine of the highest mountains in world. A short while later we reached the bottleneck and all of the fear and anxiety that I had harboured about this section of the climb was realised. Although it was steep and acutely technical, it was not beyond my abilities. I let my confidence gather and roped into the existing lines laid by the Russians in front of me. Serguey made his way ahead on the icy 300-metre pass that hangs at a vertical incline of 80°. Serguey was not using oxygen either. The air was thin and our lungs were labouring hard in this physically intense section. Serguey stopped frequently to shake his legs and feet to promote circulation.

We reached the top of the bottleneck together. The ropes were very loose so we were totally reliant on our ice axe placements. At this stage we were 10 hours into the climb and it was approaching 11 a.m. The sky was still clear and the sun had long since risen. The snow was becoming very soft underfoot, which is unusual at this altitude. I was conscious of the time and of how slowly we seemed to be progressing in this final stage. However, the next hour or so passed and we made the final traverse, leaving only the summit ridge in front of us. We waited in line to complete this pass, as the remaining section was too narrow for more than one climber to ascend at a time.

Serguey and I were still alone. I stopped and put a stake into the snow and clipped that stake onto the ropes of the traverse for added protection. I rested my weight against the ropes and looked up to the summit dome on the horizon. I imagined the leading Russian climbers; Yuri, Piotr, Arcady, Victor, Alexander Foigt and Alexander Gaponov must be near the top by now. Serguey and I were nearly celebrating. The hard work was done, we were above the bottleneck and the traverse, and I found my adrenalin rising as familiar thoughts flooded my mind. I remembered this exhilaration well from the moments before I reached the summit of Everest. As I stood on that final section I was convinced I would stand on the top of K2.

As I was speaking to Serguey, I looked up to see Jacek above us on the side of the hanging serac; he didn't move or motion to us. Serguey and I continued speaking. He was planning a toast on the summit with a small bottle of vodka that he had packed. Before he could finish his sentence, I heard a sudden swoosh above me and looked up to find only white.

I was confused. Everything was happening so fast and the world seemed to have gone silent. I was knocked off my feet and I was sliding. I was conscious that I had only clipped the karabiner to the rope and not the jumar; this meant that I had no added protection. I worried that my weight would cause the rope to snap or that I would be buried underneath the crusts of snow coming down upon me. I wrapped the rope around my right wrist as quickly as possible and waited for the sliding to stop. At first my body was in the prone position and then I somersaulted over, landing on my back and looking up into the white debris above me. What had only been a matter of seconds felt like minutes or hours. The climb below flashed through my mind; we had traversed a 10,000-foot cliff across the upper section of the bottleneck and now I could see myself free-falling over the edge. I couldn't breathe; my fear was overwhelming. I didn't feel any pain and wondered if it would hurt when I died.

When the sliding stopped, the snow felt like concrete setting on my body. I immediately tried to swim against the tide of snow and ice. My head was above the surface and I was forcing air into my lungs. I didn't see anyone around me and I wondered if I was the only survivor. I was still and the snow had settled. I dug frantically to free myself with one hand as the other was still entangled in the rope that I had been grasping with all my strength. I now realised that I was teetering on the edge of the cliff. When I cleared enough space to free myself, I dropped to my knees and gasped for air. I was frantic. Adrenalin was rushing through my veins and my heart was pumping so hard it felt like it would explode in my chest.

I reached above me and touched the cold snow. I felt no pain and shock kept me moving with rapid strokes. I looked up and was suddenly aware that I was not alone. The rope had held and Serguey came into sight. He was upside down and clinging to his own rope, which too was intact. This was the happiest moment of my life. I was alive and I was not alone. I began to imagine that we had all survived and were just spread out amongst the top layers of snow near the summit. This must have been a surface avalanche and we would all regroup and share our tales of survival. I dreamt the adrenalin in our blood would take us on to the summit and back down as planned.

Small crusts of snow and ice fell towards me as Serguey kicked his way free. He righted himself and glanced down at me. He put his hand in the air in a tight fist and smiled and I did the same so we both knew the other was okay. I made my way up towards Serguey and despite the language barrier we communicated our delight at having made it through the avalanche and ensuing fall. Above Serguey we could both see Jacek. He too was alive and well.

Although I was happy to see that Jacek had survived I felt a sudden rush of anger towards him. He was above us and had neglected the mountain code; he never warned us. I also couldn't help thinking how Jacek seemed to disappear when Ger was injured. He never assisted in the evacuation and although he probably feared for his own safety and had protected himself from the rock-fall, he had not shown any real concern about our welfare. In hindsight he might have never seen the avalanche coming but at that moment, so close to losing my life, I felt a distinct mistrust.

Serguey and I climbed up towards Jacek and the summit. Time was difficult to measure at this stage. It might have been 10 minutes since the avalanche or half an hour. There was so much going on in our minds, and our bodies were still shaken—but the proximity of the summit urged us on. We made our way up to locate the others and were met by two Russians descending. My first inclination was to think that the avalanche must have passed below them and that they had been to the summit unscathed. They were masked and it was difficult to ascertain which two climbers they were. They began to speak frantically in Russian to Serguey and I could immediately tell by Serguey's expression that something was wrong.

Serguey turned to Jacek and me and used the mountain code with his arms in an x shape above his head, signalling to us that there was danger above and not to progress. Despite this I advanced towards him because I was so close to the summit and there was this drive inside me, pushing me on towards the top. I felt out of control. I wanted so badly to be done with this mountain. All these months of work and the second year of trying were taking a toll and it felt like nothing was worth more at this moment than reaching the top. Jacek, however, seemed frozen in his tracks. He was intent on listening to what the others were saying and his face was unchanging; he didn't even seem to blink. For some reason I still believed that the men ahead had reached the summit and that they were pushing the rest of us to descend without reaching the top. I didn't want to go with them; I didn't understand them and I didn't care what they were saying. The altitude had taken a hold on me and I was totally without reason.

Despite my resolve to continue on, Serguey was adamant that we were not moving. He made his way across to me and said, 'The leader,' and then signalled with his hand across his throat that he was gone. I didn't understand him; I could not comprehend what he was saying. He spoke quickly and quietly in Russian and four more times signalled with his hand across his throat. He was telling me that Yuri, Alexander Foigt, Piotr and Arcady were gone, but I was confused. At this stage himself and Jacek began pushing me down. We had all hooked onto the same rope to abseil and they used force to make me descend.

There was an urgency about them. Serguey stamped his foot and signalled that the snow might avalanche again, this time taking all of us with it. I was breathing quickly and looked to the sky to calm myself. It was blue but there was cloud forming, telling me that the good weather would break within the next 12 to 24 hours. I still didn't realise the extent of the situation and felt defeated. I would not stand on the top of this mountain and I was so close; it was causing me great distress. My head felt light with the altitude and I was wondering how the others got lost. I tried to rationalise the situation; maybe they were blinded by the snow from the avalanche or thrown off course. But I couldn't understand why we were turning back.

There were five of us in a group at this stage and I was the first to abseil down. It was going against my instinct because I was so drunk with adrenalin and altitude but the others quickly followed and I realised that there was no turning back now. When the rope ran out near the bottom of the bottleneck, I began to return to my senses. I knew that this section is notoriously dangerous and that it would take all of my concentration and expertise to climb down without incident. Many of the climbers who perish on κ2 do so at this point. The intense technical nature of this section compounded by the composition of snow and ice make it treacherous. It must have been around 2 p.m. and the midday sun had softened the ice to such a degree that my axe placements weren't totally secure. I had to rely upon my remaining strength to knock in every axe swing with intensity and to kick all of my footing until it was secure. I was also aware that if one of the climbers above me slipped, he would fall to his death and take me with him.

I tried to move quickly but to concentrate as well. There were snow and ice chips raining down on me as the others kicked in above. Sweat was beading on my forehead and I felt thirsty. I stopped for a moment to suck on a piece of snow. My lips were cracked and I had cold sores. The cold, wind and sun were drying my mouth and throat. I knew I must not rest and thus continued on. I was unsure how long I had been descending but it could have been hours. I finally reached an area of safety where the incline had levelled to a plateau. I was just above camp four. The other climbers were all with me now; and we were exhausted.

It was Jacek who spoke first. He understood Russian and his English was by far the best. He was directly in front of me and his eyes were very serious. We were all sitting at this stage but the Russian climbers weren't focused on what was being said; they were instead examining the horizon and the cliff above us. Jacek spoke frankly and said with unquestionable conviction that the others were gone, most likely dead. He spoke their names again, Yuri, Alexander, Piotr and Arcady, and I tried to comprehend what he had told me. The two Russians who descended with Jacek, Serguey and myself were still masked and I struggled to understand who had survived and who had not. I tried to put names to faces and Jacek went quiet. Serguey rose and was peering over the edge whilst the other two, who I did not yet recognise, scanned the cliffs and passes above. There were tears in their eyes and I could clearly see the devastation the avalanche had caused. I became emotional when I realised that I had escaped the brunt force of the avalanche's path. Myself, Serguey, Jacek and the two Russians who I soon learned to be Alexander Gaponov and Victor were like logs in a river pushed to the sides as the water rushes through, but the other four climbers were taken directly downstream and off the mountain. Or worse, if they remained on the pass above, they were encased in snow and ice beneath the runoff.

At this stage none of us knew what to do. Our tents were still in place at camp four and we were conscious that the weather was changing. The adrenalin had subsided and exhaustion set in. We were all unwell and I could taste blood in my mouth. I was beginning to experience pulmonary oedema. The Russians began to look for their lost comrades but soon realised the peril we were in and how futile their search was. Yuri, Alexander, Piotr and Arcady were dead and their bodies may never be found. Mountains have a strange way of claiming lives; they often swallow people whole and leave no trace to show that they ever existed. These men would not be brought home for their families to bury; they would remain on K2 for eternity. The snow was unstable and the weather was worsening. Finally, Serguey and the others decided we must not stop here. We left everything behind and travelled fast and light down the mountain.

Whilst we were descending I felt an intense anger growing in my stomach. I could no longer look at Jacek. When I saw him I could only think of him protectively huddling himself against the peak instead of warning Serguey and me that the avalanche was coming. I am not sure if I was at all rational at this stage but memories of Jacek 'disappearing' when Ger was injured began to haunt me.

I was at camp three when I lost control. We had all left an established camp here for rest on the descent and Jacek and I were in our tent together. My heart was pounding and I was beginning to spit blood. I was conscious that pulmonary oedema could kill within hours and that

I needed to rest and descend soon. My nerves felt completely frayed. My head was sore and my chest was aching. Whilst I lay, unfit to move, Jacek began to mock me, saying that I wasn't such a great climber now, and suddenly I went at him with all my might. In hindsight it all seems a bit ridiculous, but there was so much emotion at that moment that I genuinely wanted to kill him.

In the hours since the avalanche I had utterly convinced myself that Jacek had protected himself at the expense of Serguey and me, and with his comment to incite me, I flew into a blind rage. For the moments we were entangled I fought him ferociously but thankfully sanity prevailed and after a moment or two it was all over. One of the Russian climbers broke it up. I knew then that although the five of us had survived the avalanche, nothing would ever be the same for any of us again. We would all have our own emotional scars, fear and anger to contend with.

The descent to base camp was a long and tiring process. We were all cold and shaken. There were few words said between us and we all seemed distant and deep in thought. For me the fear, guilt and sadness were nearly overwhelming. I hadn't known these men for very long but I had shared more with them in that short time than I have with some of my closest friends in a lifetime together. I felt elated for surviving but guilty for what I perceived my role in the disaster to be. It was me who had given the Russian team the forecast for good weather; it was my advice that led us on that 'final attempt'. The forecasts I had received via satellite phone from Simon had been so reliable and the risk of an avalanche seemed very low. The conditions seemed ideal for a summit attempt and I had persuaded the men that this could be our final opportunity. The very route we had chosen for the last traverse was my suggestion. From camp four I had seen a rock high above that I thought would provide us with a shelter point on the ascent, so I advised we zig-zag up the final stage of the mountain towards that rock. I now wondered if it was these decisions that led to our fate.

When we arrived at base camp, I used the satellite phone. The first person I called was Lauren. I don't think that I made much sense but I told her it was over, that I was coming home and that four others were not. I sounded distant and strange. It was around 4 a.m. in Ireland and Lauren had been awoken from a sound sleep with a start. Her voice was strained and I knew as soon as she answered that she feared the worst. Two days earlier I had sent her a text message telling her that the weather had failed me again and that my permit was expiring, so Jacek and I were descending and coming home. I had not spoken to her since I sent that message and by now she was very worried that something had happened to me. I didn't feel strong enough to speak for long and told her very little about what had happened. I phoned my mother next and will always remember her doubting it was actually myself on the line, as I sounded so distant. I told her not to worry, I was alive and it was over.

Base camp should have seemed like an oasis after the horror of the past two days on the mountain but it brought a different type of strain. This was the first time the five of us were faced with the prospect of explaining to others what had happened. Two members of the Russian expedition had remained behind at base camp when we went for the summit. One member, the team's doctor, had been unwell and the other had had a premonition that something terrible would happen on the ascent. When he told his team mates of this before we set off, they laughed at him and dismissed his fears; now we would have to verbally relive our nightmare to them as well as the liaison officers, cooks and porters. It was terrible. The traces of those we lost were everywhere. Their tents were just as they had left them; their photos, relics and mementoes of their wives and children were all as they had intended. The thought of the doctor having to phone their families and share the news was awful.

I was on safe ground, but couldn't convince my nerves of that. I was so edgy, I thought I would never sleep. When sleep finally came it was fitful and nightmares from the avalanche kept flashing into my mind. I would awaken with a start convinced I was falling. I would jump out of my sleeping bag and open the tent to be sure that I was safe.

When I had finally stripped down out of my summit gear, I realised that the rope I had clung to with such desperation when the avalanche hit had actually cut through all the layers of my outerwear and base layers and gone directly into the skin on my forearm and wrist. I never felt the pain. Without my down suit I looked thin and frail. It had been a long time since I had eaten properly or felt warm and my body was showing the strain of the previous months.

I had a small mirror in my toiletry bag and I will never forget the first time I looked at myself after we arrived back at base camp. The man looking back at me was not the same man who had set out in June to conquer this mountain. I had aged terribly. The sun and wind had chapped my face. My nose was red and the lines around my eyes were cut in deeply with dark circles. My toes were numb and black but I had miraculously escaped full-blown frostbite. With time they would regain circulation and the colour would return.

I was forced to remain at base camp for a week after the descent as our Liaison Officer was in dialogue with the Russian government about issuing the death certificates. We had to go through every detail of that fateful day whilst the information we provided was transcribed. Unfortunately this was not a straightforward process. After the doctor had notified the families of the accident, two of the wives went to see a psychic reader. The psychic told them that he had a vision their husbands were not dead but trapped in an ice cave just below the summit. He urged the women to organise a search-and-rescue team amongst the climbers who remained on K2 to locate the men's whereabouts. This was not only absurd, but also utterly devastating for the families as well as those of us who had been there when the avalanche struck. The false hope this instilled in these women and their children was heartbreaking. Those of us who had experienced the avalanche firsthand knew without a shadow of a doubt that the men were dead. However, as two of the wives now refused to accept the fate of their husbands, the issuing of the death certificates was delayed.

The women requested a helicopter be sent to the pass where the avalanche had struck to look for signs of life, but this was impossible: helicopters cannot fly at that altitude. Those of us who remained on the mountain spent our days scouring the lower passes for any signs of the men's bodies to send home to their loved ones. I have always thought that if I died on a mountain I would like to have my body returned home for burial in Ireland and I can only imagine that these men too would have liked to be laid to rest in their native Siberia. But like so many others before them, not a single trace of them was ever found.

Ironically, the date that the avalanche happened was 13 August 2006, the same date that six climbers (one of whom was Alison Hargreaves, a top British female climber) disappeared on the upper pitches of K2 during a storm in 1995. Their bodies were never recovered either.

In the end, the two wives, like so many others before them, were forced to accept the loss of their husbands and we were allowed to set off for home. The trek from base camp to Askole was a blur. We completed it in three days instead of the usual five. The weather was clear and warm. The sun felt nice on my face and I started to feel myself regaining strength beneath its glow. We arrived at the K2 Motel and immediately went to book our flights from Skardu to Islamabad. However, as luck would have it, bad weather was setting in and we were forced to make the 48-hour journey down the Karokoram Highway again.

I didn't speak much on the journey—I wasn't asleep but I wasn't awake either. The time just passed and I remained in a fatigued daze. Islamabad was hot the day we arrived. The humidity caused sweat that soaked my shirt and trousers. I said goodbye to the men who I had been through so much with. I left before the Russian climbers were able to get an outbound flight. Our final moments together were strangely normal, but beneath all of our ordinary actions, there was emotional strain. Jacek and I had remained together since our fight in the tent but had not spoken about what happened that night. We just continued with our daily routines as normal and passed the hours in transit with small talk and silent interludes.

On the day we were set to fly back to London together, Jacek and I checked in at the desk in Islamabad and he was told his ticket was not valid for travel that day. I was ushered through to security and Jacek was held back. We had a quick embrace before Jacek went back to sort out a new ticket and I went on to my gate. We said we would stay in touch or meet up again but that was the last time I was ever in contact with Jacek.

The flight to Ireland left early in the morning. I had showered and shaved before I boarded the plane and I put on my last remaining clean clothes. They were hanging off my skeletal frame and looked as if they belonged to a man twice my size. I felt nothing, not the nervous anticipation I had returning home a year ago, not the defeat I felt when we did not reach the summit, not the exhilaration I experienced after Everest. I just felt empty.

The flight landed late and Lauren had already been waiting for hours when I finally walked through the doors of the baggage claim and back into the world that I had left behind. She looked at me like I was a different person and she was right; 13 August 2006 had changed me forever.

Chapter 16 ∾

FATHERHOOD AND THE FUTURE

*'When you were born, you cried and the world rejoiced.
Live your life so that when you die the world cries and
you rejoice.'*
NATIVE AMERICAN PROVERB

In the days and weeks after I returned from Pakistan, time passed by
in a blurry haze. I slept poorly and found myself jetlagged and edgy.
I couldn't seem to reconnect with the world that I had left behind.
The first few nights in a bed were like the restless nights in my tent back
at base camp. I would finally drift off after long hours tossing and
turning and would then awake with a start, feeling confused and
excited. By the time my heart would stop racing and sleep would
return, it would be time to rise.

I still had the sensation of falling in my dreams and would feel as if
I was on the edge of the bed at 23,000 feet, teetering on a cliff. I could
hear noises that were amplified by my recollections of the sound of the
avalanche hitting. Things were loud and muffled at the same time. I
would sweat even though the cool Irish air rushed through my open
bedroom windows and my body ached constantly.

I was painfully thin and despite my best efforts to regain some of the
weight that I had lost, my appetite was minimal. Everything I could
force myself to eat ran through me before any nutrients could be
absorbed. My face was hollowed and my hair had thinned to the point
that my only option was to shave my head. I felt my body in a state of
malnutrition and never in all my years had I felt so weak. I remember
vividly the pain of my industrial accident and the devastation it caused
to my entire body, but strangely I felt worse now than I had in even the

darkest days immediately after the forklift struck me.

Finally after several weeks of being ill I went to see the doctor and was diagnosed with a type of dysentery. I had lost a total of three stone and my muscle tone had wasted away to nothing. I was put on very strong antibiotics and slowly the diarrhoea began to subside. After about a month my appetite began to reappear and with my body's healing my sleep became less fitful.

Lauren and I argued a lot when I first got back. She was angry with the decisions I had made on the day the avalanche happened. I had promised her that the expedition was over for me and that I was descending to safety and a flight home. But then I had been drawn into another attempt on the summit by the good weather and the strength of the Russian team. I had never phoned her to tell her my plans had changed and she had waited nervously for my call. When it never came she insists that she knew something was drastically wrong. When I did phone after the avalanche struck I was distant and cold. She was shaken and angry and I was too overwhelmed to acknowledge the stress that I had put her through.

Lauren has spent enough time in the mountains to know that many Russian expeditions are notoriously driven in their efforts to reach the summit. So many of them have perished in their pursuit of the world's highest peaks and the men who endeavour to climb with them often succumb to their willingness to risk it all to reach the top. For many of them it is a matter of national pride to reach a summit and so these men willingly risk life and limb to succeed in their ascents. The sacrifices that these climbers make just to be members of their national expeditions are unlike those of many other climbers from around the world. Most of these men are not wealthy. They do not come onto the mountains with large corporate sponsors or high-tech gear; they leave behind families that are often struggling to make ends meet and they are away for months at a time, pursuing not just their dreams but the success their communities and country so readily desire. Within this context of climbing, these men are put under enormous pressure to achieve. They know that returning home without the esteem of a successful summit bid is beyond disappointing.

These men are some of the most elite climbers within the international mountaineering community but they are also infamous for the risks they have taken. Many wear the wounds of their pursuits in full visibility. They have lost fingers and toes to frostbite and their ears are weathered a permanent shade of purple, or are missing pieces of flesh after the skin has frozen and rotted away—and these are the ones who have survived. Many others lie behind, interred on peaks throughout the world.

Lauren doubted my decision to pursue the summit with these men and she questioned my ability to turn back when they were pushing on. Ironically, it was the Russian climbers who had acted with clarity after the avalanche and despite their intense desire to summit, they knew the risks were far too great. They were the ones who had pushed me down instead of up, but it was only in time that I was able to explain this to Lauren, to make her realise that it was my own intense desire to be done with K2—to have conquered this mountain which had plagued my dreams—that drove me up for that final attempt.

Lauren and I had been engaged for only six months when I left for Pakistan and she had hoped to plan a big American wedding in her hometown of Boston for the following summer. We talked about extravagant and exotic honeymoons before I left and she had spent the months that I was away working, training and making wedding plans to distract herself from my absence. Three months can be a long time waiting for someone and the constant concerns about my safety had taken a toll on her as well.

After I returned, all the plans were put on hold. The strain of what had happened and the rift it had caused between us left everything in limbo. I wasn't sure our relationship was strong enough to survive what lay ahead and although I had initially vowed I would never return to K2, I was already beginning to wonder whether or not that was true. Mountaineering can be an obsessive hobby and although I had come so close to losing everything, that did not mean I wasn't willing to try again. However, they say it is darkest just before the dawn and when things seemed really rocky for us both something wonderful and truly life-changing happened.

Just five weeks after I returned home, Lauren got pregnant. We had both dreamed of having children and hoped to have a baby straight away after getting married but now this dream had come true sooner than we had imagined. I was so overcome with emotion when we got the news, I finally felt as if everything could be normal again. It didn't matter where we had been or what we had been through; we had an opportunity to make a fresh start and to bring all the goodness of us both into a new life.

Although the tension of the events on 13 August had not disappeared, Lauren and I wanted to make things work for the sake of each other and the child we would have. It didn't change her attitude towards the risks that I had taken and it didn't erase the memories of that day, but it gave us both something positive to focus on over the months that followed and it brought us closer together than we had ever been.

Although we were meant to wed in Boston in a year's time, we decided in light of the pregnancy to plan a small winter wedding in the mountains of Vermont instead. We spent Christmas in Melrose with Lauren's family and then had a quiet New Year with her parents. On 5 January 2007, Lauren and I were wed in the Green Mountain Inn in Stowe, Vermont, in front of her grandmother and parents as well as her two brothers and their girlfriends. It was a fantastic and personal way to make our vows. I had hoped some of my family would attend as well but unfortunately none were able to make the trip on such short notice. Nevertheless it was a perfect way for Lauren and me to make our commitment to each other. We had met in the snow on the world's highest peak, become engaged in a snowstorm on the top of Ben Nevis and had now wed in the snows beneath the shadows of one of New England's most beautiful mountains.

The following months passed by quickly. Lauren and I returned home to Ireland not long after the wedding and settled back into daily life. I had begun working again shortly after I arrived home from K2. It proved a great distraction from the events of the past and the anxious anticipation of the future. Both Lauren and I were tremendously excited about the baby and spent time decorating the nursery and picking names as we waited for the due date of 28 June to arrive.

One day early, at 6.34 a.m. on 27 June 2007, Conor Brendan Bannon was born. He was 8 pounds and perfect in every way. Nothing can describe the way I felt when he first emerged. I had been very involved in the birth and was there for every second of his journey. I would never have described myself as an emotional person, but at the moment of my son's birth, I was the most emotional man in the world. He changed everything for me. I was overwhelmed with tears of joy. I actually felt myself shaking as he screamed and couldn't wait to hold him in my arms.

The first moments I spent with my son against my chest were none other than the most beautiful and fantastic of my life. No summit or mountain could top the exhilaration that I felt. I honestly believe that standing on the summit of Mount Everest pales in comparison to the rush of joy that I had that day. When Conor arrived I knew that my future had taken on new meaning and that the triumphs and losses of my past were a shadow of what would come in the years ahead. However, I had not forgotten all of the friends who I had loved and lost over the years and, in honour of the finest, we gave Conor the middle name Brendan to commemorate my old mate 'Cindy' Watters.

Taking Conor home from the hospital brought the reality of parenthood home to Lauren and me quickly! We were submerged into sleepless nights and utter exhaustion but we managed to cope due to the amazing support of our family. This allowed us both a chance to return to physical training and whilst Lauren was quickly back to swimming and running, I returned to the mountains and prepared for a trip to the Alps in August.

It was a test for me to re-immerse myself in mountaineering for the first time since the avalanche, but also since taking on my new role as a father. It was difficult to leave Lauren and Conor, but I knew it was time to get back on the horse and to face the mountains once again. I spent two weeks ice- and rock-climbing on the Mont Blanc Massif and tackled many of the technical routes. We had perfect weather conditions throughout the entire trip and although I felt a bit out of shape, I had no hesitations about the ascents.

After I returned from Mont Blanc, I began to experience debilitating pains in my ankle. I had injured it several years ago whilst out with a youth group and had never sought proper medical attention. Over time it began to resolve itself but with all of my training and climbing, it never completely healed. By the autumn I could no longer ignore the pain and I saw a specialist orthopaedic surgeon, who advised me that the injury would require an operation to repair the existing damage. This news set me back psychologically and physically. I knew that recovering from the procedure would be difficult and I worried that I might not regain full mobility. In light of this, I decided to put off the operation until the spring and instead embarked upon another two further climbing trips to Scotland and a skiing trip to France after the New Year.

Not long after I saw the doctor, I received an email from Ger McDonnell telling me that he would be making another attempt on K2. He was planning an expedition for the summer of 2008 and would be climbing with Wilco and several other Dutch climbers. Although my initial instincts after the avalanche told me not to return to the savage mountain, in the year since the tragedy my feelings had already begun to change. The fact that there had never been a successful Irish summit still weighed heavily on my mind and I had distanced myself from the tragic memories of that day by looking back upon the strengths of the trip. However, with the news about my ankle, I knew that I would not be capable of making the climb that year and instead gave Ger information on summit routes and my support for his return trip.

I knew Ger was a strong climber who had a good chance at making the first Irish summit so I put any thoughts of K2 to the back of my mind in the months leading up to his departure. However, I had quietly decided that if he made it to the summit I would never return to K2; if he did not, I planned to set about the climb again in 2009.

In April of 2008 I underwent the ankle operation and began the long and tedious task of recovery. It was very difficult to maintain my strength whilst being unable to bear weight on my foot, but I did my best to train in the gym and attend physical therapy. Throughout the spring and into early summer I cycled in the hills of south Armagh and hiked whenever possible in the Mourne Mountains.

In June, Ger set out for K2 again and I followed his progress closely on the internet. He was climbing with Wilco, Rolf Bae and his wife Cecile (the Norwegian climbers I met whilst on K2 in 2005) and several other strong international mountaineers. They were a powerful team with many of them making second and third attempts on the mountain. They all had intimate knowledge of the difficulties that they would face and had planned each stage of the journey with careful thought and preparation.

The beginning of the season was filled with the usual ascents and descents to establish camps and cache supplies for a summit bid, as well as time waiting at the base camp for news of good weather to come. There were several teams making ascents that season and based on the internet reports it seemed as if everyone was working well together. Finally, on 29 July, good news came in via weather forecasts to the base camp. There was a solid weather window predicted and most of the expeditions did not hesitate to begin their attempts on the summit. On 1 August, Ger, Wilco, Rolf, Cecile, Karim (a Pakistani porter whom I met whilst on the 2005 expedition) and several other climbers enthusiastically set out from camp four for the summit. From that point on a catalogue of errors and tragedies transpired.

According to reports received after the event, when Ger and the others reached the bottleneck they found that climbers who had ascended the route earlier had laid lines in the wrong places and now many did not have enough rope with them to replace the lines onto the correct route. This would set them all back several hours. They were forced to waste precious time cutting ropes and bringing them up this very dangerous section of the climb. Once that tedious work was complete, Ger and the others were able to advance. But it was not long before they witnessed another catastrophe. A Serbian climber fell 100 metres in the bottleneck and a Pakistani porter died trying to find him. They stopped to assist and search for the men, but once it became apparent that they had died, the teams kept moving on towards the summit. This would have set them back at least another two hours.

Finally, at 8 p.m. on 1 August, 17 climbers reached the summit of κ2 and Ger was among them. His time on the top was brief as they were all running so late. He unfolded a Tricolour, posed for photos and phoned his loved ones. He then began the descent. According to reports published by Marco Confortola, an Italian climber who was with Ger, at around 9 p.m. a massive chunk of ice on the wall that overhangs the bottleneck and traverse collapsed. It swept away the fixed lines and, along with them, Rolf Bae and up to three other climbers. Rolf's wife, Cecile, was below them when the accident happened and reported seeing Rolf and several others being swept off the peak by rock and debris.

Above the collapsed ice wall were Ger, Wilco, Marco and nine other climbers. According to reports given by Wilco, panic quickly ensued.

The men were all frantic to get down but without rope they had nowhere to go. He stated that it was very dark and people started going in the wrong direction. Many traversed off the route and climbers were getting lost everywhere. He said that in the midst of total confusion everyone began fighting for themselves.

Some of the climbers made it down the bottleneck without rope by carefully free climbing and once they were down they began to organise a rescue effort. Other climbers died trying to make the free climb and some Korean climbers were killed when they tried to descend over the sheer rock face and one fell. He dangled for several hours from his rope, which remained strapped to his teammates. Although other climbers encountered the two Koreans who were struggling to hold the rope for the dangling third man, there was nothing they could do to assist them at that stage. It was pitch dark and freezing cold and amidst the total chaos, personal survival became the only focus.

Reports from Marco tell how himself and Ger decided to wait on the upper slope until daybreak. They were conscious of the chaos below and knew that an attempt to descend at this stage would be treacherous. They cut a bucket seat into the snow and rested together, trying desperately to stay awake so that they would not succumb to the cold and altitude. They were later joined by Wilco, who was suffering from partial snow-blindness. When light finally broke, the mountain was engulfed in cloud and they were near freezing. They knew that they needed to make their way down. Wilco set off first, with Marco and Ger following after him. Marco reports that he and Ger then came across the Korean climbers, and were shocked to find that they were still alive. He stated that they tried to assist them but by that stage the men were completely helpless. Marco continued to descend, but Ger remained in the bottleneck with the Koreans for an unknown length of time. Once Marco reached the bottom of this section another cascade of ice came over the top of the traverse, and with it he saw what he believed to be Ger's boots being swept away.

In all, 11 people were killed that tragic day. Despite all of the careful planning and preparations, K2 had wreaked havoc on the upper slopes again and this time the loss of human life was impossible to ignore. In the weeks after the Russian climbers were killed alongside me there was very little in the media about their deaths. However, the world could not ignore the sheer scale of the tragedy on K2 on 1 August 2008 and the media storm began immediately.

Initial reports showed Ger's successful summit and listed him only as missing whilst other climbers were immediately confirmed dead. Lauren and I were closely following the events unfolding on the net and prayed for Ger's safe return. After piecing together the reports from various teams' web pages I became more and more concerned for Ger's safety. The sheer amount of time that he spent in the 'death zone' would have been life-threatening, but this compounded by the ice-fall and avalanches made his chances of survival slim.

Two days after Ger became the first Irishman to stand on the summit of K2, his tragic death was confirmed. I have lost many friends over the years through mountaineering but Ger's death hit Lauren and me very hard. It brought back all of the memories and anguish of the avalanche in 2006 and it reconfirmed to Lauren the risks that I had taken. The massive loss of life that day showed that K2 could take even the strongest climbers by surprise.

Several weeks after Ger passed away, Lauren and I attended a memorial Mass for him in his hometown of Kilcornan, Co. Limerick. It was an amazing celebration of his life and accomplishments. His family and his partner, Annie, were fantastically proud of all that he had achieved and were very gracious. Many of Ireland's most notable climbers and explorers were present and it was a nice time for me to reminisce with friends and climbing partners. Even Wilco had made the journey, despite only recently being released from hospital in Pakistan and being in a wheelchair from the severity of the frostbite to his feet. In addition to this, all of the members of the Dutch team as well as the expedition's sponsors attended as well.

Through all the loss and tragedy that K2 has brought to my life, it still maintains a place in my dreams. This is something that many of those closest to me cannot and will not ever understand. My good friend and climbing partner Paul Clerkin sums this up best with his response to the inevitable question about why climbers pursue peaks with such high levels of risk and danger: 'For someone who understands mountaineering no explanation is necessary and for someone who doesn't, no explanation is possible.'

Although I feel confident within myself that I achieved a great deal by making it to the final traverse below the summit, and I know that physically and psychologically I was capable of making it all the way, I cannot erase my desire to ascend that final section. Even with Ger making the first successful Irish summit, my passion has not diminished. I am conscious that with my new role as a father and a husband the risks are too great to return but my ambitions remain.

It is hard to predict where these ambitions will take me in future, but I know one thing for certain; my drive towards adventure and achievement continues to grow and my dreams for the future are as ambitious as ever. I would love to have another child and to be able to share the passion that Lauren and I have for nature and mountaineering with them. I will carry the losses of my many friends and climbing partners with me and will not forget all that they lost in the pursuit of their dreams—but I will also continue to follow my own long into the future.